Making Money
on the Internet

Other computer-related Glossbrenner Books

Making Money
on the Internet

Alfred and Emily Glossbrenner

McGraw-Hill, Inc.

New York San Francisco Washington, D.C. Auckland Bogotá
Caracas Lisbon London Madrid Mexico City Milan
Montreal New Delhi San Juan Singapore
Sydney Tokyo Toronto

©1995 by **Alfred & Emily Glossbrenner**.
Published by McGraw-Hill, Inc.

pbk   1 2 3 4 5 6 7 8 9 FGR/FGR 9 9 8 7 6 5
hc   1 2 3 4 5 6 7 8 9 FGR/FGR 9 9 8 7 6 5

Library of Congress Cataloging-in-Publication Data
Glossbrenner, Alfred.
        Making money on the Internet / by Alfred and Emily Glossbrenner.
             p.   cm.
        Includes index.
        ISBN 0-07-024049-3 (H)   ISBN 0-07-024050-7
          1. Business enterprises—United States—Communication systems—
    Case studies. 2. Internet (Computer network) 3. Internet
    advertising. 4. Information networks. I. Glossbrenner, Emilly II. Title
        HD30.335.G55   1995
        658.4'038—dc20   94-48312
                                                                    CIP

Acquisitions editor: Brad Schepp
Editorial team: David M. McCandless, Managing Editor
               Joanne M. Slike, Executive Editor
Production team: Katherine G. Brown, Director
                Rhonda E. Baker, Coding
                Lisa M. Mellott, Coding
                Wanda S. Ditch, Desktop Operator
                Lori L. White, Proofreading
                Joann Woy, Indexer
Design team: Jaclyn J. Boone, Designer   0240507
             Kathryn Stefanski, Associate Designer   WK2

Contents

Part 2
The tools at hand

Introduction

The naked emperor

Forget the hype. Forget the breathless cover stories in leading news and business magazines, and the articles in major newspapers that somehow *never* get around to offering any hard numbers. Forget the segments on CNN and *MacNeil-Lehrer* that appear to predict an online "point-and-click" future for the selling of goods and services.

It's all a crock!

You don't have to have a "presence" on the Internet or risk losing sales to your competitors. You don't need some elaborate "home page" on the World Wide Web, complete with photos, fonts, and graphics. And the Internet will *not* forever change the way you do business, as many in the press would have you believe.

 # The problem with the press

Your co-authors have been watching and writing about computers and technology since the 1970s, and, with one or two exceptions, the general-interest press *never* gets it right. For us, this is profoundly disturbing. After all, if the press can so often be so wrong when reporting on subjects we know a great deal about, how trustworthy is it likely to be when covering subjects about which we know absolutely nothing?

It's an important point. And a good lesson for us all: We should take everything we read or hear—even this book—with a grain of salt and then make up our own minds. The difference is that if the press gets it wrong on international politics or on its analysis of why the Federal Reserve board raised or lowered interest rates, it doesn't much matter. Not in the overall scheme of things.

But if the press is wrong in promoting, even unintentionally, the idea of doing business on the Internet, you as a businessperson could be persuaded to invest (and ultimately lose) some serious money. Not to mention a lot of effort, energy, and time.

That's why the single most important truth you can take away from this book is this:

> When it comes to making a fortune on the Internet, the Emperor truly has no clothes! Without the proper guidance, you are far more likely to *lose* a fortune than to make one. That's because most of what you've heard and read in books, articles, and on TV about making money on the Internet is wrong—and demonstrably so.

There are thousands of people out there who are working overtime to persuade you that if your business is not online, you're out of it, now and forever more. These are the people who seek out the attention of the press, particularly the technology-illiterate press, and succeed in getting stories run that reflect their viewpoint.

The fact that these sources own businesses that charge companies a hefty fee for establishing a presence on the Internet is, of course, irrelevant. About as irrelevant as the fact that the main source for a story on a recent "infestation" of mice, rats, or cockroaches in the area just happens to be a local exterminator.

 It's not what you've been told

The truth is this: There is money to be made on the Internet. There is time and effort to be saved. There are ways—many ways—for the wonderful technology of *online*, as the field is now called, to enhance absolutely everything about your business. But the method and means are definitely *not* what you're being told.

That's why we wrote this book. We have been there, and we know what a bill of goods businesspeople are being sold. Whether you're on the Internet, Prodigy, America Online, or CompuServe, you are not going to find a pot of gold at the end of the online rainbow. Not without a lot of hard work, imagination, commitment, and some financial investment.

If you're willing to bring those things to the table, maybe you'll make some money. Maybe you won't. The online "market" is just as uncertain and unpredictable as any other. What this book will do is show you your options, starting with a consideration of whether your business should be online at all, on up through the creation of a multimedia home page on the Internet's World Wide Web.

Here's what you get

The chapters in Part 1 will quickly and conversationally bring you up to speed, both as a businessperson and as a consumer and user of online services. These chapters will lay out the playing field.

The chapters in Part 2 zero in on the Internet itself and on the major features it offers. Woven throughout, of course, is commentary designed to address the questions and concerns of a businessperson interested in using these features to market a product or service. Chapter 12 introduces you to a wide variety of companies that are already using the Internet to sell their products. Not all of them are

winners, but they are included because we believe that one of the best ways for you to create your own uses for the Internet is to see how others have done it.

⇨ Don't buy this book!

Okay, that subhead is a little over the top. The truth is, we would love to have you buy this book.

Your co-authors often lie awake nights thinking of how we might spend the $1.50 the publisher will pay us six months or so after you make your purchase. Your contribution, suitably adjusted for inflation, is what we live for.

Still, the major purpose of this book is to provide guidance, so it seems appropriate to say who is most likely to find it of interest and of value.

Basically, this is a book for entrepreneurs, whether they happen to be working within the confines of a corporation or working without a net running a small business of their own. We will show you what online sales and marketing is all about. We will show you how to avoid the traps and how to be truly *smart* in your approach. And we will give you all the resources, contacts, phone numbers, and other information you need to quickly get up to speed.

⇨ Our job, your job

In fact, we'll go even further. As the authors of over 30 books about computers, software, and the online world, we can flatly state that by the time you finish this book you really and truly will *understand*. But you've got to do your part. Namely, you've got to read *every* word!

We have written this book on the assumption that you are an enthusiastic, curious person who wants to learn more. We do not assume that you are now or ever have been online. You are simply a bright bulb who has been paying attention during the last year or so

and who wants to find out whether there's anything to be gained from this online, Internet thing.

Come with us, and we will take good care of you.

If you are a more advanced user, you are welcome here as well. But we know your impulse will be to skip over the things you think you know. That's fine. Just remember that each chapter has been written on the assumption that you've read all of the chapters that come before it. In other words, if you choose to start with Chapter 8, don't blame us if you encounter something that you don't fully understand.

That just about does it. If we haven't scared you off yet, we'll see you at the start of Chapter 1.

1

How to make (or lose) a fortune

THE *electronic universe*—CompuServe, America Online, Prodigy, Delphi, GEnie, plus the world's 60,000 or so bulletin board systems and the globe-girdling Internet—is truly a miracle of rare device. It's an exciting place that people travel to for many different reasons.

But it is not at all clear that any significant number of them go online to shop, at least not for ordinary merchandise or services. After all, as you will see yourself in the next chapter, going online is anything but convenient.

Nor is it clear just where an online session fits in the typical person's day. Do they do it after work, while dinner is turning in the microwave? Do they do it late at night instead of watching—or even while watching—*Letterman*? And since choosing to do one thing usually means choosing not to do something else, what other activities do they give up in order to have time online?

It's important to think about these questions before even considering ways to make money on the Internet and the rest of the electronic universe. It's also important to see things in perspective.

Lessons from the past

In business, as in life, success depends at least in part on learning from past mistakes, whether they were made by you or by someone else. That's why it is so vital for you to realize that the craze for doing business on the Internet is merely the latest manifestation of a phenomenon that dates back more than a decade.

The first personal computer, the Altair 8800, appeared in 1974, but for all practical purposes, things didn't really get started until the introduction of the Apple II+ in 1979. From that time on, businesses have been bedazzled by dreams of the pot of gold supposedly lying at the end of a phone-line rainbow.

⇨ Here's the pitch

Just think of it! All the upscale families in America will have personal or "home" computers. They will dial a number to go online with a distant mainframe computer, where they can shop till their heart's content—reading descriptions of your products and placing their orders by tapping a few keys.

The system runs 24 hours a day and requires virtually no human intervention. So you won't have to pay a bank of phone operators to enter customer orders and credit card information. That means your order processing costs will plummet as your profits go up. With the right software, you won't even have to check the computer every day to pick up all those orders that have piled up during the night. Instead, the orders will be instantly zapped by computer to the warehouse.

Sounds wonderful, doesn't it? Well, that's the basic theme of the siren song that has lured so many companies onto the rocks and cost them tens—even hundreds—of millions of dollars. The problem is that this model violates the most fundamental law of successful selling—taking a "you" approach with your prospective customer. All the benefits are on the company's side. When impartially examined, it is clear that this approach offers the customer virtually nothing.

After all, why would any sensible person go to all the trouble of turning on a computer and dialing into some online system to read about and order your product? The color catalog that comes in the mail presents much more information. And what could be easier than using a toll-free 800 number to place an order? It's the same merchandise offered at the same price. Why would any prospective customer shop online?

In most cases, online shopping simply doesn't make any sense. That's the message that consumers have conveyed again and again over the years.

 # A trip through time

The year was 1986, and what we now think of as the world of online services like shopping, news, and home banking was called *videotex* (no final *t*). It was the year of the first Big Crash in consumer online services. On March 21, Viewtron, a Miami-based home videotex system created by Knight-Ridder Newspapers, suddenly shut down. It turned out that over a year and a half the company had invested more than $55 million and succeeded in attracting only about 3,000 subscribers.

This came almost immediately on the heels of the March 7 demise of Gateway, a videotex service created by the Times Mirror Company that cost that firm nearly $30 million and ended up attracting fewer than 1,000 subscribers. "We found that our subscribers only used the service sporadically," said James H. Holly, president of Times Mirror Videotex Services. "Our goal was to have an average revenue of $20 per month per user. We just didn't see anything close to that. People would sign up for the service, try it out a few times, and then just drift off."

One can argue that a lot has happened in the past eight or nine years to change the dynamic of this marketplace. Certainly the fact that Viewtron subscribers had to buy a special $600 AT&T Sceptre terminal and pay subscription fees of $20 to $40 a month had something to do with Knight-Ridder's stunning lack of success. (But wouldn't you have thought that an idea like this would have been crushed in the egg by any executive who had an ounce of common sense?)

These days, computers and modems are priced like commodities. Nearly everyone can afford one. And they can do so many things— word processing, home finance, multimedia, education, and so forth—that it is not a question of buying one merely to go online. Surely that bodes well for the concept of online shopping. Maybe. But don't hold your breath, and don't believe most predictions.

⇨ All aboard!

In June of 1983, for example, the consulting and research firm Booz Allen & Hamilton proclaimed that a huge home information systems market was only 24 to 36 months away. The prediction, based on a two-year, $2 million study, affirmed that as early as 1985 a $30 billion market would exist, with consumers willingly paying $32 to $35 a month for the convenience such systems would offer (bill paying, information, home security, games, etc.). The message was clear: "You better get aboard now because this train's leaving the station."

Other experts and wise folks added their voices to the din. That same year, Creative Strategies predicted that sales of videotex services would grow more than 90 percent annually, reaching $7 billion by 1987. Communications consultant Gary Arlen, president of Arlen Communications, Inc., and member of the board of the Videotex Industry Association predicted (*Business Week*, 27 February 1984) that videotex could be a $30 billion industry by the mid-1990s. The U.S. Commerce Department's 1986 Industrial Outlook predicted that videotex could be used in "20 to 50 million homes by 1995."

⇨ Sorry, wrong number

All the pundits and experts were similarly optimistic. And all of them were wrong. Seriously wrong.

As Herbert Brody pointed out in his article "Sorry, Wrong Number" (*High Technology Business*, September 1988), sales in the online market in 1987 totaled a mere $113 million—not even close to the $7 billion predicted by Creative Strategies. And, according to SIMBA Information's *1994 Review, Trends & Forecast*, worldwide sales of online services totaled $11.3 billion in 1993, a far cry from the $30 billion being predicted a decade ago.

As for the total number of users, at the end of 1993, there were an estimated 7.7 million subscribers to online services, again, according to SIMBA Information, an affiliate of Cowles Business Media based in Stamford, Connecticut. Neither this number nor the original U.S.

Commerce Department's prediction of 20 to 50 million users by 1995 included Internet subscribers, so it really is an apples-to-apples comparison.

 # How many subscribers?

But that 7.7 million figure is really quite soft since it was derived by adding up the subscribership numbers reported by the leading commercial online systems. What most people don't know is that in the online world, there are no standards for calculating and reporting subscribership. For example, at GEnie, the online service offered by General Electric, the policy is to count everyone who has *ever* subscribed. Those who have cancelled their accounts are simply considered "inactive" subscribers.

Prodigy, in contrast, calculates subscribership the way a magazine estimates its readership. Just as the publishers of *Time* or *Newsweek* assume that more than one person in a household reads each issue, Prodigy assumes that each account is used by more than one family member in each household. Thus, when they claim two million subscribers, that does not mean that there are two million people paying Prodigy's fee of $9.95 per month. According to some reports, the actual number of accounts may be closer to *one* million rather than two.

CompuServe's numbers are pretty solid, since each account is charged at least $2.50 a month, and the company does not apply any multiplier. Thus CompuServe really does have the 2.3 million actual, paying subscribers it reported in late 1994. But even that number cannot be accepted without adjustment when calculating the total number of subscribers in the industry. That's because many people subscribe to more than one system and are thus counted twice or more.

 # And what about the Internet?

The soft number problem is not limited to the world of commercial online services. It also applies to the Internet. In the August 22, 1994, issue of *InfoWorld*, for example, Bob Metcalfe—the inventor

of Ethernet, founder of 3Com Corporation, and publisher of the magazine—offered some valuable insights. He was reacting to the recent report by Anthony-Michael Rutkowski, executive director of The Internet Society, that the system had between 20 and 30 million users. Here's what Mr. Metcalfe said:

> Hey, I'm an Internet enthusiast, but these numbers are crazy. *The New York Times* was right when it ran a front-page story on August 10 questioning the actual number of Internet users. Could this skepticism lead to Internet backlash?
>
> A weak link in Rutkowski's chain of estimates is the assumption that there are on average 10 users per Internet host computer. This is a holdover from when the Internet was made up mostly of VAX Unix hosts, each of which had many users.
>
> Considering that most computers today are personal, the average number of users is closer to 1 than 10, even accounting for the few really big ones. So, the Internet might have as few as 3.2 million users.

Mr. Metcalfe goes on to point out that at the 1993 meeting of the Internet Society, everyone was told that the Internet had 20 million users and a growth rate of 10 percent per month. "At that rate, the Internet should now [August 1994] have 60 million users, not just 32 million . . . The National Research Council recently put the Internet not at 60 million, 32 million, or even 20 million, but at 15 million users, which is down from a year ago."

Certainly no one would want to underestimate the difficulties of calculating the number of people using the Internet. After all, the Net doesn't have a corporate headquarters. But, at the same time, it would be just plain foolish to base *your* projections for making money on the Internet or elsewhere in the electronic universe on any of the published subscribership figures.

Naturally, the fact that comparing the subscribership numbers reported by the leading online systems is like comparing apples to oranges to pears to passion fruit is rarely noted whenever a magazine or newspaper runs one of those charts. But now you know the truth.

The subhead of the Herb Brody "wrong number" article cited earlier was "Market-research firms routinely mispredict the course of technology businesses. Why do executives still listen?" Why indeed? Particularly when, like your local TV weather personality, the same pundits and industry experts are once again predicting sunny skies—without acknowledging for a moment that the last time they said it would be fair, it rained cats and dogs.

⇨ IBM & Sears: The Prodigy project

One reason why executives still listen to predictions of the success of online shopping is that the dream of a pot of gold simply will not die. Indeed, it has been given new life in recent years, thanks to the success of TV "infomercials" and the QVC home shopping network. Yet, as *Business Week* (November 14, 1994) reported:

> So far, online shopping has not been a winner for network operators such as Prodigy and America Online. Forrester Research figures that online shopping will generate only about $200 million in revenues this year—not even a drop in the $1.5 trillion bucket U.S. consumers spend in stores and mail-order channels.

There is no better example of the persistence of the pot-of-gold vision than Prodigy Services, the system operated by IBM and Sears. It all began in 1984.

That was the year that a number of formidable corporate combines were announced. A full frontal assault on the online/videotex market was underway. RCA, J.C. Penney, Bank of America, and others formed various alliances that appeared to offer a wonderful synergy. The goal was to bring shopping, financial, and other services into the home.

Among these was a firm called Trintex, a three-company joint venture that originally included IBM, Sears, and CBS. The notion was that IBM would supply the technical expertise and computers. Sears would supply the merchandise that would be sold to subscribers. And CBS

would provide the news and entertainment content that would attract subscribers in the first place. In 1986, CBS dropped out after spending nearly $20 million on the project and facing a reported possible additional investment of $80 million.

The mission, according to Prodigy

In any event, Prodigy is important to look at because it is the one service that was created specifically to sell things online. According to literature supplied by the company, Prodigy is aimed at baby boomers in two-income households who are starved for time and frustrated by a lack of control over their lives.

It is also aimed at "home-bound elderly, young people without cars, and people with physical disabilities" who find "many transactions, such as grocery shopping, a formidable task." Plus "the newly retired, college students, single parents, and professionals working at home." And apparently, everyone else whose needs can be satisfied by "a service that's delivered through their regular telephone lines" and that has been "designed to become second nature." Like breathing out and breathing in. Or "as familiar as the TV set" and "as easy to use as a microwave or a VCR."

The brochure, aimed at potential advertisers, concludes by saying that "With its vivid color and compelling graphics, the Prodigy service has a distinctive style and personality that has to be experienced to be fully appreciated."

What's wrong with this model?

Fair enough. Prodigy has some very pleasant, innovative features. In mid-1994, for example, it began to include sound and voice files as options on some of its menus. That means that anyone whose computer is equipped for sound can point and click and (in about 30 seconds or so) hear, say, the week's featured author talking about her latest book. Or a featured performer playing a sample from his latest recording.

There are news stories and news photos, an encyclopedia, electronic mail, online "clubs" devoted to many different subjects, and lots more. All of it presented on graphical screens that, while no longer state-of-the-art, are far more interesting and fun to use than plain text.

The point here is that graphics, photos, fonts, and artwork—the same elements you are being told are essential if you want to sell your product on the Internet—have been used by Prodigy since 1984. Those are the basic elements of the World Wide Web *home pages* that magazines and TV programs love to show when discussing doing business on the Internet. (See Fig. 1-1 for a typical Prodigy screen and Fig. 1-2 for a sample Internet home page.)

Figure 1-1

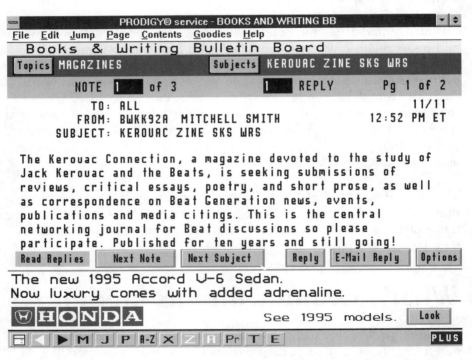

Though its graphics are no longer state-of-the art, Prodigy screens like these appear almost instantly.

Figure 1-2

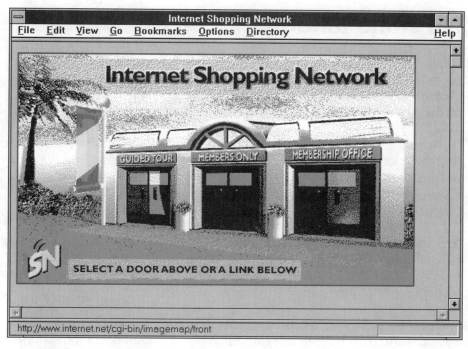

This Internet home page looks great. Trouble is, more than two minutes are required for this image to appear. (The company has since replaced it with a much simpler one.)

But Prodigy has something the Internet does not—an advertisement on *every* screen. Whenever you are on Prodigy using a feature of any sort, the lower one-sixth of your screen displays an ad. The ad may or may not be related to the subject of the feature you are using. You won't necessarily see an ad for a Ford or GM car when you are using an automobile-related feature. Then again, you might.

Indeed, you might see ads that have been chosen specifically for you. Prodigy keeps track of what you do on the system. So if you used an automobile-related feature the last time you were on, it assumes you are interested in cars and will show you car ads during your next session.

 # No stone unturned

Okay. Ready for the payoff? On November 17, 1994, the CNN program *Moneyline* aired an interview with Scott Kurnit, Executive Vice President, Prodigy Services. When asked about the current state of the service, Mr. Kurnit said, "At this moment we are not profitable."

Not profitable. After more than 10 years and after investing more than $1 billion! After attracting somewhere between one and two million users. After using fonts and pictures, graphics and sound, and after presenting users with millions of screens of ads. Still not profitable?

Prodigy has, in short, tried everything. It has left no stone unturned in its well-financed efforts to create an interactive shopping service and thus seize the pot of gold its backers apparently still see at the end of the online rainbow.

And yet some twit of a reporter, who didn't know what a modem was six days ago, has the temerity to tell you that if you don't immediately invest hundreds or perhaps thousands of dollars setting up a World Wide Web home page or otherwise establishing a presence on the Net, you and your company are going to be left in the technological dust. Meantime, other instant experts enthusiastically claim that companies are making fortunes selling on the Internet.

It is entirely possible that we've missed it. But to our knowledge, none of the companies that advertise on Prodigy has ever come forward to rave about all the sales the system is generating. None of the companies that have rented space in CompuServe's Electronic Mall or in the GEnie equivalent over the past five or six years has done so either.

The most any company spokesperson will say is that "We are generally satisfied with the performance . . ."

Why it does or doesn't work

At this point we should emphasize once again that we are not saying that online advertising, marketing, and sales don't work. Far from it. What *we are* saying is that you should not believe the hype and the misinformed news stories designed to convince you that there's a fortune to be made by selling your product or service online, and that the best way to make that fortune is to invest a sizeable sum in creating a snazzy home page on the World Wide Web.

We're fully aware that some of you will have only the vaguest notion of what the online world and the Internet are all about. That will have changed by the time you finish Part I of this book. (At which point, you may want to come back and read this chapter again.) For the moment though, let's accept a general, "lowest common denominator" definition for doing business online, and let's explore in broad terms why it does or does not work.

Information exchange

Forget about graphics, fonts, and photos. They may or may not be involved. For now, limit your thoughts to plain text, displayed in whatever font is built into your potential customer's computer.

We can thus say the following: Anyone with a product or service to sell can do so online. The systems you can use include CompuServe, GEnie, the Internet, and others. In every case, you can provide prospective customers with merchandise descriptions and give them the option of placing an order for a product immediately.

That's our lowest common denominator-style definition for doing business online. In the end, it all boils down to an exchange of information. The prospect asks for and receives information about the item you offer. The information you provide can take the form of text, graphics, photos, or even sound. The prospect absorbs what you provide and decides whether to send you the information that says, "Yes, I'd like to buy that item. Here's where to send it, and here's how I will pay for it."

This is nothing new. It is the basis of any business transaction. And, whether you're selling fresh fruit from a pushcart in nineteenth-century Baltimore, books from a stall in modern Paris or New York, or computer components from a World Wide Web home page on the Internet, the challenges are the same.

Where to find you & why bother to visit

Whether your potential customers are on online, on foot, or on the road, they must somehow learn about your place of business. Then they must be persuaded to expend the effort and energy needed to get there.

That means it's not enough to simply open a store. You've got to advertise. You've got to tell people that you're there and where to find you. And, not surprisingly, you've got to do so in TV, radio, and print ads, plus in your direct mail and any other non-online means you are now using to reach your market.

It also means that you've got to give your prospective customers some reason for making the trip. You will understand this much better once you've made the trip yourself. As you'll discover, reaching your store requires your customers to turn on their computers, load communications software, tell the software to dial a particular number, and then enter a command or two to get to your online place of business. Or to reach the place where they can send you electronic mail requesting additional information.

If you have never done this yourself, you have no business even considering trying to make money on the Internet or on any other online service. Only by personally expending the energy and effort required to reach an online store or facility on any online service can you fully appreciate the incentives you're going to have to offer to get people to come to you.

The Seven Rules of successful online selling

We will explore options and alternatives later in this book, and we will do our best to guide you. But you will find the experience most profitable if you keep the following seven "rules" in mind. Don't worry if you're not familiar with all of the terms or concepts discussed here. Read the Seven Rules and absorb whatever comes easily. Then read the rest of the book and come back here after you've had a little more experience.

Rule 1: Make it worth the trip

Rule Number 1 of successful online selling is that you've got to make it worth the trip for a person to seek out and visit your store. You've got to give online users an incentive to pay you a visit.

It doesn't take that much. If your company can save $10 by taking an order online instead of via your toll-free phone number, split the difference with your online customers and offer the merchandise for $5 *less* than the person would pay ordering by phone. You'll be surprised at how many people will eagerly make the trip to save a mere $5.

Consider putting online merchandise on sale or running special promotions. Is there some item you can make available *exclusively* via your online store? What about a service or convenience that's not available any other way?

For example, imagine giving customers the power to specify the features they want in a TV or VCR, and having a computer scan your inventory for just those units that match that profile. That's service! In many instances, that's reason enough for a user to make the effort. You won't have to offer any financial incentive at all.

The biggest mistake you can make is to assume that online selling is just like selling through mail-order catalogues. The next biggest

mistake is assuming that online selling will ever free you of the expense of printing and mailing a catalogue or whatever other advertising and promotion you may be doing right now. As long as any competitor is offering merchandise comparable to yours via print ads, color catalogues, and toll-free phone numbers, you will have to do likewise.

And don't forget, with a catalogue, you can go to your customer. It arrives, unbidden, in the mailbox. When you're online, your customer must be persuaded to come to you. All of which reinforces once again the need to make it worth the trip.

Rule 2: Integrate your online efforts with everything else

It's amazing, but true: In most issues of *Wired* magazine, a publication devoted almost exclusively to the Internet and cyberspace, you will have to look high and low to find a print ad that includes the advertiser's e-mail address or World Wide Web site.

There may be exceptions, but for most businesses, the Internet and the electronic universe will never replace conventional means of advertising, marketing, and sales. It is thus just plain stupid to invest time and money establishing an online presence and fail to integrate it with everything else you're doing.

At the very least, every print ad should include your e-mail address on the Net, as well as your land address, voice phone, and fax phone numbers. You should put your e-mail or Web site address on your letterhead and on business cards as well.

And, once you've got things set up, you should make a real effort to use your print and conventional efforts synergistically with your online presence. There are all kinds of ways to do this, but here's a quick example:

> If you want to get prospects to come to your online site, consider running a trivia contest in your most successful print publications. Put the questions in the ad and tell readers that they've got to go

online and go to your electronic location to play. Perhaps every correct entry will be placed in a random drawing for some prize. Naturally, once they are at your location, there will be items for them to buy and other things to do.

⇨ Rule 3: Keep it fresh

So many companies in the past have assumed that if they offered some information or created an online feature, that there was no need to keep an eye on it. Internally, the online area is assigned the lowest priority. Some staffer is supposed to take care of it, but only if time permits. Which it rarely does.

This is a huge mistake. Neglect of this sort not only hurts sales, it creates an extremely negative impression in the minds of prime prospects—those 20 percent of customers who account for 80 percent of your sales.

For example, assume you're in the model airplane kit business. You create an online presence that lets users instantly get informative descriptions of your product line. They can easily place orders when they see something they want. And they can get transcripts of interviews with masters of the field and download pictures of prize-winning models.

This is not a difficult thing to create. So, assume you do so and then just walk away. Or, more accurately, assume you fail to assign someone to maintain this feature and make it a top priority.

What will happen is this: Once the word gets out about your site and what you offer, you'll get a good initial boost as model airplane enthusiasts gravitate to your feature. They love it! Fantastic! Great job!

But when these same people check in two weeks later, they will expect changes, updates, and new information. If no one has updated the product descriptions and price list . . . if no new interviews or images have been added . . . if, in short, it's the same-old, same-old, you're in trouble! Okay, two weeks is a very short time. Maybe they'll

cut you a break. Particularly if you are the only model airplane kit company online at the time.

They'll wait another two weeks—making a month between the time they first checked you out and now. Surely, your company will have uploaded a new interview or two or a batch of new images.

No? It's been four weeks, and nothing has changed? So long, guys. We're outta here!

Possibly never to return. Through plain, stupid neglect, you have just alienated your prime, platinum-plated online customers. To persuade these folks to give you another look, you'll have to do something spectacular. And you'd better hope that none of your competitors has come online in the meantime.

Rule 4: Start small & keep it simple

Do you know why you so often see newspaper and magazine illustrations that look like Fig. 1-2, the original World Wide Web home page for the Internet Shopping Network? The answer is that it's pretty. Far more attractive than the screens of plain text that used to illustrate most online articles.

No one can blame an editor, reporter, or art director for wanting to produce a visually pleasing page. The trouble is that in so doing, they have created a serious misconception. The image of the storefront you see in Fig. 1-2, for example, looks great on the screen—but it takes over two minutes for it to appear when coming in on a 14.4 (14,400 bits per second) modem.

Don't worry about the technical details right now. Focus instead on the fact that, as wonderful as they are, the graphic images you see here, on TV, and in newspaper and magazine articles take one heck of a long time to appear on a user's screen. People who use the Internet from locations at large companies, government agencies, and college and university computing centers usually will see an image like the one in Fig. 1-2 in just over one second, thanks to their high-speed connections to the Net. But those connections are at least 100 times faster than a 14.4 modem can deliver, and 50 times faster than a 28.8 (28,800 bits per second) modem, the fastest modem available.

Bottom line: Under the best of circumstances, each image like the one shown in Fig. 1-2 will take between one and two minutes to appear on your prospective customer's screen. And, since most computer users today operate at only 9600 ("ninety-six hundred") bits per second, each such image could take as much as three minutes to appear!

People will try this once or twice. But the novelty soon wears off. Especially if you are paying a connect-time charge for each of those minutes.

That's why we strongly suggest that you think small and simple. We'll show you later how easy it is to get a really big bang for your online buck using just plain, easily created—and instantly delivered—text!

 Rule 5: Hire an expert

There are many, many things you can do yourself on the Net. Or, if you personally can't do them, they can be done by someone you assign. But—just as a desire to be freed from worrying about ad copy, design, layout, and media schedules may have prompted you to hire an advertising agency—you may be better off hiring an expert to handle your Internet/online activities.

You'll find lists of people and firms you can check out later in this book. (You might even give us a call!) You will also learn how to plug in and look at what other firms in your line of work are doing. If you like a particular service, you may want to hire the people who created it.

You may be the smartest, cleverest person in the world. But like everyone else, you only get 24 hours to spend each day. So, even if you know you have or could easily acquire the necessary knowledge and skills, think about concentrating on what you do best and hiring the rest.

Our friend Robin Raskin, editor of *PC Magazine*, once recounted the remark an eminent scientist made to her at dinner: "If I was ever in close competition with another scientist, and I wanted to get a year ahead, I'd just go out and buy him a computer." As Ms. Raskin commented, "True words, but if I really wanted to put someone on idle, I'd add an Internet connection to the gift!"

Rule 6: Test it personally—always!

One of the most amazing things about the current collection of advertising and marketing efforts on the Net is how bad so many of them are. Many of them just don't work. You can follow the instructions and click on something and nothing will happen. Or, worse, something unintended will happen. You can sit there for what seems like hours as some large graphic image insists on being displayed, with no option to get out and no option to specify "text only" before you get in.

In short, there are lots of very rough edges to many online efforts. And some are so rough that it is impossible to believe that anyone from the company sponsoring the ad or the online presence has ever actually tried it out.

Don't make that mistake. Make sure that you and everyone in your group signs on and pretends to be a prospect. Keep notes on what is confusing and what should be improved. Think of it as a debugging process of the sort *every* software product must go through. Hire the experts, if appropriate, but don't let them "publish" your material until you and your group have thoroughly, and personally, checked it out.

Rule 7: Make the commitment!

Finally, the absolute worst thing you can do is to attempt to market your goods or services on the Internet or via some other online system without first making the commitment to doing so. Indeed, commitment is the essential element in all of the Seven Rules.

You can't do this kind of thing off-the-cuff and have a hope of being successful. You and your company have got to take the time to make a thorough study of online options and alternatives.

You'll have to assign the online marketing and sales project to some specific person—even if that person is yourself. And you will have to make it clear that this is a primary task, not just one more thing on the "to-do" list. You will have to monitor progress and results and fine-tune things as necessary. In brief, making the commitment means treating the online effort not as a poor stepchild but as a full-fledged member of the family.

If you are not willing to do this, you should close this book and put it back on the shelf for someone else to find, for it will do you no good.

On the other hand, if what we have said here is of interest and you are indeed willing to make the commitment, then we will really enjoy working with you, sharing our knowledge and insights, and generally showing you how to make the most of the online medium in general and the Internet in particular.

We firmly believe that the informed, intelligent, and committed use of the Internet and the online medium can boost sales and improve the image of any business or profession or anyone else with something to offer. The trick is in offering it the right way!

2

Crucial concepts made simple

How the online world works

AS a magazine reader, there is no need for you to know how ad pages are produced and inserted into your particular copy of your favorite magazine. Nor do you need to be aware of postage rates, ZIP code sorts, or anything else that is part of the mechanics of producing and delivering the magazine and its advertising.

The same thing would be true about the mechanics of the online world if you were a typical user interested in the features offered by America Online, CompuServe, the Internet, and the rest. But you're not a typical user. You're seriously considering using these mechanisms to market and advertise your product or service.

If you want to do so with confidence, you've got to know how the online world works. You've got to know about text and graphics and communications speeds. And you've got to have a broad overview of the landscape your customers will be traversing.

Understanding & overview

We'll give you a quick tour of the online world in the next chapter, and after taking it, you will have a much better idea of where everything fits. In this chapter we'll concentrate on the essential mechanics. And—we promise—we won't force you to learn a lot of mindless technical detail. We can start with the fact that computers can exchange information over the telephone. At this point, that is surely obvious. But you need to know a little more about it than this.

How do computers communicate?

All computers communicate using on/off signals or pulses that, for our convenience, we humans refer to as 1s and 0s. Physically, those pulses can consist of literally anything. They can be two different voltage levels or the presence of a hole or the absence of same in a punched card or piece of Mylar tape. They can be regions of a disk that are either magnetized or not magnetized or the pits and plateaus of a laser-read CD-ROM.

All that matters is that there be two, and only two, distinct signals and that the computer have some way of receiving them.

When it comes to sending two distinct signals over the phone line, a piece of equipment called a *modem* is needed. The modem translates the voltage pulses used inside the computer into sounds that are suitable for sending over the phone line. It also reverses the process when receiving data, translating sounds into voltage pulses.

The bandwidth problem

Modems come in all shapes and sizes. Some are designed to be inserted into the computer as a circuit board. Others are free-standing boxes that are connected to the computer by a cable.

The most important characteristic of any modem, however, is its speed. Modem speeds are often loosely referred to as their baud *rate, though* baud *technically applies only to 300 baud units. Fortunately,* bps *(bits per second) is gradually replacing* baud *as a modem's speed designation.*

Available speeds range from 300 bits per second to a high of 28,800 bits per second, which is usually expressed as 28.8 kilobits (thousand bits) per second or 28.8 kbps. Often it is pronounced "twenty-eight eight," just as 14.4 kbps, the next speed down, is pronounced "fourteen four." Modems are classified by their top speed, but, with very few exceptions, all modems can handle every possible slower speed. They are downward compatible, *in other words.*

Not too long ago, the standard top modem speed was 2400 bps. But as modem prices have fallen, we can confidently say that 9600 bps ("ninety-six hundred") is now the standard. This will change over time as people migrate to the 28.8 kbps standard that was officially announced in June 1994.

For those of us who began life online with a 300 baud acoustic coupler (foam cups you put around the mouth- and earpiece of a telephone handset), this is wonderful. The trouble lies in the science of physics. A speed of 28.8 kbps is generally considered the maximum speed ordinary copper telephone lines can handle. And it is not nearly enough.

Think of those brain-teaser puzzles asking you to calculate the amount of time required to fill a swimming pool if the water is flowing through a pipe of a specified diameter. Well, the maximum diameter of the pipe feeding computer data into American homes permits a top data flow of 28,800 bits per second. And not everyone has such a pipe.

There are data compression techniques one can use to boost the effective throughput. But the bandwidth *(the diameter of the pipe) is still limited by the physical characteristics of copper wire. Not until the nation has been completely rewired with fiber-optic cable will there be enough bandwidth to pump graphic images and sound and all the other wonderful things you've heard about into the home at an acceptably fast speed.*

What about pictures & graphics?

Computers have two modes: text mode and graphics mode. As we will see in a moment, sending and receiving text is easy for a computer, even for one operating at 2400 bps. Graphic images, however, are another story. Graphic images take much longer to transmit than plain text. Much, much longer.

You will understand why this is so if you think of your computer screen as consisting of hundreds of thousands of tiny picture elements or *pixels*. Each pixel consists of three dots (red, green, and blue), and each of those dots can be controlled individually. The *intensity* of each pixel can also be controlled. In short, four computer bits—one for each color and one for intensity—are required for each pixel when you're in graphics mode.

That sounds reasonable. After all, it means that the typical 16-color, 640 × 480 pixel VGA screen can produce very pleasing images. For photographic quality, you've got to go to 256 colors, but let that go for now.

Here's the key point: The total number of pixels on a standard 640 × 480 screen is 307,200. Each pixel requires four bits of data. That means that filling an entire screen with a graphic image requires over

one million bits. (The exact number is 1,228,800 bits, which you get by multiplying 307,200 by 4.)

✳ Unacceptable, even at the fastest speed

We already know that the fastest data speed possible for the vast majority of your customers is 28.8 kbps. In the best of all possible worlds, then, nearly 43 seconds will be required to transmit the 1,228,800 bits needed for one full-screen graphic image.

The majority of users will find 43 seconds far too long to wait, and that's the *best* possible speed. In the real world, lots of things conspire to slow things down. For one thing, the software procedures and protocols needed to transport such an image add a considerable amount of overhead in the form of additional bits of data.

There are also delays introduced by noise on the phone lines and the need to retransmit faulty data. There is the fact that the computer sending the image to your customer may be handling several other people at the same time. It may have to divide its attention on a round-robin basis, doling out portions of bits to each person in turn.

There are other complications as well. All of which leads to the fact that, in the *real* world, even with a connection operating at 28.8, your customers could easily find themselves drumming their fingers for two minutes or more, waiting for the image to appear. If they were to click on a button to go to the next page of your online catalog, they might have to wait another two minutes for the next image to appear.

You can reduce the time required to paint a page by using fewer and smaller graphic images. But most users who are on at 28.8 will still find them maddeningly slow. And, as we've said before, 28.8 is as good as it gets.

✳ The really bad news

Now for the really bad news. At this writing, most of your potential customers have modems with a top speed of 9600 bps. For them, given the inevitable delays, five minutes or more will be required to receive a single full-screen graphic image. If two minutes at 28.8 is

unacceptable, five minutes or more at 9600 is outrageous. No one's going to sit still for it.

There's really no need to get any more technical. All you have to know is this:

➢ Color graphic images in their native form require a lot of bits. Paint and screen-capture programs use data compression techniques to cut in half the amount of space required to store an image as a file on disk. But that doesn't do you any good here.

➢ The bigger the image, the longer it takes to transmit. So, if you're going to use images, keep them as small as you can while maintaining their effectiveness. But once you start cutting down on the graphics, you naturally start to lose whatever benefits graphics add. At that point, you may wonder whether any kind of graphic images are worth the bother.

➢ Most users today have 9600 bps modems. Since even a small graphic image can take too long to transmit at 9600 bps, be sure to always offer customers the option of using your online feature *without* graphics.

The case for text-only

This is a technical chapter, it's true. But, like everything else in this book, it is informed by the concept of doing business on the Internet and in the online world.

That's why we can say that graphics are fine, even exciting, when used intelligently. And there are ways to use the Internet and online resources to send your prospects graphic images *without* making them wait for the images to appear. But fundamentally, the reality of the marketplace being what it is, you will be much better off if you stick to text.

That's because you can convey a tremendous amount of information as text in a very, very short time. You can zap text to your customers within seconds of their request. We're not kidding: Your customers will have no sooner hit the Enter key to send their e-mail requests to you than your text will appear in their online mailboxes. We will show you how to set things up to make this happen later in the book.

 Pre-positioning the heavy armor

Here's why text can be pumped through so fast, even when people are connecting at 2400 or 9600 bps: The concept is the same as that used by the U.S. military in pre-positioning tanks, heavy armor, and artillery abroad. With that equipment already in place, activating it requires but a simple secure phone message, delivered in seconds: "Move the 87th tank division to position X-57 on the map right now."

No heavy lifting and no long delays are required to get the tanks shipped halfway round the world. They are already there, ready to be activated with a simple command.

Yes, it sounds like a stretch, but this is exactly the concept that makes it possible to transmit text so quickly over the phone lines. If each text character had to be transmitted as a *graphic image*, we would be in big trouble. That's because each character consists of numerous pixels, depending on its size and typeface. And, as we already know, you've got to plan on sending four bits for each and every pixel (red, green, blue, and intensity bits).

But suppose you pre-positioned in the receiving computer the list of which dots in which pixels had to be turned on and at what intensity for each character. Suppose each of these sets of individual instructions for creating a character were given a number. In that case, you could cause any text character to appear by simply sending the distant computer the character's number.

The character number acts like a kind of shorthand. The computer receives the number and goes to a look-up table to retrieve the instructions needed to create that character on the screen. Then it does so, with blindingly fast speed.

The point is that the actual bit-by-bit instructions for creating said character do not have to be sent out over the phone line. All you've got to send is the character number, which, for technical reasons, requires only 10 bits.

It is worth noting that the actual appearance of the character on the screen—its size, color, typeface, and style—depends entirely on the look-up table the receiving computer is using at the time. After all, just think of how many ways one can "write" a capital *A*. Every computer comes with one or more fonts burned into a silicon chip. But those instructions can be replaced or supplemented by software fonts of the sort you see in Microsoft Windows and the Apple Macintosh.

ASCII & the binary numbering system

Now that you've got the "pre-positioning" concept, here are the actual details. First, thanks to the magic of the binary numbering system, any number can be expressed as a series of 1s and 0s. So computers can easily send and receive numbers.

Second, because it is in everyone's best interest for computers of all makes and models to be able to communicate, the industry as a whole long ago adopted a standard. The standard is called ASCII (pronounced "as-key"), short for American Standard Code for Information Interchange.

The ASCII code assigns a number to every upper- and lowercase letter of the alphabet. It assigns a number to most major punctuation marks (period, comma, colon, etc.). And it assigns a number to some 26 control codes ranging from Control-A through Control-Z.

Thus, thanks to the ASCII code, if you are a Macintosh user and you enter a capital *D* at your keyboard while chatting online with a DOS/Windows-using friend, you can rest assured that your Mac will send your friend an ASCII 68 and that your friend's machine will know that it should respond by painting a capital *D* on the screen.

Similarly, if you as a businessperson want to offer your product catalog as a text file on the Internet, you can key in the information and store it as a text file in full confidence that everyone will be able to read it, regardless of the computer they use.

Caveats, of course

There are caveats, of course. First, we are assuming that your text file will be in English. Reaching non-English-reading users requires a special effort that is beyond the scope of this book.

Second, we're assuming that you've limited yourself to just plain text characters. For technical reasons, computers communicate using eight-bit packages called *bytes*. In the binary numbering system, eight bits—a series of eight 1s or 0s—can express any number from 0 through 255.

But the universally accepted ASCII code set runs from 0 through 127, exactly half of the total possible numbers that can be communicated using eight bits. As it happens, the 128 numbers of the "standard" ASCII code offer more than enough slots for all the letters, numbers, punctuation marks, and control codes most users will require.

Thus—and here's the key point—no universally accepted standard applies to the ASCII code numbers ranging from 128 through 255. Computer makers have been free to do what they will with these 128 "high" ASCII codes. In the world of IBM-compatible machines, for example, the ASCII codes from 128 through 168 are devoted to foreign characters, including the sign for the British pound and the one for the Japanese yen. After that come a lot of shading and box-drawing characters, followed by codes for mathematical symbols.

Naturally, the Macintosh is different. If you're a DOS/Windows user and you send your Mac-using friend an ASCII 227, which shows up on your screen as the Greek letter pi, there's no telling what will appear on your friend's screen.

The lesson is this: If you want your words to be easily readable by the largest number of people, make sure that what you offer consists of nothing but plain, pure, ASCII text. (Check your word processing software manual for instructions on how to save a file in plain ASCII text mode.)

Pre-positioned graphics: Prodigy & America Online

We've discussed one-of-a-kind graphic images that must be transmitted bit by bit. And we've discussed the universally accepted and implemented ASCII code system that greatly speeds up information transmission by pre-positioning the instructions needed to put any character on the screen within every computer.

Now we need to discuss *pre-positioned graphics*. If you have read this far, the concept will seem simple.

Suppose you equip every potential customer with a special program that includes software-based instructions for drawing or painting certain basic shapes on the screen. The instructions might even consist of formulas that will produce the same shape in different sizes, depending on the specific variable that gets plugged into the formula at the time. Finally, suppose that each of these sets of instructions is given a number.

If you are an online service like Prodigy or America Online, you can make some really nice graphic images appear on your customers' screens very quickly. All you have to do is send the customers' software the number of the basic shape you want to use and the size variables for that shape's formula.

Just as is the case when working with text, the receiving computer looks up the shape's number in its look-up table and responds by quickly painting the shape on the screen. Only a handful of bits must be transmitted to do this, yet the resulting image can occupy so many thousands of pixels that many minutes would be required to send it as a graphic image.

This is indeed how Prodigy and America Online work. The results are not photographic, but they are visually pleasing. Both systems can show you photographs as part of a feature—say a picture in the news or an exhibit at the Smithsonian—but, as you might imagine, those photos take a long time to appear.

And now you know why! You can also deduce that this approach is the reason you must use each system's proprietary software to gain access. You can't just dial up with any old communications program.

⇨ Summary & overview

The next item on the agenda is to lay out a map of the electronic universe. We want you to have an overview of the options available to you and to your prospective customers and gain a sense of where everything fits.

But we've just covered a lot of territory, so a short summary would seem to be in order. The essence of that summary is this: Text is fast, but graphics are slow—and likely to remain so for the foreseeable future. You can satisfy your personal and corporate ego by setting up a wonderfully graphic home page on the World Wide Web, but doing so is not likely to satisfy most of your potential customers.

You will definitely want to try this yourself. Indeed, we encourage you to do so—otherwise you'll never know how bad things can be. Buy a 28.8 modem and set yourself up with a SLIP or PPP connection as discussed in Chapter 5. Use the software supplied by your service provider—Mosaic, NetScape, NetCruiser, or some other *browser* package.

Then check out the World Wide Web home pages offered at the following addresses:

CMP Publications, Inc.
http://techweb.cmp.com/corporate

Internet Shopping Network
http://shop.internet.net

Silicon Surf
http://www.sgi.com

Each of these companies offers a state-of-the-art implementation of the graphical approach made possible by the World Wide Web. Put yourself in the shoes of your typical best customer and imagine how that person would react if it were your product or service being offered at these Web sites.

⇨ The Internet in perspective

Your co-authors have visited each of these Web sites—at a connection speed of 28.8 kbps. And we have found them cleverly done, visually pleasing—and completely unusable. Even at 28.8, the images do not appear fast enough to make visiting the sites anything but a painful experience.

You can see what they're getting at. You can see the vision they have in mind. It would be wonderful if the graphics appeared almost instantly. As it is, you'll be tempted to take a nap as you wait for a single screen to get painted.

People will try a World Wide Web site home page once or twice to see what it's like. But no one in his right mind—even with a top-of-the-line 28.8 modem—will regularly spend time there. Especially if the connect-time meter is running.

We would go even further. Unless your company is in the business of selling something like "Cottontail Brand Smart Pills," the kind of person who would willingly spend minute after minute waiting for images to appear on a World Wide Web Internet page is not likely to be among your prime customers!

But again, try it yourself. And give yourself every advantage: a PPP connection (instead of the slower SLIP connection), a 28.8 kbps modem, and a real hot-rod of a Macintosh or Pentium-based machine with "local-bus" graphics.

→ It ain't no black-and-white TV!

After all the criticism we've leveled, it wouldn't hurt to once again state that using the features offered by the online world in general and the Internet in particular can be very, very profitable. There is money to be made, but it's not easy money. And that has been our point so far.

We feel we are honor-bound to drive home the point that—despite everything you read in the media—the Internet is far from a mass market medium. It has some very powerful features, but, in general terms, the Internet is not ready for prime time.

If the Internet were a person, it would react to all the attention it has received like someone who had been spirited off to a time bubble on another planet the moment of its birth in 1969 and only returned to Earth in 1991. In effect, the Internet is a 25-year-old "child" that has grown and developed in its own private environment. But it's been a part of what most of us consider the real world for only the last four or five years. During which time it has experienced a phenomenal, destabilizing growth rate.

Sure, it's huge. With perhaps 20 million users, the Net is 10 times bigger than CompuServe. But 20 million users worldwide is a tiny fraction of the five *billion* people populating the globe. And Internet users are likely to remain a small fraction of any market for years to come, due to the relatively steep entrance requirements.

To a marketer, those entrance requirements connote desirable demographics. But it is worth noting that, while computers and modems and software may be truly cheap and getting cheaper, they've got a long way to go before they can match the $65 currently charged for a 12-inch black-and-white television. And they will never match the $15 street price of a Sony clock radio. Yet both of these appliances can transmit the typical advertising messages we all know and love.

Your prospect, in contrast, will have to invest at least $1,200 in computer hardware just to own the tools needed to get online. And

he or she will have to be knowledgeable enough or dogged enough to find you in the ether and to read and respond to your message.

Fortunately, it's not as if you're asking people to invest that kind of money solely to connect with the Net. As we all know, computers can do so many things, and they have become so essential, that more and more people are buying them. And these days, most systems come equipped with modems and communications software. Your prospects may not know how to *use* this gear, but at least they don't have to make a special purchase.

Everything *but* the Internet

THE bulk of this book is devoted to the Internet and to showing you how you can make money using its facilities. But as you will have gathered, the Internet is but one part of a much larger online picture. In our opinion, anyone considering using the Internet for commercial purposes needs a sense of where it fits in the overall scheme of things. There's also the fact that you should not necessarily limit your online marketing efforts to the Internet alone. You may also want to consider systems like CompuServe or Prodigy, or even setting up your own bulletin board system.

So that's what we'll look at here. We'll look at the online world—what we've been calling the *electronic universe* in books and articles since 1982. The electronic universe begins with the 5,307 databases available on 812 online systems, as reported by the latest edition of the authoritative *Gale Directory of Databases*, published by Gale Research, Inc., in Detroit, Michigan. (Ask your local reference librarian if there's a copy on the shelf; you'll find it an eye-opener.)

These databases include such familiar systems as Dialog, Lexis/Nexis, Dow Jones News/Retrieval, as well as many other far more obscure entities. Like HORSE, a system from Bloodstock Research Information Services in Lexington, Kentucky, that can supply you with the pedigree and racing record of every thoroughbred in North America since 1922.

The Gale figures include the leading consumer services like America Online (AOL) and CompuServe. But they don't cover the 60,000 or so independently owned and operated bulletin board systems (BBSs) in North America. Each BBS consists of at least one computer connected to a modem and phone line. The computer runs BBS software that automatically answers the phone and guides callers to various features.

Then, of course, there is the Internet—linking tens of thousands of individual networks and thus serving tens of millions of users. Many of whom access the Net via Prodigy or Delphi or one of the other consumer-oriented systems. For, any more, everything is quite literally "connected."

Now that we've managed to thoroughly overwhelm you, let's pull back and see if we can impose some order on this apparent chaos.

Order out of chaos: Five main categories

The two fundamental features of the online world are *information* and *communication*. But like the simple components of an atom of helium, these two features can be combined and presented in an apparently infinite number of ways. There's no need to split hairs, however. In general, there are five main categories of online systems used by consumers, businesspeople, and professionals:

➤ Information-only systems

➤ Communications-only systems

➤ The Big Five consumer online systems

➤ Bulletin board systems (BBSs)

➤ The Internet

Information-only systems

People have been using online systems to search for and retrieve information for decades. The information can be anything from the full text of the *Wall Street Journal* to population figures from the Census Bureau. Indeed, those 5,000 or so databases cited a moment ago contain just about *every* kind of information you can imagine, on any topic you'd care to name.

Although TrademarkScan, a database owned by Thompson & Thompson, includes graphic images of as many as 40 percent of the marks on file with the U.S. government, virtually all of the "industrial-strength" information available online is exclusively text. It also tends to be quite expensive.

The patent databases on Dialog, for example, cost upwards of $120 an hour. Standard & Poor's costs $60 an hour, and Books in Print is $30 an hour. Users are also charged anywhere from 40 cents to $4 for each complete record they display on their screens. That's why many people hire *information brokers*, professionals who know how and where to find the information you need at the lowest possible price. (If this is of interest, you'll want to see *The Information Broker's Handbook—2nd Edition* by Sue Rugge and Alfred Glossbrenner, published by McGraw-Hill.)

Communications-only systems

On the communications side of things, there are systems that specialize in transferring messages. The leader here is MCI Mail, which can take a message you transmit and send it to your recipient as an e-mail message, a fax, a telex/TWX message, a cablegram, or a laser-printed paper letter delivered by the post office or an overnight delivery service. If you like, you can even have the paper letter printed with your letterhead and finished off with a facsimile of your handwritten signature.

The Big Five consumer online systems

The third general category of online system is a hybrid. It is a system that offers both communication and information features. This is the category we will call *consumer online systems*, and under it you will find America Online, CompuServe, Delphi, GEnie, and Prodigy. It is these "Big Five" systems that account for the bulk of the six to seven million people who are now online, exclusive of the Internet.

Bulletin board systems (BBSs)

Bulletin board systems form a fourth category. Each BBS is, in effect, a mini-CompuServe or mini-America Online. Current BBS software is so sophisticated that it can easily fool users into thinking they are on one of the commercial consumer systems. Indeed, although the vast majority of boards are free, run as they are as hobbies by their *sysops*

(system operators), any number of entrepreneurs have been attracted to the field. And many of them are doing quite well, thank you, charging quarterly or yearly subscription fees.

The Internet

The fifth and last category is the Internet. To put it mildly, the Internet is something else again. The systems that it connects offer industrial-strength information as powerful as the databases on Dialog or Nexis, communications features on a par with MCI Mail, and hybrid features like real-time chat, file transfers, and interactive games of the sort formerly available only on the Big Five systems. And access is essentially free!

All of which sounds fantastic, until you remember that the Internet is not a single, integrated online system. There's no central office you can complain to. There is no toll-free "help" line to phone when you have a problem. Nor is there any easy, centrally organized way to locate the information or features you want. The Internet is the antithesis of "user friendly," and it's basic interface looks like something out of the late 1970s.

The Internet is *not* the "Information Superhighway" that the experts envision. At best, it is an early prototype. And, although we long ago got sick of highway metaphors, there is one that remains valuable. Think of CompuServe, Prodigy, America Online, and the rest as individual Disney Worlds. These companies control everything you see once you enter their magical little "towns."

The Internet, in contrast, is not a town at all. It is the high-speed interstate highway that runs by the towns' front doors—and the front doors of tens of thousands of other computer systems. It was built by taxpayer dollars, so, at this writing, there are no tolls or entrance fees. The Internet, in short, is the transport mechanism that makes it possible for people to "visit" a location and to ship information from one location to another.

The Internet itself has no more to do with what you encounter at a given location than the U.S. Interstate Highway Commission has to do with how hot the chili is at some roadside diner off I-95.

⇨ The relevant players

For the purposes of this book, we're going to sweep the first two categories—Information- and Communications-only systems—from the board. They have no role to play in marketing goods and services to consumers. That leaves the Big Five, BBSs, and the Internet, each of which can be important in an online marketing strategy. Indeed, one could easily write an entire book about how each of these types of systems could be used to sell online.

For reasons that will become obvious, however, we feel that the Internet is the place to start any marketing effort. But you really do need to have some idea of what consumer online systems and BBSs are all about, if for no other reason than that most of their subscribers can reach *you* via the Internet! And vice versa, of course.

Thus, we will devote the remainder of this chapter to the Big Five consumer online systems and BBSs, and spend the next chapter on the Internet. Though not the main focus of this book, all of these systems can be considered tools for selling, marketing, customer service, and building good will.

⇨ The Big Five consumer online systems

Once again, here are the top five consumer-oriented online systems: America Online, CompuServe, Delphi, GEnie, and Prodigy. America Online is the only independently owned and operated system. It is the only online system you can buy stock in directly, which is why it gets a lot of ink on the nation's business pages. CompuServe is owned by H&R Block. Delphi is owned by Rupert Murdoch's News Corporation, the same company that owns the Fox television network and many

other properties. GEnie is short for General Electric Network for Information Exchange. Prodigy is owned by Sears and IBM.

⇨ What do these systems offer?

The Big Five consumer online systems are a lot like the leading television and cable networks in what they offer. They've all got news, weather, and sports, plus an online encyclopedia to help kids with homework. They offer online games of varying quality, plus shopping services of one sort or another. On every system, users will find shareware software to download, graphic image files, and real-time "chat" (like CB radio from a keyboard).

They will also find hundreds or even thousands of *special interest groups* (SIGs) or clubs devoted to topics like organic gardening, wine tasting, or IBM's OS/2 software. There's no charge for joining such SIGs. And all of them offer message boards where members can discuss topics of interest; file libraries from which members can download text, graphic, and program files related to the SIG's focus; and a conferencing area where members and special guests can "chat" in real time.

✳ E-mail via the Internet

All of the Big Five offer electronic mail as well, including the ability to send and receive messages via the Internet. That means two things. First, it means that any subscriber to one system can send mail to any subscriber of any other system using the Internet as the "common carrier."

Second, it means that if you and your business have a location anywhere on the Internet—which is to say, if you have an Internet e-mail address—all seven million subscribers to the Big Five can communicate with you and vice versa. It's as simple as sending any kind of e-mail.

Unfortunately, like Dorothy in *The Wizard of Oz*, many of these folks may not know that plugging into this power is as easy as clicking together the heels of their ruby slippers. So you may have to educate them. You may have to include specific instructions for

sending mail to your address in your print ads. But that's not too difficult. (There is also the slight problem that CompuServe charges its users 15 cents for each message received via the Internet, although that policy may change under user pressure.)

 # CompuServe

The oldest of the Big Five systems is the CompuServe Information Service (CIS). The company that gave it birth was started in 1972, a time when mainframes ruled the world. That company's purpose was to offer remote data processing services to banks and other firms that could not afford to buy their own in-house computers. The trouble was that activity dropped off sharply at the end of every business day, leaving the CompuServe mainframes sitting there gobbling up electricity with no work to do.

So someone came up with the idea of letting consumers who owned what passed for personal computers in those days have access during the evening hours and on weekends. The speed was 300 baud, and acoustic couplers were the rule. Downloaded data was recorded on an ordinary cassette tape recorder. And at $5 an hour, it was sheer heaven.

Undoubtedly because of its computer hobbyist origins, CompuServe offers the most and the best information on hardware and software items. Indeed, hundreds of computer-related companies have opened special areas on the system that are used for customer support. If you need the latest software drivers or program patches, you can usually get them by going to the area operated by the software house or manufacturer and downloading the files directly into your own computer.

CompuServe has many other wonderful features as well. But, from the standpoint of online marketing, you should check out the company's Electronic Mall. Like everything else on CompuServe, it is text-based. No image or pictures magically appear on your screen.

CompuServe compensates for this in at least two ways. First, the glossy, four-color magazine it sends each month to subscribers always

contains a special section devoted to Electronic Mall merchandise. Second, in 1994 the company began offering the CompuServeCD, a CD-ROM-based "multimedia extension" of the service. This allows CompuServe to bypass the bottleneck of the phone line and deliver images of products and features, as well as sound clips and musical clips from forthcoming records.

The cost is $7.95 per issue and at this writing, the CompuServeCD is published every other month. Often it comes with a coupon good for $5 of online time, making the actual cost $2.95.

The company has also tried to compensate for the fact that it is a text-based service by offering software packages like WinCIM and the CompuServe Navigator, which present a Windows- or Mac-like front-end with buttons, icons, and bars. Unfortunately, it is impossible to disguise the fact that what is pouring in over the phone line is plain text—the same text that someone using a regular communications program would see. (See Fig. 3-1 for a look at CompuServe's main menu.)

Figure 3-1

```
CompuServe Information Service
15:49 EST Friday 25-Nov-94 P
Last access: 15:18 24-Nov-94

      Copyright (c) 1994
    CompuServe Incorporated
       All Rights Reserved

CompuServe    TOP

    1 Access Basic Services
    2 Member Assistance (FREE)
    3 Communications/Bulletin Bds.
    4 News/Weather/Sports
    5 Travel
    6 The Electronic MALL/Shopping
    7 Money Matters/Markets
    8 Entertainment/Games
    9 Hobbies/Lifestyles/Education
   10 Reference
   11 Computers/Technology
   12 Business/Other Interests

  Enter choice!
```

CompuServe's main menu.

It's not at all clear that this much matters. After all, Microsoft Windows isn't any easier to use than DOS—it just looks better. The same thing applies to truly graphical systems like Prodigy and America Online. Ultimately, people usually like what they get used to. So if the icons and buttons of a CompuServe front-end program persuade people to learn to use the software, it doesn't really matter that they do a relatively poor job of masking the text-based nature of the system.

CompuServe is based in Dublin, Ohio, a suburb of Columbus. For more information, call CompuServe at 800-848-8199.

GEnie

GEnie was created for the same reasons that gave birth to CompuServe. In the evening hours, the world-spanning network operated by General Electric Information Systems (GEIS) had clock cycles to burn. So they hired Bill Louden, one of CompuServe's original employees, and gave him the freedom to go CompuServe one better. Which he quickly did.

GEnie offers all the basic features you will find on CompuServe, but in less depth. Although, as you can see from Fig. 3-2, GEnie is text-based, it has carved a special niche for itself as the premier system for online games. Bill Louden, who is no longer with the company, once explained this fact to us quite simply: "I know what makes money."

Figure 3-2

```
GEnie                          TOP                    Page    1
                        GE Information Services

        1.   About GEnie              2.   New Members' Information
        3.   Hot & Happening Events On GEnie   4.   Communications (GE Mail & Chat)
        5.   Computing Services       6.   Travel Services
        7.   Finance & Investing Services   8.   Online Shopping Services
        9.   News, Sports & Features   10.  GEnie Games
       11.   Career/Professional Services   12.  Business Services
       13.   Leisure Pursuits & Hobbies   14.  Education Services
       15.   Entertainment Services   16.  Symposiums on Global Issues
       17.   Research & Reference Services   18.  Leave GEnie (Logoff)

       Enter #, <H>elp?
```

GEnie's main menu.

People do indeed spend hours at a time playing Air Warrior, Orb Wars, CyberStrike, and a host of conventional card games. In every case, subscribers must download a special program to play these graphical games. The program, as you may have guessed, contains the graphic images and instructions needed to paint the screen. It's pre-positioning again.

Interestingly, Rupert Murdoch's News Corporation has purchased Kesmai, the company responsible for Air Warrior, GEnie's most popular game. So Air Warrior is now available on Delphi, which was also recently acquired by the News Corporation. And in what can only be called a truly cool move, Delphi has set things up so that GEnie Air Warrior enthusiasts can play Delphi users in real time, while each is online with his or her respective system!

The bad news about GEnie is that it has been a victim of corporate neglect. As far as we can tell, the parent company has put nothing new into it in years. With the 1994 hiring of Mark Walsh, a dynamic new president for GEnie, all this promises to change. Hopefully the neglect hasn't done irreparable damage, but frankly, we have our doubts.

GEnie is based in Rockville, Maryland, a suburb of Washington, D.C. For more information, contact GEnie at 800-638-9636.

Delphi

Delphi was created in 1983 because Wes Kussmaul had made a small killing in the stock market. Mr. Kussmaul and his associates never let business concerns block their elemental creativity. As a result, Delphi has always been a delight because you never know what new feature or innovation you will find when you sign on.

It is also the system with what is arguably the worst text-based interface in the business. (See Fig. 3-3.) Its mail system is archaic and difficult to use, and the rest of the software that runs the system, while fine in its day, has really begun to show its age.

Yet Delphi has something that—even today—none of the other Big Five systems yet offers, namely *full* Internet access.

Figure 3-3

```
Welcome to DELPHI
Copyright (c) 1994
Delphi Internet Services

Logon at   : 25-NOV-1994 16:08:15
Last Logon : 25-NOV-1994 15:53:45

MAIN Menu:

Business and Finance      Member Directory
Computing Groups          News, Weather, and Sports
Conference                Reference and Education
Custom Forums             Shopping
ELECTROPOLIS (Games)      Travel and Leisure
Entertainment             Using DELPHI
Groups and Clubs          Workspace
Internet Services         HELP
Mail                      EXIT

MAIN>What do you want to do?
```

Delphi's main menu.

All five now offer e-mail access to the Net. In late 1994, CompuServe and Prodigy added newsgroups as well. America Online has long offered access to Internet newsgroups, but not to *all* such groups. (Although subscribers are never informed of the fact, the many newsgroups with sexual content are not available on this family-oriented service.) AOL also has a Gopher, and in late 1994 they gave subscribers the ability to transfer files (FTP) from Internet sites.

If we haven't lost most of you by now, we'd be greatly surprised. Rest assured that you will become well-acquainted with each of these Internet features by the time you finish this book. The point is that, despite its lousy look and feel, Delphi stands out because it's the only one to offer full Internet access.

Certainly this will change. But it is just as certain that the other members of the Big Five could offer full access to their subscribers tomorrow if they really wanted to do so. There are no huge hardware or software problems to be solved. Clearly, the go-slow approach is a deliberate attempt to stave off the Internet for as long as possible. Yet, truth be told, no one really knows whether offering full access will actually hurt a system's business. It might just help.

Clearly that's what Delphi concluded. Thus, at a time when all the other Big Five systems were deliberately dragging their feet, Delphi began offering its subscribers access to every major Internet feature, including the World Wide Web in nongraphical form. Australian press baron Rupert Murdoch looked down and saw that this was good, so in September 1993, he bought the company. He renamed it Delphi Internet Services. And shortly thereafter, the now ubiquitous ads offering five free hours on the Net via Delphi began to appear in magazines and newspapers everywhere.

For the time being, Delphi has clearly tied its future to the Internet. But it has many other interesting features, including one that lets subscribers create their own special interest groups (SIGs) for a small fee. The SIGs can be devoted to any topic a subscriber finds of interest, and, should it attract enough traffic from other Delphi subscribers, the company will actually pay the SIG's creator a royalty.

What we find most exciting of all, however, is the Rupert Murdoch connection. Newspapers, magazines, the Fox Television Network, the Internet, and multiplayer, multimedia-style online games like Air Warrior—combined with Delphi and the financial wherewithal of the parent company—could add up to a truly awesome service some day.

Delphi is based in Cambridge, Massachusetts. For more information, contact the company at 800-695-4005.

Prodigy & America Online

As you know from our previous discussions, Prodigy and America Online are *graphical* services. The only way to gain access is to use their special software, which they give away freely. These are the systems that pre-position instructions for drawing graphical shapes on their subscribers' disks, which virtually eliminates any delays in painting screens.

Prodigy uses a system called the North American Presentation-Level Protocol Syntax (NAPLPS, pronounced "nap-lips") to transmit and display its text and graphics. NAPLPS was hot a decade ago, and Prodigy has done a nice job with it, but as you see in Fig. 3-4, the

Figure 3-4

Prodigy's NAPLPS graphics in action.

size and resolution of its graphics and type make it resemble an old Color Graphics Adapter (CGA) screen.

AOL, on the other hand, offers the higher resolution and more colorful graphics made possible by the Video Graphic Array (VGA) equipment that is now standard among PC users. (See Fig. 3-5.) AOL *looks* like Windows or the Apple Macintosh. Which, of course, is no accident.

✳ Similar systems, different approaches

Both systems have something to offer. Both have interesting, unique features. The National Geographic feature on Prodigy, for example, and the Smithsonian Museum feature on AOL are simply outstanding. And, it is probably fair to say, both are after essentially the same audience—the upscale, college-educated person with one or more

Figure 3-5

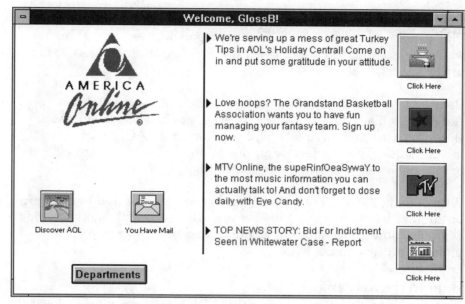

America Online's greeting screen.

kids who owns and uses a home computer but doesn't really know much about it.

Neither offers the breadth and depth of information you will find on CompuServe. For its part, Prodigy has assigned the responsibility for maintaining and offering a collection of downloadable images and shareware software to ZiffNet. And, of course, the Prodigy model is television—offering features that will get people to voluntarily look at your screens, and then make sure that a portion of each of those screens is devoted to advertising some product or service.

No one would argue about the fact that magazine and newspaper publishers, radio and TV network executives, and the executives at Prodigy concentrate primarily on the advertising they publish. Sure, everyone will protest that it's the *content* they are most interested in, but we all know that isn't true. Without advertising, the entire enterprise collapses. So, necessarily, the main role of the content is to set up the audience for the advertisers.

❋ And success & profits?

This is neither bad nor good. From our perspective, all that matters is what works. And, to date at least, the Prodigy approach has yet to prove itself.

Believe it or not, the same can be said about America Online. Advertising plays almost no role on AOL at all. The system has a shopping area and an area where you can order AOL-brand merchandise. The product descriptions and order forms are all text-based, however, just as they are on Prodigy.

When you boil it all down, the shopping services offered in one form or another by each of the Big Five are *all* text-based. And knowing what you now know about how long it takes to transmit a photograph, you know why.

❋ Behind the screens at AOL

The reason we question whether the AOL model has worked has to do with capacity and accounting. Capacity problems can be solved by adding more computers, modems, and phone lines. AOL has done so repeatedly while experiencing a growth rate that took it from 300,000 subscribers in July 1993 to over one million a year later.

Understandably, there was no way to make sure that capacity always matched demand. Consequently, during 1994, there were times when it was impossible to log on to AOL because all its available slots were in use. In the industry, the joke became that AOL stood for "Almost Online."

So far, our experience has been that AOL has been able to solve such problems within about two weeks in each instance. But there's no way of telling whether this will be a pattern for the future.

The second niggling doubt about AOL has to do with its accounting methods. As *Forbes* reported in an October 24, 1994 story called "What profits?":

> In its published financial reports, America Online is solidly profitable. But look closer and the picture is less rosy.

America Online's biggest expenditure is the cost of attracting subscribers . . . America Online sends out millions of pieces of mail solicitations and works deals with computer manufacturers to give away a free trial subscription with *every* computer sold . . . For fiscal 1994, subscriber acquisition costs amounted to $37 million—over $40 per new subscriber. With subscribers paying an average $15.50 a month . . . it costs about three months in revenue to buy a new subscriber.

Basic accounting question: Is that $37 million subscriber acquisition figure an expense against income? Or is it an investment undertaken to create an asset?

AOL chose to capitalize all of those costs for fiscal 1994 and amortize them over 18 months. But as the *Forbes* article points out, "Had the $37 million been expensed as incurred, America Online would have lost around $6 million after taxes. But by capitalizing and amortizing, the company was able to report net income of $6.2 million, or 76 cents per share."

The article concludes by suggesting that the "asset" of a subscriber base AOL has created could quickly desert it, once new systems from Apple, Microsoft, and others come up to speed.

✳ We've got faith in Steve!

We don't know what to think. All we can suggest is that, when you combine this fact with the games all the online systems play with their subscribership numbers and with the controversy over whether the Internet has anything even close to the supposed 30 million users claimed for it, it's probably wise to be skeptical of all statistics in this area.

In our opinion, America Online really is the wave of the future. It's smart, it's good-looking, and, thanks to the personal involvement of its president, Steve Case, it seems possessed of a vision of where it wants to go. Frequently AOL users will see a button labelled "Letter from Steve" on their greeting screens. Such letters take the form of a scout leader addressing the assembled campers and explaining what's going on at AOL, where the system is headed, and what to look for in the future.

This is the kind of thing the other systems do with a press release mailed out to magazine and book writers. But Mr. Case addresses his troops directly and thus brings them into AOL's electronic family. Though we've never met, spoken, or corresponded with Mr. Case, we have the greatest confidence in AOL's future as long as he (or someone like him) remains in charge.

A quick cost comparison of the Big Five

	Monthly Fee	Includes
America Online	$9.95	5 hours free, round the clock; $2.95 for each additional hour.
CompuServe	$8.95	Unlimited basic services round the clock; about 60 e-mail messages; $9.60 for each additional hour.
Delphi	$10.00	10/4 Plan: 4 hours free; $4.00 for each additional hour. Surcharge of $9.00 per hour for access via Tymnet or SprintNet during weekday business hours.
	$20.00	20/20 Plan: 20 hours free; $1.80 for each additional hour. Surcharge of $9.00 per hour for access via Tymnet or SprintNet during weekday business hours. (A one-time fee of $19.00 applies to this plan.)
	$3.00	Full Internet access for $3.00 more per month with either of the above plans.
GEnie	$8.95	4 hours free; $3.00 each additional hour. Surcharge of $9.50 per hour for prime-time access. Surcharge of $6.00 per hour for 9600-bps access.
Prodigy	$9.95	Basic Plan: 5 hours free; $2.95 per hour for each additional hour.

Bulletin Board Systems

At its most basic level, a Bulletin Board System (BBS) is nothing more than a phone line, a modem, and a computer running BBS software that lets it automatically accept incoming phone calls, prompting the caller for name and password. In fact, many communications software programs these days include a *host mode* feature that lets you set your own system to automatically answer the phone.

Turn your computer and modem on, load your comm software, activate host mode, then take off for the weekend. Regardless of where you are, if you've got access to another computer and a modem, you can call up your desktop machine at the office and run it as if you were sitting right at its keyboard.

Naturally, no one who runs a BBS is going to give that kind of access to the public at large. That's why callers are prompted for their names and passwords. Or, if they are first-time callers, they are taken through a registration process, during which they can specify the password they want to use. Many boards charge subscription fees to callers who want full access.

Sometimes these fees are set merely to help the board's sysop cover expenses. But a growing number of boards are profit-making enterprises, charging as much as $75 a year for perhaps 10 hours of access per week. Any number of these enterprises have purchased small satellite dishes to enable them to receive things like the text from all Internet newsgroups, news, weather, and sports, plus the feed from *USA Today*.

In any case, whether the board is commercial or totally free, once callers are admitted to the system, there is no telling what they will find. The one thing we can say for certain is that the types and general design of the features will be very similar to what the Big Five systems offer.

 # Who knew?

And that is very much our point. You can be on a BBS and truly not be able to tell whether you're logged onto a multimillion-dollar system like CompuServe—or some guy's Macintosh or IBM-compatible computer. In fact, if you limit yourself to text, what you see on the BBS is likely to be much more pleasing than the screens offered by CompuServe, Delphi, and GEnie. That's because BBSs often highlight words or instructions in different colors and make frequent use of block graphics.

And, speaking of graphics, take a look at Fig. 3-6. These graphics appeared instantly on our screen, thanks to the Remote Imaging Protocol (RIP) created by TeleGrafix Communications, Inc. RIP graphics were introduced for DOS/Windows and Macintoshes in 1993, and more and more communications programs and BBSs are offering them. The point being that "working the boards"—as using BBSs is called—doesn't mean giving up pleasing visual screens.

Figure 3-6

RIP Graphics can make BBSs look like America Online!

According to our friend Jack Rickard, editor and publisher of *BoardWatch Magazine*, there are approximately 60,000 BBSs in North America alone. They offer a wide range of features, starting with electronic mail. Though its articles seem to go on forever, *BoardWatch* is the single most important publication to have if you are interested in this field. For more information, call 800-933-6038.

 BBS-based "networks"

The least sophisticated boards let you exchange mail only among other users of the board. You sign on on Tuesday and leave a private message for John. John signs on over the weekend, picks up your message and sends you a reply. Simple. But many boards are part of one or more special networks that have been created for the transfer of mail.

The most famous such network is FidoNet, a system that makes it possible for you to call your local FidoNet board in, say, Miami, and send a message to someone living in Portland, Oregon. You make a local call to your board and your friend makes a local call to her board. Both of you send and receive messages as if you lived only a few blocks apart. The magic occurs late at night—as all the best magic does—when all the BBSs on the FidoNet system stop taking callers and instead call each other to exchange messages. This is called *mail time*, and it lasts for about an hour.

Created by Tom Jennings, FidoNet is a technological wonder. But that's not why we bring it up. The fact is, many FidoNet "node" BBSs are connected to the Internet. So you could send an e-mail message to anyone whose FidoNet address you know, using your preferred Internet e-mail connection.

No one's saying it's necessarily simple or easy. But there can be no denying that there are one heck of a lot of links *from* anywhere *to* anywhere. That's why it doesn't take long to spread the word about almost anything—whether it concerns some wonderful special deal you're offering or some problem with your product.

 # Other BBS features

Most BBSs also offer *conferences* of some sort, which are very much like the SIGs, clubs, and roundtables found on commercial systems in that they make it easy for people to ask questions and discuss specific topics of interest to them. BBSs also usually have large file libraries packed with public domain and shareware software. Sometimes these libraries actually exist on CD-ROM, instead of on the board's hard disk drive.

It's not unusual for a multiline BBS to offer real-time CB-radio-like chat among users. Often there are games to be played once you pass through the "door" leading from the BBS software to some other location on the host system. Some BBS sysops also sell products of one sort or another. Many offer real-time interactive games. And many are devoted to some particular interest, whether it is saving the whales or the glories of eating red meat.

 # Corporate applications

More to the point for our purposes here, any number of companies have set up their own bulletin board systems to make it easy to support and interact with their customers. Naturally, they tend to be computer-related companies.

Recently, for example, we needed a printer driver (a small but essential piece of software) to make XyWrite work with our H-P LaserJet printer. We called the company, and its voice-mail system notified us that there was a XyWrite BBS we could call. We did so and had the needed file located and downloaded in about three minutes. In another five minutes, it had been installed and tested, and we were on our way.

Yes, this required a level of knowledge most of your customers do not have. But that doesn't mean you can't use the same technique. All it means is that you or someone you trust is going to have to design everything for the lowest common denominator. That means including step-by-step instructions for accessing the BBS in your voice-mail

message. (You can't just provide your BBS phone number and expect your customers to know what to do.)

It means very carefully designing the system that they will see when they do call. And it certainly means making sure that whomever you hire to prepare this system anticipates the questions and needs of your typical customer.

⇨ The most crucial point

All of which leads to what is probably the most crucial concept in this entire chapter:

> If you want it to work, you've got to make the commitment!

You've heard that before, and you're going to hear it again in one form or another as we go through the next several chapters. That's because commitment is fundamental.

It doesn't matter whether you are opening a store on one of the electronic shopping malls offered by many of the Big Five systems, or setting up your own customer-support BBS, or establishing a presence of some sort on the Internet. If you are not willing to allocate sufficient time and money to the project and to put some single individual in charge, then you might as well not be involved at all.

On the other hand, if you really are willing to make that commitment—and let's face it, we're not talking about a huge amount of money here—then you will be amazed at what can be done and how little it will cost.

Without being slaves to chronology, we can say that you now have a pretty good idea of the layout of the electronic universe _before_ the Internet became available to ordinary human beings and before very many of those human beings became aware of the fact. In the next chapter, we'll introduce the Internet and its major features, and help you understand how it fits into the electronic universe.

4

Enter the Internet

All the basic features

WHEN thinking about the Internet—where it came from and what it is today—it is impossible to avoid the hothouse metaphor. This notion is important for all kinds of reasons, as you will soon see. But basically, for more than a decade the commercial systems like those discussed in the previous chapter, plus the nation's BBSs, developed in the national marketplace.

Unbeknownst to most of their subscribers, however, another system, funded by the U.S. government, was developing and growing behind closed doors. If you happened to be a defense contractor, a military officer, or a computer-wise university student or professor, you were well aware of this network. But if you did not fall into one of those categories, you probably never heard of it. And even if you did know about it, you couldn't get access unless you belonged to one of those groups.

⇨ The year everything changed

Then, in 1991, everything changed. The U.S. government effectively broke down the wall that separated this system from the rest of the world and more or less let everybody in. Those of us who had heard about the system were amazed at what we saw. Everyone else was either confused, or dumbfounded, or making plans to get onto the system as soon as possible.

The system we're talking about, of course, is what we now call the Internet. Discovering it was like discovering some long lost civilization that had been growing and developing on its own on the moon or in some other isolated area.

⇨ Perfect timing!

The Internet seemed to come out of nowhere, and its advent instantly redrew the boundaries of the electronic universe. In retrospect, public access became available at just the right time. If the same thing had happened two years earlier, it is doubtful that it would have made such a splash.

As it was, by 1991, the prices of the modems and computers needed to get onto the Net had fallen dramatically (as they continue to fall). There was an audience of tens of millions who had been developing their computer skills over the last decade or so. Prodigy and CompuServe were advertising on television, raising the general awareness of the online world.

Most powerful of all, perhaps, was the Information Superhighway metaphor that caught the nation's fancy. In the "giving credit where it's due" department, Vice President Al Gore had been working for this concept for many years in the senate. Although no one really knows what this Information Superhighway will consist of, the globe-girdling Internet is clearly the closest thing to it now in existence.

⇨ They gotta have a deal

Actually, we may be overestimating the influence of that metaphor here. Our recollection is that what motivated most new Net users was that it was *free*. Indeed, we should warn you that, despite their terrific demographics, in our experience, many online users are extraordinarily cheap.

Like someone who races from one supermarket to another clutching coupons clipped from the Wednesday food section of the paper, many online users are only happy if they think they're getting a deal. Just as the coupon clipper doesn't count the time, effort, and gasoline required to pick up all those "bargains," many online users fail to factor in inconvenience, frustration, and time when calculating their savings.

There's no better example of this than the headlong rush of many of them to the "free" Internet. Men and women who only a few months ago would groan and moan about how difficult it was to use CompuServe, Delphi, or GEnie now demanded instant access to the Internet. No wonder many at the Big Five commercial services were worried.

⇨ Why the Big Five are worried

To these users it did not matter that the Internet is a kingdom built on the most obscure, bytehead, complex and confusing, UNIX-based commands you have ever seen. People who only yesterday could not be bothered to learn a few simple CompuServe commands—like keying in M for "take me back to the previous menu"—are eagerly diving into Internet features for which not only are the commands obscure, but they've got to be entered in the right case!

On the Internet, for example, keying in the command menu is not the same as keying in MENU or Menu. Case counts. And so do the myriad esoteric moves you must make to get a file transferred from an Internet site to your own computer.

This is very much the situation as it exists today. The Internet is not some freestanding entity. It is part of the whole matrix of the online industry that, as we will see repeatedly, has developed its own culture and ways of doing things. Many old Internet hands are not at all pleased to see the hordes of Delphi and America Online users invade "their" territory.

Offering full Internet access to the subscribers to the Big Five systems clearly has the potential to upset relationships they've been developing with information providers for a decade. After all, if subscribers are spending all their time using the Internet, they're not going to be spending time and money using the system's other features. Offering Internet access is also likely to add to their customer support costs as subscribers call the toll-free customer support numbers at CompuServe or GEnie for help in using Internet features.

Thus, it's reasonable to assume that many executives at many commercial systems secretly wish that the Internet would just go away. Or that the withdrawal of government funding, which is already taking place, would raise the cost of access. That would provide the commercial systems with some cover for charging a premium for Internet access.

Where did the Internet come from?

Though it may seem surprising, the system we know today as the Internet is a direct by-product of the Cold War. In the early 1960s some bright bulb in the United States Department of Defense realized that in the event of a thermonuclear holocaust, a single bomb or two could effectively eliminate any form of communication or "command and control" between the Pentagon and military installations around the world.

As it often did in those days, the government called in the Rand Corporation and hired its experts to think about the problem and present one or more solutions. In 1964, the results of their thinking became known. The Rand experts proposed a new concept in system structure. Instead of a hub-and-spoke system in which, if the hub—the Pentagon—is destroyed and the nodes at the tip of each spoke are cut off, they suggested a network without a hub or "boss." It would be composed of peer-to-peer interconnections that put no single system in charge.

If the old system was a *wheel* in which all communication from one spoke to another flowed through the central hub, the new system was a *sphere* in which the node on the end of every spoke was connected to every other node, plus the Pentagon center, through multiple links.

The invention of "networking"

You can destroy a wheel by bombing its hub. But how many bombs is it likely to take to sever every connection in a ball of fishnet? Practically speaking, it cannot be done. If Site A wants to relay a message to Site Z, and it finds that a dozen sites in between have been destroyed, it just keeps trying until it finds a site that is still active. The message is transmitted to, say, Site T, which keeps trying to find a path to the site that is nearest to Site Z, the ultimate destination.

This is pretty neat, but when you look a bit deeper, it's even neater still. For the reality is that the computer at Site A does not send the entire message to Site T. The first page of the message might go there, but the second page might go to Site D, which would be equally vigorous in finding the next step on the path toward Site Z.

The two pages might arrive at Site Z in reverse order, but the computer at Site Z will know how to reassemble them correctly.

Packet switching is the key

All of this sounds like a lot of work, and it is. But since everything takes place at computer speeds, the actual time required can be minimal. The concept that makes it all possible is *packet switching*.

Packet-switching technology was designed and developed in 1969 by Bolt, Beranek, and Newman (BBN) working under contract for the Defense Department's Advanced Research Projects Agency (ARPA). The network that was created was called the ARPANET. In 1973, the name became DARPANET, the initial *D* standing for *Defense*.

Packet switching is the same technology used by SprintNet, Tymnet, the CompuServe Network, and many other companies that offer access to the Big Five and nearly every other commercial online service—including privately owned bulletin board systems. Indeed, many of these public packet-switching networks were created by former BBN employees.

Packet number & address

The concept involves chopping any file or message into uniformly-sized packets, stamping each with an address and packet number, and firing it out into the network. (Nondata filler characters are added when necessary to round out the number of bytes in a packet, ensuring that each is identical in size.)

Once these packets are in the network, the route they take to reach their destination differs with network conditions that change each fraction of a second. If the source is Columbus, Ohio, and the destination is Los Angeles, Packet 1 might go down to St. Louis, up to Portland, Oregon, and then down to Los Angeles. Packet 2 might go to Miami, and then to Las Vegas, and then to L.A. All of the computer nodes on the network have been programmed to seek the best route for each packet at any given moment.

 # Consumer benefits

This is great from a national defense perspective because it makes it all but impossible to take out the entire network. But there are consumer benefits as well.

When you call someone on the phone, an actual circuit is set up between you. The circuit remains in existence for the duration of your call. But think of how many pauses there are in normal human conversation. During those pauses no data is exchanged, but the wires and equipment used to create that circuit are not available for anything else.

Packet switching, in contrast, sets up a "virtual circuit" that makes very efficient use of the phone lines. Theoretically, all the wires and all the equipment that make up the network are in use all the time. Sitting in front of your computer in L.A., you can't tell that no direct, physical connection exists between you and CompuServe's computers in Columbus, Ohio. The results and performance are the same as if you had indeed called CompuServe directly.

Thanks to packet switching, with the exception of most BBSs, users of most online systems can connect with a distant computer by making a *local* phone call to their nearest SprintNet, Tymnet, or other packet-switching node.

⇨ Content & features

In the commercial world, the protocol or set of rules and procedures adopted to make packet switching possible is called X.25 ("X-dot-twenty-five"). This is a universal standard, promulgated by an arm of the United Nations which, for reasons we need not worry with, labels all standards either X or V "dot something."

The protocol used by the Internet is called TCP/IP, short for Transmission Control Protocol/Internet Protocol. TCP defines the way in which packets are to be handled, while the IP portion does the same for the addressing of those packets. Anyone who plugs directly into the Internet today—as opposed to going through one of the Big Five systems or an Internet service provider, must use software that supports TCP/IP.

⇨ The end of the Cold War

We well remember having lunch with a communications consultant friend many years ago and hearing him say that a directive had gone out to all scientists using the ARPANET not to store their notes on the system. Apparently it was not at all uncommon for Soviet scientists to somehow gain access to the network and download copies of those notes.

Or maybe someone at the Pentagon was merely speculating that this could happen. We didn't pay all that much attention, for, while we knew about the ARPANET, we also knew that ordinary people couldn't gain access to it and, thus, this was but a fascinating footnote.

With the Cold War over and the Internet now open to the public, it does indeed seem possible that really good computer experts in other countries could find a way to tap private files stored on the Net. Perhaps someday someone will write a book about the Net during the Cold War that will be the equivalent of the books about the Ultra machine that gave the Allies access to all of the Third Reich's secret codes during World War II.

The Internet thus began as a high-speed rail line linking key sites at the Pentagon, defense contractors, and colleges and universities. But other networks were developing independently at the time. It wasn't too long before these other networks began seeking permission to connect themselves to the high-speed lines or "backbone" network of the ARPANET.

There's no need to rehearse every step of how the Internet grew. You should know, however, that the ARPANET was taken down in June 1990, but hardly anyone noticed because, by that time, most of its functions had been taken over by the National Science Foundation (NSF) and its network, NSFNET.

The key point is that, before it became available to ordinary citizens in 1991, the Internet had become a "network of networks" that spanned the globe. Colleges, universities, companies, and government agencies worldwide hooked up to the Net. The Internet had thus ceased to be a network dedicated to a particular purpose (defense).

 Five key Internet concepts

It had become, instead, the electronic equivalent of the U.S. interstate highway system. The Internet, in short, isn't an "end," it is merely a means to an end. Physically, it is just the *transport* mechanism that links tens of thousands of locations (computer sites or networks). That's Concept Number 1.

Concept Number 2 is the essential oneness of every location on the Net. Thanks to the speed of computer communications, the distance from any single point on the Net to any other is essentially the same, which is to say, zero. Geographical distances make no difference. From your computer on a farm in Idaho, you can pull in information from a computer located in Hong Kong one second and switch to a computer located in Paris the next—and never notice the difference!

Concept Number 3 is that no one controls the Net. It is true that until now the U.S. government has provided the bulk of the funding for

the backbone links. But the Net has taken on a life of its own. If the U.S. government were to completely withdraw its support tomorrow, the effect on the Net might be the equivalent of a series of nuclear blasts. But the Net would survive. After all, that's precisely what it was *designed* to do!

⇨ Community standards

Finally, while the Internet may be the modern equivalent of the Wild West, even in Tombstone Territory unwritten community standards controlled the way most folks behaved. People who violated those standards were shunned. The modern day equivalent on the Internet is for violators to be *flamed*. Which is to say, subjected to strong verbal criticism via e-mail and in public forums.

That's Concept Number 4, and it is the most important concept of all for would-be electronic marketers. There are innumerable doctoral theses waiting to be written on the phenomenon of the development of the Internet electronic community.

⇨ The evolution of the community

For example, someone comes up with an idea, with a way to push the envelope of the network structure. The next thing you know, *newsgroups* have been created. Newsgroups, as we will see, are essentially "piano rolls" of messages, one tacked on to the next, in which discussions can take place over time. Net users like the idea, so the number of newsgroups mushrooms. Of necessity, the community independently establishes a procedure for creating and approving newsgroups. And in typical Net fashion, the process is very democratic.

No government committee in Washington, D.C., sat down and deliberated over whether newsgroups should be created and how they should be implemented. The Net decided, debated, created, and implemented. And no one could stop them.

People from all over the world could register their opinions, make their arguments, and participate in the process. It didn't make any difference who you were.

⇨ When you're on the Internet, no one knows . . .

You may recall the now famous Steiner cartoon in the *New Yorker*. The one that showed a mutt sitting in front of a computer screen and, paws on the keyboard, saying to another dog nearby, "On the Internet, nobody knows you're a dog." Well, on the Internet, nobody knows your name, age, gender, or nationality. All they know is what you say, and if what you say makes sense, everyone will listen to you.

The ingrained prejudices and other baggage all of us bring to any human encounter no longer exist. The Internet, e-mail, and other forms of electronic speech are the closest thing this side of heaven we are likely to come to absolutely pure, soul-to-soul communication.

This process has taken place again and again on the Internet, and over time, as with any group of serious, hard-working human beings, standards of behavior have evolved. Unwritten agreements have developed on what is acceptable and what is not.

⇨ Respect the culture

It is completely irrelevant whether you personally agree with those standards or not. You violate them at your peril. The Internet is a community of users that has been developing for over two decades. It is true that most members of this community have benefited from free, taxpayer-subsidized access. So as a taxpayer you may feel that it's your network too. That may be technically true. But again, it is irrelevant.

The best way to approach the Net as a businessperson is with the same regard for culture that would inform your approach in a non-American country. In Japan, for example, it can be important to

know that white, not black, is the color of mourning. If you're invited to dinner at a business associate's home in Germany, it is a faux pas to bring flowers to his wife since it is considered a sign of romantic interest.

The list of tiny, but significant, differences goes on and on. Culminating, perhaps, in the colossal blunder made by a major American electronics firm that invested millions in Christmas promotions in a certain European country, all of which was designed to culminate on December 25.

Trouble was, no one bothered to check local customs. If they had, they would have discovered that in this particular culture it is St. Nicholas's feast day, December 6, on which children receive their Christmas presents. Needless to say, millions of dollars were lost as a result of this stupid blunder. And it all could have been a success had the marketers taken the time to investigate the local culture.

A place for everything, & everything in its place

We want to help you avoid similar blunders on the Internet. As you'll discover, the Internet is open to anything. But everything must generally be in its appropriate place. That's Concept Number 5. What upsets veteran Internet users is not that you have placed an ad or some really wild sexual fantasy on the Net.

There are places for all of these things. What bugs them is that you've placed your ad for business stationery, your accounting services, or your quickie incorporating service on a newsgroup designed to let small-business owners exchange tips and tricks. Your logic is, "Hey, a group that is read by precisely the people I want to reach! I'll just upload a few ads."

Their reaction is, "Get the hell out of here! You are welcome to place your ad in any number of business/advertising groups on the Net. But not here. We, the users of this newsgroup, do not want to discover

that every fourth message in the queue is some kind of advertisement. So get thee gone!"

The main Internet features

We could have relegated this cautionary advice to the back of this book and simply plunged ahead to present the Internet's main features. The reason we did not do so is the firm conviction that learning to use a system's features is not nearly as important as becoming aware of its culture.

For example, to many Americans—including at least one of your co-authors—the ultimate culinary experience is a thick, juicy, charcoal-broiled steak with a baked potato, sour cream, bacon bits, and chopped chives, washed down with a frosty mug—make that a pitcher—of beer.

But if you were to present this wonderful, fat-filled feast to someone in Southeast Asia, they would probably throw up. Just as you might balk at an Asian dish that featured meat from animals that, in America, are considered family pets.

So, as we take you through a survey of the main features of the Internet, remember the five concepts and remember that "culture counts."

What can you do on the Net?

Now, with all of that out of the way, let's look quickly at the main Internet functions. You should realize that there may be any number of other functions and features developed by people on the Net. After all, literally millions of people around the globe are thinking about ways to use the Net for one thing or another. And anyone can invent a feature.

But right now, users of the Internet, and those special people like university computer center managers, have generally agreed on the following eleven features:

➢ Electronic mail

➢ Newsgroups

➢ Mailing lists

➢ File transfers via FTP

➢ Archie

➢ Telnet

➢ Chat (IRC)

➢ Gopher

➢ Veronica

➢ WAIS

➢ World Wide Web (WWW)

We'll look at many of these features in detail in the chapters that follow. But, since it is important to get an overall sense of the Internet and what it offers, we will take just a moment to give you thumbnail sketches of each feature here. There are sales and marketing implications—both positive and negative—for each of them.

Just bear in mind that most of these features were designed, programmed, discussed, implemented, and ultimately adopted by the Internet community as a whole with no official input from government agencies. Nonetheless, they do tend to be designed around the lowest common denominator. Which is why, in their native state, most Internet features look like something from the early 1980s.

⇨ Internet e-mail

Everyone with an account on any system connected to the Internet automatically has an Internet e-mail address. Subscribers to

CompuServe, GEnie, MCI Mail, AOL, and many other systems can exchange mail with friends on different systems or on Internet-connected systems. All that is required is the correct Internet address, like **Alfred@Delphi.com**, our address on Delphi.

Unfortunately, Internet e-mail messages must be no longer than 64K and must consist of nothing but "standard" seven-bit ASCII text. No "extended characters." Eight-bit binary files, like graphic image files, can be sent. But they must be converted to 7-bit ASCII first and converted back to their binary form by the receiver. The software needed to do this is free, but you've got to know where to find it, how to get it, and how to use it.

 USENET newsgroups

Newsgroups (most people drop the "USENET") are essentially ongoing conferences devoted to a specific topic. They began as a way of discussing and conveying the latest news about the Internet. Hence, the name. But they have grown far beyond the focus of the Internet.

Today, there are over 10,000 newsgroups devoted to *every* topic you can imagine—and many that you would not want to imagine. There are no membership requirements for any group. Anyone who can read a newsgroup's message is free to add comments to a given *message thread* or list of messages and replies that constitute the discussion.

The main drawback is that at any given time, a newsgroup will be able to show you only a limited number of messages. Previous messages will have "scrolled off" the board, unless some user has taken the time to collect previous messages into an archive file somewhere.

Mailing lists

Mailing lists are similar to newsgroups, but they are far less interactive. The items uploaded to a list are more likely to be articles

and longer pieces rather than the short comments that typify newsgroups. Also, while one must key in a command or two to read the latest newsgroup messages, the material sent to mailing list members automatically arrives in their electronic mailboxes.

In most cases, getting your name added to a mailing list is as simple as sending an e-mail message to a given address.

 # Files via FTP

The uploading, downloading, and transfer of files is probably closer to the heart of the Internet than any other function. The files in question could be anything from a piece of music to a graphical image to the full text of a Supreme Court decision. The main Internet technique for locating and downloading files is called FTP, short for File Transfer Protocol.

Basically, you "FTP" to some system, use the DIR command to see what's there, and then use the GET command to tell that system to transfer the file to your computer or to your "workspace" if you are accessing the Internet via a system like Delphi. You then download the file from your workspace into your own system.

That's the "raw mode" way of doing things. Fortunately, software is becoming available to shield most users from this bytehead approach. The recently added FTP feature on America Online, for example, is simply terrific. It completely shields users from all of the bytehead nonsense they would otherwise have to tolerate.

 # Archie

Archie is the name of a file-finding system based on the word "archive." It works like this: Someone at the major FTP sites on the Internet periodically keys in DIR and captures the results in a file. Those results consist of nothing but the name of each file and its directory or *path* location on the system. There are no keywords or descriptive paragraphs for each file, only its name.

That list of files is then shipped off to the Net's *Archie servers*. These are computer sites that have agreed to offer the Archie program and to compile incoming file lists from remote systems.

When everything goes as planned, you, the consumer can connect with one of these Archie sites and search its database of filenames for the file you want. The program running at the Archie server will tell you the name of the file, the system or systems that have it, and the subdirectory you will need to go to to get it.

With that information, you can then use FTP to log onto a given system and get the file.

Nice in theory. And, surprisingly nice in practice. We have used Archie servers many times to good effect. But your search focus is still limited to the name of the file, the least informative element. And not all of the sites keep their Archie listings current.

 # Telnet

This function allows you to access certain areas of a remote computer system as if you were actually sitting at the keyboard of one of its consoles. Or, to put it another way, "telnetting" to a site is a lot like signing onto CompuServe or some other online system. Everything you see on your screen, everything you can do, is controlled by a program running on the host system you have dialed.

"Telnettable" systems include libraries, universities, government agencies, and private systems. In libraries you can call up the card files. In universities you can look into campus directories and library files, access databases, and see what's new on campus.

Internet Relay Chat (IRC)

This is the Internet version of the real-time chat features offered by each of the Big Five consumer online systems. Like those systems, it resembles text-based CB-radio conversations. And the content is equally vapid.

Maybe someone will indeed find a way. But, in general, it is difficult to see how to make a buck out of real-time online chat of any sort. Appearing as a guest in a special interest group somewhere online might be effective. But that's about it.

Consequently, we're not going to waste much time on IRC. But you should know that the same technology that makes IRC possible is used to play MUDs (Multi-User-Dungeons) and other home-grown fantasy games. The games are all text-based, of course.

Gopher

A *Gopher* in Internet-speak is a menu system. The two most important things to remember about Gophers are these: First, *every* Gopher is unique. The Gopher software arrives at a site as an empty shell, which the system administrator then fills in with appropriate menu items, submenu items, and so on.

Second, the Gopher menus can include just about any kind of Internet feature. That's because each item on the menu consists of a line of text describing what you'll get when you select that item, plus Internet commands needed to accomplish it. The commands are hidden from the user, of course, but they can relate to everything from FTP file transfers to Telnet sites to displaying a local text file.

If you're a bit confused at this point, don't worry. Gopher is probably the best feature on the Net, and we'll have a lot more to say about it later. For now, just remember that Gophers give users a way of using Internet features by picking items from a menu.

Veronica

Finding the information or feature you want on the Net is the fundamental challenge. We've seen how Archie helps you find the locations of a given file by letting you search the file directories of leading FTP sites. Well, Veronica does the same for the items on Internet Gopher menus.

Dedicated people at sites with Gopher menus all over the Net regularly send their menus to other sites that have agreed to run the Veronica software. The menus that get sent include everything—both the visible text and the hidden commands lying behind each menu item.

When someone logs onto a Veronica site and does a Veronica search, what gets searched is the database of Gopher menus. This database is what Net users call *Gopherspace*.

Using this database, Veronica then assembles a customized menu for you. If you have told Veronica to search on, say, "Supreme Court," every item on this customized menu will contain that search phrase. When you select any item on that menu, Veronica, like Gopher, will issue the hidden Internet command to take you to the described location or run the described program or whatever.

A program called Jughead (what else?) also exists. But Jughead is much more limited. Jughead is used to search the line items on a *single* Gopher menu system.

We know this sounds confusing. You'll feel a lot better about it later. For now, here is a word of advice: If you decide to rent space on a Gopher menu or set up a Gopher of your own, make sure that you mention your company name or product in the single line that describes your Gopher item. Don't just say, "Product description and price list." Say "XYZ Company product description and price list." That way, anyone doing a Veronica search can search on "XYZ Company" and find your item.

⇨ WAIS

Pronounced "ways," WAIS is an acronym for Wide Area Information Servers. It is yet another attempt to help people find what they want on the Net. Where Archie searches a database of filenames, and Veronica searches a database of Gopher menu items, WAIS lets you search the actual text of a document or group of documents. But it does so in a manner that *eliminates* the complex AND/OR/NOT Boolean logic and nested expressions used by people who search

databases for a living. Its goal is to turn every user into a "super searcher."

This is a nice idea that works quite well. It relies on a technique called *relevance feedback* that assumes several iterations will be needed before you find exactly what you want. You can ask for what you want using anything from "natural language" English to Boolean operators to dBASE-style data fields.

The system makes a first cut and shows you what it found. You look at the actual text and when you see a paragraph or article that's close, you, in effect, say, "Yes, you're getting there, bring me more stuff like this paragraph right here." Usually you don't have to do this more than two or three times before you find exactly what you're looking for—assuming it is part of the WAIS database.

The main drawback is that the feature can only be used at a WAIS site. Such sites contain documents that have been indexed using the WAIS software. Just as is the case on Dialog or Orbit or some other major commercial online information systems, it is these indexes that you actually search with WAIS.

The WAIS software and concept was created by Brewster Kahle when he worked for Thinking Machines in Cambridge, Massachusetts. In 1992, Mr. Kahle left Thinking Machines to form his own company, WAIS, Inc. The new company markets WAIS server software to any organization wishing to make its text resources available online and to do so in a way designed to let users search for just the information they want.

The main caveat when using WAIS is that both commercial and freeware versions exist. The freeware version was distributed starting in 1991 to help make people aware of the product. Unfortunately, it is so weak that it really creates a false impression of what the full-strength version of WAIS is all about.

For more information on WAIS, call 415-617-0444 or send an e-mail message to **Info@WAIS.com**. You can leave the subject line and the message blank, if you like. Or, if you have a specific question, feel

free to put it into your message. At this writing, responses are still being handled by a human being, not a mail server.

It is worth noting that, while WAIS has a head start, others are entering this area. Most notable so far is a company called InfoSeek. Contact them at **info@infoseek.com** or call 408-982-4463.

Also, watch for Navisoft, a company formed by David Cole, who ran Ashton-Tate back in the good old days. These and the other companies that are sure to appear may never become as well-known as WAIS—such is the power of getting there first—but they will certainly be competitive.

The World Wide Web (WWW)

Finally, there's the World Wide Web, often called just "the Web." From a business standpoint, this is the Internet feature that has gotten most of the attention among the laymen's media. Why? Because it's pretty. Web pages make good illustrations in magazine and newspaper articles.

And with the power that videotape has over time, they make for an exciting series of quick-cut images on the national news. Never mind the fact that the series of images the reporter shows you in 30 seconds actually took 30 minutes or more to appear on the computer's screen. Never mind that the reporter somehow fails to report this fact to the viewing audience.

The result is the distinct impression that the World Wide Web really works, which, as you're going to see yourself, it manifestly does *not*!

✳ Images & hypertext

The essence of the Web is images and hypertext. Like CompuServe, Delphi, and GEnie, the Internet is a text-based service. Of necessity, it is designed for the lowest common denominator—the plain 7-bit ASCII text that every make and model of computer can understand.

The Web is the only Internet feature that even remotely resembles America Online or Prodigy or Windows or the Macintosh. But it does

so not by pre-positioning images but by transmitting them in real time. Which takes forever at 28.8 kbps and below.

The hypertext features of the Web are far more important than images, however. Indeed, it is here that the Web really shines. (After all, you can use the Web in nongraphics, ASCII text mode, if you want to.)

Remember how the Gopher menu system lets people use an Internet feature by merely selecting an item on the menu? Remember how we have said that on the Internet the physical location of an item and the geographical distance that separates you from it do not matter? Well, the Web takes this to its highest level.

There is no menu system, there is just text filled with "hot-button" words. Imagine reading an article about the Boston Tea Party. You're reading along and come to a sentence that talks about Sam Adams and his role in this affair. But you notice that the name "Sam Adams" is highlighted, indicating that it is a hypertext *hot link*.

You decide you want to know more about Sam Adams, so you click on that hot link. The article on the Boston Tea Party disappears and is replaced by a biography of Samuel Adams. This article might be physically located halfway around the world from the article on the Boston Tea Party. But you neither know nor care. Whatever it is, it's all right *here*!

Certainly this article on Sam Adams will be filled with hot links, too. One of which might be "Thomas Jefferson." You click on that and get a biography of Jefferson, but you notice that "Barbary Pirates" is among the hot links, so you click on that, and in that article you find a reference to "Algiers," so you click on that, and so on and on until your curiosity is satisfied for the moment.

No wonder Mitch Kapor, founder of Lotus Development and chairman of the Electronic Frontier Foundation, has called this the Internet's "killer application." If you're an information junkie— indeed, if you have but an ounce of curiosity about anything—you could disappear in the Web for hours.

Unfortunately, the Web as it exists today is merely a preliminary sketch. The Boston Tea Party example presented here was invented on the spot. As far as we know, no such article and no such hypertext links actually exist.

We passionately hope that one day they will. And we hope that we live to see that day. But so many things have to be built or moved into place to make this dream possible that it would be unwise to hold your breath waiting for it.

We will give you much more information about the Web in later chapters. For now, however, you can rest assured that, despite the hype, there is no need for setting up a highly graphical Web home page. After all, as of the beginning of 1995, only about three percent of Internet users have the capability of viewing such pages.

Conclusion

At this point, you should have a pretty good idea of the boundaries of the online playing field and the nature of the terrain. You should also have a pretty good *general* idea of what the Internet is, where it came from, and how it fits into the current online picture.

You have also developed at least a nodding acquaintance with the Net's major features. The point we need to make in closing this chapter is that not all Internet features are suited for business applications. The main features of interest to anyone wishing to make money on the Internet are e-mail, newsgroups, mailing lists, Gopher, and the World Wide Web. Consequently, those are the features we'll focus on in Part II.

If you want to know more about the other Internet features cited here, among the many available books are two we've written: *Internet 101: a College Student's Guide* (published by McGraw-Hill, Inc.) and *Internet Slick Tricks* (published by Random House). For prices and ordering information, see Appendix B.

For now, there's just one more bit of business to attend to before launching into Part II, and that is the mundane but crucial step of getting you connected to the Net. That's precisely what we'll do in the next chapter.

5

How to get
"well connected"

AT this point, you have a pretty good idea of what the electronic universe is all about. Now you have two problems. The first is how to go online in general—how to set things up so you can dial up CompuServe, Prodigy, or your local BBS. The second is how to connect to the Internet. In this chapter we'll help you solve both problems.

What it takes to go online

If you've read the first four chapters, you already know a great deal about going online. You know about modems and bit-per-second rates, the ASCII code set, and lots of other things. Therefore, we won't have to spend much time on Problem 1—How to go online.

In addition to a phone line, you will need a modem and a communications software package. If you bought your personal computer relatively recently, it is entirely possible that it came with these two items as part of the deal.

If not, we recommend that you buy a 28.8 kbps external data/fax modem. The cost will be under $200 at this writing, and possibly even lower as you read this. You want a 28.8 because that's the fastest speed available, and the price difference between this and the next model down (14.4) is negligible.

The international designation for a 28.8 kbps modem is V.34, pronounced "vee dot thirty-four." The product literature will cite other "V" designations, which is fine. The key thing is to make sure that your unit supports V.34. Do not be lured into buying a "V.FAST" unit claiming 28.8 kbps. Such modems were manufactured before the V.34 standard became official in June 1994. As such, they represent the manufacturer's best guess on the final standard, and may not be 100 percent compatible with all other true V.34 modems.

And just why is that?

Data/fax—why not? The *data* form of online communications is what you're interested in. But these days, modem makers throw in the software and circuitry needed to send and receive faxes from your computer almost for free.

Once you've got a text or image file in your computer, you can send it to any fax machine in the world. And you can accept faxes from fax machines as well, recording the message on disk as a file and viewing and printing it after the transmission is over.

You want an *external* unit because it can be used with *any* computer system. With the right cable, you can use the same modem with a PC, a Mac, or a laptop computer of any type. External modems are also easy to control: If the thing starts acting up, just reach over and turn it off and then on again.

Finally, external modems have lights to show you what's happening. When you're running a communications program, for example, the SD (send data) light will flash each time you hit a key. That can be reassuring when you're trying to find the source of a problem, since it tells you whether or not your information is "getting out the door." If it is—if the light flashes—then the problem lies with the phone line, the packet-switching network, or the online system you've been connected to.

When to go internal

The alternative to an external modem is an *internal* unit, which is basically a modem on a circuit board. These boards fit into your Mac or PC just like any other add-on board, but, of course, they're system-specific. They are neat and clean and occupy zero desk space, but having tried both over the years, we still prefer external units.

Again, this is just our opinion. If you have a desktop system, the only good reason to buy an internal, card-mounted modem is if your computer is not equipped with the necessary high-speed UART chip.

Before the data bits whizzing around inside your machine can be sent to the modem, the parallel, eight-abreast formation they normally use must be changed. Eight-at-a-time parallel must be changed to one-bit-at-a-time serial.

The UART or Universal Asynchronous Receiver/Transmitter chip is what makes this conversion. The UART chip is the heart of any communications card or serial card or port. Trouble is, the old 8550-model UART chips can't work any faster than 9600 bits per second. If you want to plug in a 28.8 external modem, you will need a comm port equipped with a 16550A UART or a 16C550 UART, both of which can operate at a top speed of 115,200 bits per second.

If you're in doubt about what you've got, ask your favorite computer guru. Or run the program UARTID.EXE, available on the Glossbrenner's Choice disk called Utilities 9, System Configuration Tools. (See The Glossbrenner's Choice appendix for information on ordering this disk.) The program will check your serial communications ports and tell you what it finds.

If it finds a 16550A UART chip, then you can indeed operate at 14.4 or 28.8 with the appropriate external modem. If it doesn't, then you will have to either replace the serial port connection—at a cost of about $25—or go with an internal modem, which has the necessary high-speed UART built in.

PCMCIA for notebooks & laptops

Most notebook and other portable computers come with a serial port, so you can plug in a conventional external modem if you want to. You would not want to lug such a unit around, however. Alternatively, you might be able to equip your notebook with an internal modem. No muss, no fuss. Just plug in the phone line whenever you want to communicate. It's neat, but then you are always carrying your modem with you as part of your computer.

The PCMCIA modem-on-a-card solution solves both problems. (The acronym stands for Personal Computer Memory Card International Association.) It's light, self-contained, and detachable. You don't have

to take the modem with you unless you want to. And if you do want to, it can be carried someplace else. All of that is to the good.

The downside is the expense: PCMCIA modems tend to cost more than comparable external or internal models. And there's the convenience factor. An internal modem may add a bit of weight to your system, but it eliminates the need to think ahead. Who knows where you'll be before day's end or how many times you will want to be able to go online? If you've got an internal modem, you may not even have to worry about bringing along a phone cord, since you can simply unplug a telephone and plug in your computer at many locations.

Two other considerations. First, you may have to pay a bit more for a notebook equipped with a PCMCIA socket. Second, battery life. Internal modems and PCMCIA modems alike draw the power they need from your computer. If the computer is plugged into an electrical outlet, no problem. Otherwise, they will both drain your battery.

Buying the "old-fashioned" way

Here's an example of the state of the art in non-Internet selling. After using a 9600 modem on one system and a 14.4 modem on the other, we decided we had better see if things like World Wide Web pages appeared markedly faster at 28.8. So we called PC Connection in Marlow, New Hampshire, at 800-243-8088 and ordered a Zoom modem. From past experience, we know both companies to offer superb products and service. The total cost, including shipping, was $185.

The call was placed shortly after midnight, and the modem was delivered to our home office in Yardley, Pennsylvania, just 10 hours later from the PC Connection warehouse in Wilmington, Ohio, courtesy of Airborne Express. The $5 shipping charge would have been the same, regardless of the number of items in the order, all of which would have been delivered with the same incredible speed.

If this weren't a book about electronic sales and marketing, we would not have gone into such detail here. As it is, you've got to ask yourself how an online Internet presence can possibly add anything to a performance like that!

 # What you need to know about any comm program

The commands, keystrokes, and mouse clicks differ. But the communications or *comm* programs for *every* computer offer the same essential functions. At the most basic level, a comm program opens a channel between your keyboard and your modem, allowing you to "talk" to the modem directly when you are in *terminal mode*. Once you are in terminal mode, you can key in AT or at, and the modem should respond by displaying "Okay" or "OK" on your screen. (The AT command essentially says "Attention, modem.")

If you have a modem connected to your machine and you do the AT bit and get no response, check each of the following, if applicable:

➤ Your cable connections. Everything plugged in firm and secure?

➤ Your power connections, if you're using an external modem.

➤ The COM port address. DOS/Windows machines can support four or more communications ports—typically COM1 through COM4. If your modem does not appear to work, make sure that your communications software is set to "talk" to the port the modem is connected to.

If you are a new user, set your comm software to talk to COM1 through COM4 in turn. After changing each setting, get into terminal mode and key in AT. If you get no response, tell the comm software to address the next higher COM port. If you try all four and still have no "Okay," call in a computer guru.

Or, if you are not a comm novice, check the modem or software manual for references to "jumpers" or DIP (dual-inline-package) switches. The key point is that the port your comm software addresses must be the same port to which your modem is attached.

 # The tools you've got to work with

The most crucial point when communicating with any remote system is that your settings match the settings of that remote system. You don't need to know what the settings mean. All you need to remember is that there are just two general settings: 7/E/1 and 8/N/1. Translated, that means "7 data bits, Even parity, and 1 stop bit" and "8 data bits, No parity, and 1 stop bit."

Your best bet is to start with 7/E/1. If it does not work, try 8/N/1. The Help file or printed manuals that came with your software will tell you how to control these settings.

Now let's take a moment to introduce you to the most important features offered by any comm program.

✳ Capture buffer

In computer talk, a *buffer* is simply an area of memory set aside to serve as a temporary holding tank. When the tank fills up with incoming text, the software dumps it to disk, using a filename you have previously specified. If you don't open your capture buffer or otherwise tell your comm program to "log to disk," all incoming text will simply scroll off the screen, never to be seen again.

Generally, it's a good idea to open a capture buffer each time you go online with any system. That way you won't have to worry about whether you've captured something or not. When you sign off, if there is nothing you want to look at again, simply delete the capture file.

✳ Dialing directory or phone book

Most comm programs let you record frequently dialed numbers in a phone book or dialing directory. That means you can key in something like Alt-D and be presented with a list of numbers. Pick a menu item off the list and the program will automatically dial the number. (You key in a single menu item number, and the software does the rest.)

✳ Scripts

Many comm programs today let you prepare *scripts* that tell them to dial a number, wait for a particular response, and, only when they see such a response, issue some command. With the right comm program and the right script, you could issue a single keyboard command and have the software dial up an online system, download any mail messages in your mailbox, and sign off. And you could arrange to have this done at any hour of the day or night—automatically.

✳ Upload/download protocols

A *protocol* is nothing more than an agreement between two machines on how they will handle the delicate task of transferring an error-free copy of a file from one system to another. A number of protocols—often called *error-checking protocols*—exist. Among them, XMODEM is the lowest common denominator, while ZMODEM is unquestionably the best. In between are Kermit, YMODEM, and XMODEM 1K.

The reason you need to know about protocols like these is that, unless you have what's called a SLIP/PPP connection to the Internet (about which a lot more later), you will be dealing with an intermediary, like Delphi. You can use Delphi to log onto an FTP site and download a file. But the file does not go from the site directly into your own personal computer. It goes instead into your "workspace" on Delphi. Once the file is in your workspace, you must leave the Net and download the file into your personal computer using Zmodem or some other protocol.

✳ Terminal emulation

To this day, the vast majority of online, personal computer communications is based on the old mainframe-and-terminal model. That model is simple to understand: You've got a big, expensive, powerful mainframe computer located in a climate-controlled "glass house" somewhere, and you've got any number of dumb terminals scattered about.

The dumb terminals consist largely of a keyboard and a screen and have very little processing power of their own. But each does have certain characteristics. The most common set of characteristics are

those embodied by the DEC VT-100 model terminal. Thus, many of the sites you log into on the Internet will expect you to "be" a VT-100. Your comm software can almost certainly produce a convincing illusion, but you've got to tell it to do so.

If you plan to access the Internet often, you'll want to make "VT-100 emulation" the default setting for your comm program. This will not interfere with most of your other online activities, but it will simplify things greatly when you telnet to some location on the Net.

 # Where to get your software

The basic functions of any communications program are simple. Far simpler than those of a word processing or spreadsheet package. After all, it's essentially a matter of opening the communications port and sending and receiving data using industry-standard procedures.

That's why comm programs are a dime a dozen and why the ones you'll find sold commercially are loaded with features you will never use. After all, when the essential function is so simple, how do you justify charging such a price unless you offer a veritable smorgasbord of features?

Communications software, in short, is not a problem. Your modem maker will almost certainly include not only a basic fax program but a basic comm program as well. Microsoft includes a program called Terminal with Windows 3.1 and promises to include an *even* more powerful comm module in its forthcoming Windows 95 (formerly known as Chicago).

There are scads of *shareware* comm programs—fully functional software made available for free with the caveat that if you like and use the program, you are honor-bound to send its author the requested registration fee of $25 or so. (Many of the Internet programs you may have—programs like Mosaic and Trumpet WinSock—began as shareware or are still shareware.)

As for AOL and Prodigy, the two systems that require you to use their own proprietary software, they basically give their programs

away. Often you don't even have to ask—the disk will arrive in the mail like an unsolicited mail-order catalog.

 # Connecting to the Net

If you work for a large company, you can no doubt have all of these niggling technical details taken care of by someone else. But that could be big a mistake. If you don't put yourself in the shoes of your ideal online customer—and go through whatever he or she must go through to get online—you are sure to develop a false sense of what it's really all about.

It may be a radical notion, but we strongly recommend that you assume that you are a typical consumer and that you decide that you're going to get yourself online without any help from the computer experts at your company. It is not *that* difficult. But for most people, it is not as easy as calling up your corporate microcomputing or LAN department and asking them to take care of it for you.

 # Available connections

Now, about making that all-important Net connection. You and your potential customers have essentially three alternatives:

> ➤ Dedicated, hard-wired, high-speed connection

> ➤ SLIP/PPP dial-up connection

> ➤ Third-party shell or dial-up connection

Unless you're a very big company, the first alternative is out of the question. Dedicated T1 or T3 connections, as they are called, carry hefty installation fees and high monthly costs. It's true that they move data at blindingly fast speeds, but in the course of a year you can easily spend many thousands of dollars on such lines.

All of which may be appropriate for *other* corporate applications of the Internet. But all of which are totally unnecessary for marketing, selling, and generally making money on the Internet.

 # A node on the Net?

A dedicated connection makes you a full-time node on the Net. This is the kind of connection universities, corporations, and government agencies typically have. A SLIP or PPP connection makes you *appear* to be a node on the Net. You will have your own, personal *domain name*, like **firecrystal.com** or **mycompany.org**, just as if you had a dedicated connection. Indeed, none of your customers can tell the difference when they look at your SLIP/PPP connection address.

The acronyms stand for Serial Line Internet Protocol and Point-to-Point-Protocol. All you really need to know, however, is that a PPP connection is the faster, more advanced option, and that you will need either a SLIP or PPP connection to be able to run Mosaic and other graphical World Wide Web browsers. These days, the cost for such a connection is about $20 a month.

That's for using the Net as a typical caller. If you are a businessperson interested in marketing your products or service on the Internet, the same company that provides you with your SLIP or PPP connection may have a rate card covering various other services it can offer. (Please don't worry; we will get to these in good time. But there is more groundwork to be laid right now.)

Your access or service provider will almost certainly supply the communications software you will need to use a SLIP or PPP connection. You will not be able to use your favorite conventional comm program. In our case, we've had a very good experience with VoiceNet (voice phone: 215-674-9290), which supplied a package of excellent shareware programs that certainly seem to function as a unit.

We also had a good experience with Netcom Online Communications Services (voice phone: 408-554-8649) and its proprietary NetCruiser integrated software. It was an absolute breeze to install and set up. But these are just two of the many providers out there. You'll find a

list of major national Internet service providers at the end of this chapter.

⇨ Shell or dial-up connections

The quickest, easiest, and possibly least expensive way to get onto the Internet is to do so with a *shell* or *dial-up* account. The best examples are the Big Five commercial systems: America Online, CompuServe, Delphi, GEnie, and Prodigy. You simply cannot beat the convenience of companies that have long been in the business of putting people online.

Eventually, all of the Big Five systems will almost certainly offer subscribers access to all the major Internet features. But, as noted earlier, only Delphi does so at this writing. In all five cases, there is also the matter of software. As you know, you must use AOL's and Prodigy's software to access their systems. But you can access CompuServe, Delphi, and GEnie with any ordinary communications program.

Either way, however, you cannot run Mosaic, Cello, or the other famous programs you may have heard of. That's not to say that the Big Five won't one day offer software comparable to Mosaic, or even some special version of Mosaic itself. But right now, these systems display World Wide Web pages in text mode only. No special fonts. No photos and graphic images.

One way around this is to go with a company like Pipeline (voice phone: 212-267-3636). Pipeline's Internaut software for Windows and Macintosh lets you use Net features from a simple dial-up connection. There's even a fully graphical Web-like browser.

Pipeline founder James Gleick (author of *Chaos*) is determined to make the Internet accessible to "normal, interested, non-university, non-UNIX-speaking . . . individuals like himself." To encourage the skeptical and fainthearted, Pipeline offers the TIW (Toe in the Water) plan for a low rate of $15 a month, which includes five free hours ($2 for each additional hour). For more active users, Pipeline offers the IIMO (Internet is my Oyster) plan for a flat rate of $35 a month. And

for businesses, there's a Corporate rate of $20 per month plus $2.00 for each hour of connect time.

⇨ And the winner is . . .

For most businesses, the only kind of connection that really makes sense at this point is a SLIP or PPP connection, preferably PPP. That means you'll be in for a set-up fee of about $35 and a monthly charge of $20 to $35. For that, you can expect to get as many as 90 hours of usage, with hours after that being billed at around $1.50 an hour.

It is true that you can send and receive e-mail using the Internet facilities offered by the Big Five and other dial-up services. But you won't have your own domain name. If you are the XYZ Company, your address will be **xyz@aol.com** or **xyz@compuserve.com**. If you want to be **Jane@xyz.com**—that is, if you want to be able to use **xyz.com** as your domain name—you will have to get either an expensive dedicated connection or a SLIP/PPP connection.

⇨ Only SLIP/PPP has the features you need

Even more important, if you want to be able to really use the features of the Net to market your product or service or to automatically flash information to potential customers, you'll need that same kind of connection. The Big Five generally make it easy for you to *get* information from the Net, but they aren't designed to let you *give* information to potential customers.

With a SLIP/PPP connection, you can set up your own FTP site to let customers download files; use a *mail server* to automatically fill customer information requests by zapping back an e-mail message; become a part of a Gopher or create one of your own; create your own World Wide Web home page; and so on.

Naturally, your service provider will charge extra for these options, but prices tend to be reasonable. If they aren't, once you're on the

Net, it's easy to shop around. Don't forget, you will want to have your own account at a provider that's only a local phone call away. But your FTP site, Gopher, and what-not can be located *anywhere* on the Net, wherever you get the best price.

How to find a service provider

Now let's look at the points you should consider when shopping for Internet access via SLIP/PPP. This is not a life-or-death decision. As long as you haven't committed a lot of time, effort, and money to a given service provider, as long as you haven't yet put your Internet address in your advertising, it's easy to cancel your account with one provider and open a new one someplace else. (Though it adds to the complexity, you may even be able to keep your same domain name.)

If the Internet and online communications is completely new to you, the first step is to get an account on Delphi, America Online, or both. (As noted, the other members of the Big Five will be along, but let's keep it simple.) Plunge in and get your feet wet. Find out what the Internet is all about without the distraction of having to set up a lot of software.

Using the Net itself!

Once you're on the Net, you can make use of the Net itself to locate a service provider. One quick and easy way to do this is to use Delphi or AOL to tap into the newsgroup **alt.internet.access.wanted**. There you will find lots of tips, advice, and requests from Internet users around the world. The only trouble with this approach is that you're taking pot luck that someone will see and be able to answer your request, or that the answers you need have already been posted.

For a more organized approach, follow the instructions for getting the POCIA and InterNIC lists of service providers presented in the sidebars nearby. In addition, you may want to consult the list of national access providers at the end of this chapter and the more exhaustive list presented in Appendix C.

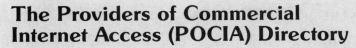

The Providers of Commercial Internet Access (POCIA) Directory

Celestin Company in Port Townsend, Washington, maintains one of the most complete and regularly updated lists of Internet service providers. They call it the Providers of Commercial Internet Access (POCIA) Directory, and it's widely available on the Internet and commercial online service.

*You can request the latest copy of the directory (as well as additional information on Celestin Company and its products) using e-mail. To do so, send a blank message to **cci@olympus.net**. Or, if it's more convenient, contact us at Glossbrenner's Choice and we can send it to you on disk for a small charge. (See the Glossbrenner's Choice appendix at the back of this book for details.)*

The POCIA Directory is organized by area code. Here's an example of the kind of information you will find for each company providing access within a particular area code:

```
201  Carroll-Net              201 488 1332  info@carroll.com
201  The Connection           201 435 4414  info@cnct.com
201  Digital Express Group    301 220 2020  info@digex.net
201  INTAC Access Corporation  800 504 6822  info@intac.com
201  InterCom Online       X226-212 714 7183  info@intercom.com
201  Internet Online Services  201 928 1000  help@ios.com
201  Mordor International BBS  201 433 4222  ritz@mordor.com
201  NETCOM On-Line            408 554 8649  info@netcom.com
     Communications Services
201  New York Net             718 776 6811  sales@new-york.net
201  NIC - Neighborhood       201 934 1445  infor@nic.com
     Internet Connection
```

*If you have access to the World Wide Web, look for the POCIA Directory at Celestin Company's Web site at **http://www.teleport.com/~cci**. The version available there includes pricing as well as contact information for each of the companies on the list.*

The InterNIC Information Services List

InterNIC Information Services is the organization that keeps track of and registers e-mail domain names. You will probably want to have your service provider register your chosen domain name with InterNIC. The process takes about three weeks and most providers charge a handling fee of about $50 to $100 for this service. As long as no one else has registered the same domain name, things should proceed with no problem. (Should you ever decide to change providers, you should be able to keep your domain name by having your new provider update the information on file with InterNIC information.)

The InterNIC offers all sorts of information to help new users get started on the Internet. To request a copy of their Network Service Providers list, call, fax, or send postal or electronic mail to the following locations:

> *InterNIC Information Services*
> *P.O. Box 85608*
> *San Diego, CA 92186-9784*
> *619-455-4600 (voice)*
> *619-455-4640 (fax)*
> *E-mail: info@is.internic.net*

When requesting the Network Service Providers list, be sure to include your name, address, telephone number, fax number, and/or e-mail address.

⇨ How to choose a provider

The ideal Internet access provider should meet all of the following criteria:

> ➢ Reachable via a local phone call

> ➢ Connection speed of 28.8 kbps

> ➢ PPP connection since it is faster than SLIP

> ➢ A full range of features that let *you* put your information on the Net, including mail server, Gopher, FTP server, World Wide Web home pages, and possibly a list server.

> ➢ Telephone support

There are two other important points that are difficult to quantify. First, the main weakness of many Internet access providers is a lack of sufficient incoming phone lines to handle demand. Nothing is more frustrating than to be all set to go online and face nothing but a busy signal each time you dial. In our opinion, no price is low enough to make this tolerable.

Unfortunately, your prospective service provider is not likely to make a big deal of the fact that by 9:00 a.m. all the available incoming lines are busy and that they remain that way until the wee hours of the morning. Complaints about such things are one thing to look for on the newsgroup **alt.internet.access.wanted** cited earlier.

Second, there's the matter of the software. At this writing, the past practice of sending you a bunch of raw programs that you have to configure—in detail—yourself is no longer acceptable. The nightmare stories you may have heard about setting up a SLIP/PPP connection should be a thing of the past.

The only way to cope with potential perpetual busy signals or byte-head software is to give the provider a try and cancel if the service is not satisfactory. You can get a preliminary indication, however, by requesting a copy of the company's brochure and the materials it sends to new users. If that conventional printed material looks good, the company probably cares about providing good service.

Costs

Prices vary widely, of course. And they can and do frequently change. At this writing, however, a one-time set-up fee for a business account of $50 and a monthly charge of $35 seems about right. For this you should get a certain number of hours of connect time, with each additional hour being billed at a very low rate. The VoiceNet account we mentioned earlier gives us 90 hours per month, with a charge of $1.50 for each additional hour.

If you want to set up a mail or list server, an FTP site, or a Gopher to serve your prospects and customers, there are other set-up and monthly charges. A set-up fee of $50 and a monthly fee of $20 to

$50 seem typical for each of these services. Ditto for putting up your own World Wide Web home page, though your initial cost is likely to be higher since the provider will probably have to spend some time preparing the page or pages based on the material you supply.

 # Conclusion

We can conclude with two words of advice. First, do make an effort to get into the Net and "play" before committing to anything. Put yourself in the shoes of your customers and see things through their eyes. Check out what your competition is doing. Get a sense of what these features are all about.

Second, when you do pick a service provider, think in terms of building a relationship. Most service providers have technical expertise that can save you a lot of time now and in the years to come. In other words, use the tools we've given you in this chapter to find someone good, then stick with 'em!

Major Internet access providers

The majority of Internet access providers serve rather small areas, and, though they may be very good, they are typically very small organizations. The providers listed here, in contrast, have nodes you can dial located all over the United States. In each case, we've given you the company name, voice phone or phones, and Internet e-mail address.

Alternet
800-488-6383
703-204-8000
alternet-info@uunet.uu.net Advanced Networks and Services (ANS)
313-663-7610
info@ans.net

CERFnet
800-876-2373
619-455-3900
help@cerf.net

CICnet
313-998-6103
info@cic.net

Colorado Supernet
303-273-3471
info@csn.org

Delphi Internet Services
800-695-4005
617-491-3342
info@delphi.com

HoloNet
510-704-0160 (voice)
510-704-8019 (fax)
support@holonet.net

JVNCnet
800-358-4437
market@jvnc.net

Msen, Inc.
313-998-4562
info@msen.com

NEARnet
617-873-8730
nearnet-join@nic.near.net

Netcom Online Communications Services
800-501-8649
408-554-8649
info@netcom.com

Pipeline
212-267-3636
info@pipeline.com

PSINet
800-827-7482
703-620-6651
info@psi.com

The World
617-739-0202
info@world.std.com

E-mail

The most *useful* feature

CHAPTER 6

YOU already know this but it bears repeating: The statement "Your business has got to have a graphical World Wide Web home page if you want to be on the Internet" may not be the Big Lie, but it is certainly the Big Fib. Sometimes the simplest tools are the most effective, and that's definitely the case with e-mail. So we won't criticize the misguided mania for graphics again.

Except . . . How's this for a way to get ahead of your competition: Tell them, "Oh yeah, our Web page is doing great. You just can't beat the World Wide Web for moving product!" Let your competitors expend all their time, energy, and money on a Web home page— while you quietly devote all your resources to e-mail and related features.

The big payoff

We can say this because we know that whatever you devote to e-mail is sure to pay off. And we're not just talking about conventional electronic mail in which a letter comes in and someone reads it, prepares a reply, and sends the response to the person.

As we'll see in Chapter 7 when we look at *auto-responders*, you can easily set things up like this: Prospective customers *anywhere* in the world see your special "info" address in an advertisement. They want to know more. So they log onto the Internet, tap a few keys, and within minutes (sometimes within *seconds!*) they receive in their mailboxes your product descriptions, price lists, company "backgrounder," press releases, or whatever other information you want to provide.

Talk about instant gratification. Talk about customer interaction. And no human intervention is required, thanks to the *mail robot* or *mailbot* or *auto-responder* software provided to you by your Internet service provider or someone else for as little as $25 a month.

There's a lot more you can do as well, all without straying very far from the essential e-mail concept. But let's get basic Internet e-mail

down first. Then we'll look at how to set up an auto-responder in Chapter 7.

⇨ Basic e-mail, all systems

There are some wrinkles, but if you've used e-mail of any sort, you already know what to do:

❶ Prepare your message with your favorite word processor, but make sure that you save it in "nondocument," "unformatted," "ASCII," or whatever other term your software uses to refer to plain text.

❷ Sign on to your chosen online service and get into its mail program.

❸ Tell the program you want to send mail, and respond to the resulting prompt with the e-mail address of your recipient.

❹ Transmit your previously prepared text file, and then enter the required command to tell the system that you have completed your message.

❺ The system may ask if you are satisfied with your message. If you say you are, the message will be sent.

❻ Finally, to read mail someone has sent to you, sign on to the system, get to the mail feature, open your comm program's *capture buffer* so the text you are about to receive will be recorded on your hard drive, and then choose the option to read your mail. Usually, you will be able to key in a reply on the spot, if you feel so moved.

⇨ Points to watch

The specific details differ, but all e-mail works in essentially this way. There are also some key points to remember about all e-mail systems. First and most important: plain, 7-bit, ASCII text is the lingua franca of electronic mail. That essentially means that only the characters you can type from your keyboard can be used.

Many beginners make the mistake of thinking that the perfectly formatted messages they create in WordPerfect, Word, or some other program are what will be displayed on their correspondents' screens. Unfortunately, if you fail to save your message in plain ASCII text, your correspondent will see your text interspersed with "garbage" characters on the screen.

If you *must* send someone a WordPerfect or similar document with all its special codes and formatting intact, you must send it as a *binary file*, and you cannot use Internet e-mail to do so. At least you cannot do so easily. (More on this later.)

Second, you can get PC or Mac software that will automate much of the process just outlined. That software will include a text editor or word processor for preparing your messages offline, and it is smart enough to prompt you for the subject line and e-mail address you want to use.

This makes it possible for you to prepare a batch of letters and then tell the software to sign on and automatically mail them. If the program finds that you have mail in your mailbox, it will automatically pick it up and notify you of the fact. Then it will sign off.

Needless to say, this is the most efficient way to handle e-mail.

Since you compose offline, with no connect-time meter ticking, no cost is involved. Plus you have the time to write a really thoughtful letter, if appropriate. On the other hand, if most of the letters you get require only a quick response, you may be better off telling your software that you want to read each message in turn and respond to it on the spot.

⇨ Getting Internet-specific

The key thing to remember about electronic mail on the Internet is that it was designed decades ago, and it is aimed at the lowest common denominator. Over the years, the Internet community has

added its own little twists and quirks, all while staying faithful to the lowest common denominator.

Thus, you can use only the 128 characters that form the "standard" 7-bit ASCII code set. Each message can be a maximum of 64K long. That's the equivalent of about 35 double-spaced pages, which is really plenty of room for a message.

If both you and your correspondent are using a mail program that supports the MIME (Multipurpose Internet Mail Extensions) protocol, then you can indeed exchange binary files. However, at this writing, relatively few programs include MIME support.

Practically speaking, the only way to send a graphic image, a formatted word processor file, a program, a sound file, or other binary file is to first convert said file to *text*. This is typically done with a program called UUENCODE/UUDECODE, versions of which are available for most computers. (DOS/Windows users can get such programs from Glossbrenner's Choice.)

This is the same process that habitues of the sex-oriented newsgroups use to post their favorite X-rated pictures. The process does indeed work, but it significantly increases the overall amount of data that must be sent, often resulting in multiple, sequentially numbered messages of 60K or so.

Frankly, if you must get a binary file to someone, it's best to send it on floppy disk via FedEx or some similar service, or use one of the Big Five consumer systems instead. The Internet's mail system simply was not designed to handle binary files, so use one of the Big Five (or MCI Mail) instead.

Dot-crazy addresses on the Net

Now let's consider those crazy Internet mail addresses that are starting to appear in company ads and in magazine and newspaper articles. The tip-off that it's an Internet address is the "at" sign (@). Internet addresses consist of two parts: the stuff to the left of the "at" sign and the stuff to its right.

As an example, consider the address **grendel@beowulf.heorot.com**. (By the way, mail addresses are one of the few exceptions to the rule that "case counts" on the Internet. You're free to use any combination of upper- and lowercase letters in an e-mail address, regardless of how the creator or owner of the address presents it.)

If Grendel were giving you his address, he would say, "I'm Grendel at Beowulf dot Heorot dot Com." But Internet computers read this kind of address from right to left. So the address tells them (and us) that the location is a commercial system called Heorot on a computer called Beowulf that's part of that system. And Grendel is the "logon" name of the individual person.

The information to the right of the "at" sign is called the *domain*. Internet addresses all follow the *Domain Name System* of addressing. Most addresses you'll see end in one of the following *zone* name extensions:

.com   U.S. commercial businesses

.edu   U.S. college and university sites

.gov   Governmental bodies

.int   International bodies, like NATO

.mil   Military organizations

.net   Companies or organizations that run large networks

.org   Nonprofit organizations and others that don't fit elsewhere

Moving to the left, following the zone is the organization's name—in this case, Heorot. If the organization is a large one, it may have several computers or network servers, each with its own name. In this case, the computer at the Heorot organization where Grendel hangs out is called Beowulf.

The Internet mail system effectively "reads" these addresses from right to left. The computers that route and transport the mail know

that it is their responsibility to deliver a message to the "highest" subdomain in the full domain name, in this case, the Heorot system. After that, it is the responsibility of the subdomain name system to take over routing and transport within its own network.

Getting a list of country codes

We should add here that e-mail addresses for users outside the U.S. typically end in a country code. *For example, .AU is Australia, .KH is Cambodia, and .NP is Nepal. Internaut Larry Landweber maintains a complete list of such codes. To get a copy, FTP to **ftp.cs.wisc.edu**; Path: /connectivity_table/. Look for a file called Connectivity_Table.text.*

If you expect to send and receive a lot of international e-mail, you might also want to get a copy of the document called "FAQ: International E-mail Accessibility." (FAQ stands for "frequently asked questions.") In addition to the list of country codes, it includes information about the level of service available in each country (full Internet access, e-mail only, etc.), and where to find further country-specific information if you need it.

*The International E-Mail FAQ is posted regularly on the newsgroups **comp.mail.misc** and **news.newusers.questions**. Or you can request a copy by sending e-mail to **mail-server@rtfm.mit.edu**. Leave the subject line blank, and in the message area key in the one-line message* send usenet/news.answers/mail/country-codes.

⇨ IP addresses & when to use them

The Domain Name System is actually a mask that hides the *numerical* addresses the Internet Protocol (IP) actually uses. Somewhere along the way to our friend Grendel, one or more Internet *nameserver* computers will convert the Domain Name System address **grendel@beowulf.heorot.com** into something like **Grendel@123.45.67.89**. This might translate as "network number 123.45, and computer 67.89 on that network."

For computers, it's easy. For humans, it's not. So the Domain Name System was invented to let us use plain English to specify the same thing.

Most of the time, you will have no problem using the domain name version of an e-mail address. But if a letter gets "bounced back" to you as undeliverable, it may be necessary to use the numerical IP address instead. Before resending, check the address on the bounced-back letter to make sure that you did indeed type it correctly in the first place. If you did, then it is a sure sign that some nameserver system along the way does not yet have that domain name mapped to the proper numerical IP address.

Send the letter again using the IP address. If it still comes back, phone to let your correspondent know that the address does not appear to be working.

Encrypt your text for privacy

Electronic mail is not private. At least not theoretically. In practice, so many messages flow on the Net each day that it is highly unlikely that anyone is reading yours.

Technically, though, someone could read your stuff. After all, if the National Security Agency has the ability to pluck a single phone conversation out of thousands taking place on a microwave link, and if the Central Intelligence Agency can determine what people in a room across the street are saying merely by monitoring the diaphragm-like vibrations of the window panes, how can anyone assume that the Internet is secure?

In point of fact, no one does. That's why it is best to assume that if something can be done, it will be done, eventually, by someone, somewhere. The way to play it safe is to encrypt any truly sensitive e-mail messages you send to colleagues via the Net. And it is so easy to do, once you and your correspondent have the right program. Here are several you might consider:

- *PGP (Pretty Good Privacy) is the famous "public key" RSA encryption program written by Phillip Zimmermann.*

- *PC-CODE by Richard Nolen Colvard includes a version of what he calls super-encipherment, in which "each character of plain*

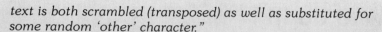

> text is both scrambled (transposed) as well as substituted for some random 'other' character."
>
> • *The Confidant by Stan W. Merrill encrypts files so thoroughly that a National Security Agency supercomputer might be needed to figure it out. Yet your recipient will find the text simple to restore because you have supplied the program and the key.*
>
> *You will find all three programs on the Encryption Tools disk from Glossbrenner's Choice. These programs are for DOS/Windows users. Similar programs exist for Mac users.*

Sending mail to other networks

No discussion of the basics of Internet e-mail would be complete without highlighting one of its often overlooked benefits: Namely, that it lets each subscriber to one of the Big Five consumer online systems communicate with every other subscriber. If you're on GEnie, you can use the Internet to send mail to someone on Delphi. If you're on Delphi, you can use the Net to send a message to someone on Prodigy or CompuServe. (And folks on all of these systems can send messages to your auto-responder, if you have one.)

For those of us who have been tracking the online field for the past decade or so, this is nothing short of remarkable. The interconnectivity of systems is something the United Nations has been striving to get established via the X.400 standard for nearly 10 years!

But for most of those years, the X.400 concept, as it was called, got nowhere. It wasn't until public pressure literally forced virtually every online system to offer Internet e-mail that the interconnectivity dream was finally realized.

You will also hear of an X.500 standard. This is the foundation upon which people hoped to build a master directory of e-mail addresses. That hasn't taken place, either. Instead, there are numerous privately maintained directories that offer basic listings free of charge. You'll learn all about them in Chapter 8.

 # How to do it!

Many subscribers to the Big Five systems, MCI Mail, and most Internet service providers are still not aware of the connectivity that exists today to allow the exchange of e-mail among the various systems. Here's a quick primer.

❋ **America Online (AOL)**

To send mail to someone on AOL, remove any spaces from the person's AOL user name and add **@aol.com** to get an address like **jsmith@aol.com**. (If you don't know the user name, your best bet is to call the person and ask.) To send mail from America Online to someone on the Internet, just put the person's Internet address in the "To" field before composing your message.

❋ **CompuServe**

CompuServe users have numerical addresses in the form **12345,678**. To send mail to a CompuServe user, change the comma to a period and add **@compuserve.com** to get an address like **12345.678@compuserve.com**. (Keep in mind that most CompuServe users must pay a minimum of fifteen cents for each message received from the Internet.)

To send mail from CompuServe to someone on the Internet, use an address in the form **>INTERNET:jsmith@company.org**. Both the greater-than sign (>) and the colon (:) are required.

❋ **Delphi Internet Services**

To send mail to a Delphi subscriber, use an address consisting of the person's Delphi user name plus **@delphi.com** to get an address like **jsmith@delphi.com**.

To send mail from Delphi to someone on the Internet, the form is **internet"jsmith@company.org"** (the quotation marks are required).

❋ **GEnie**

To send mail to a GEnie user, add **@genie.geis.com** to the end of the GEnie user name, for example: **jsmith@genie.geis.com**.

To send mail from the GEnie Mail system to someone on the Internet, use the person's Internet address plus the constant **INET#**. The address will look like this: **jsmith@company.org@INET#**.

✳ MCI Mail

To send mail to someone with an MCI Mail account, add **@mcimail.com** to the end of the person's name or numerical address. For example: **555-1234@mcimail.com** or **jsmith@mcimail.com**. (You're better off using the numerical address if the person has a relatively common name, since there can be no doubt about the John Smith at 555-1234, but considerable doubt about JSMITH.)

To send mail from MCI Mail to an Internet address, at the "To:" prompt, key in the person's name and (EMS). At the resulting "EMS:" prompt, key in internet. At the resulting "MBX:" prompt, key in the recipient's Internet address.

✳ Prodigy

To send mail to a Prodigy user, add **@prodigy.com** to the person's Prodigy user ID. For example: **jsmith@prodigy.com**. (As with CompuServe, Prodigy users must pay extra for Internet e-mail.)

To send mail from Prodigy to an Internet address, you'll need Mail Manager software, which is available for download from Prodigy. After composing your message offline using Mail Manager, send it to the person's normal Internet address, like **jsmith@company.org**. No special punctuation is required.

⇨ E-mail "signatures"

It is common practice among many long-time Internet users to append a *signature file* to every e-mail message or newsgroup posting they prepare. You can think of these as the rough equivalent of personal or company letterhead. Though, as you can see from the examples shown in the nearby sidebar, many signatures include some wry or funny quote, as well as a person's name and e-mail address.

On many UNIX-based systems, users can create a signature and store it in a file called ".signature." When they post a message to a newsgroup, the system will automatically get that file and tack it onto the end of the message.

E-mail programs, like the shareware Windows-based Eudora program that may have come with your access provider's start-up kit, let you do the same thing for the e-mail letters you create. You prepare a file once and record it on disk. Then Eudora, or whatever program you're using, automatically adds it to the end of each letter you write and send.

 # Keep it simple

If you are using the Net for business, creating an e-mail signature is a really good idea. But a number of cautions are in order. In general, you don't want your signature to run much beyond six or seven lines. As long as you don't try to be cute, that's plenty of space to convey the essential "letterhead" information.

Think in terms of two columns. One on the left for your land address and one on the right for your e-mail, phone, and fax numbers. If there's room, you might include an advertising tag line or motto. The key thing is to avoid going overboard and thus irritating your correspondent.

For example, if we were to create a signature for our book-writing business, it might look like this:

```
--------------------------------------------------------------
Alfred and Emily Glossbrenner      Voice: 215-736-1213
699 River Road                     FAX:   215-736-1031
Yardley, PA  19067-1965            Internet: Alfred@Delphi.com

        "We write the best computer books in the world!"
For more information, send a blank message to books@infomat.com
--------------------------------------------------------------
```

No reasonable person receiving a message with a signature like this is going to object. After all, it contains information that is crucial to anyone who might want to buy your products or services, presented

in a clean, clear, concise way. It is every bit the equivalent of an electronic letterhead.

Practically speaking, however, there is really no limit on the number of lines you can use as your signature. After all, the Internet mail system and the newsgroup system don't see it as something apart from your message or letter. It's all text, as far as they're concerned. And some non-business people do take advantage of this to express themselves or to show everyone how cleverly they have created pictures using nothing but standard text characters or "ASCII art."

Signatures on parade

Here are some signatures drawn from the collection assembled by Glen Robbins. It is simply amazing what people with time on their hands can create using nothing but plain, 7-bit, ASCII text. They're a lot of fun, but flashiness of this sort is not likely to be appropriate for most businesses:

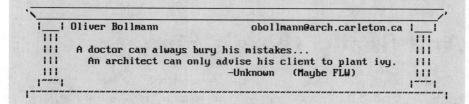

```
"Hey Rocky!
Watch me pull some intelligence
out of the Internet!"
"But that trick never works."
"This time for sure."
boba@gagme.wwa.com
```

*If you'd like to see the entire collection, log onto the Gopher at **wwa.com**, select "Scarecrow's ASCII Art Archives," and then select "The Scarecrow's Funnies (humorous ASCII art)" from the menu that will appear.*

You might also be tempted to take a look at the item on the menu identified as "The Scarecrow's Sig Gallery." This is a binary file, and

```
  _____
   \           \---------__      __          _____/  /_____/
    \           \----\\\\\\  //_ _ \\   //////-------/  /_____/ IBM
Artist, _____\----\\!! (( ~!~ ))) !!//------/_____/ Amiga &
Stand up     \_____\---\\ ((\ = / ))) //----/_____/ Macintosh user
 Philosopher and \____\--\_))) \ _)))---/____/ Computer Modeling/
Aspiring computer  \__/  (((      (((_/ Engineering student  Phil
Nerd. (413) 549^i4541 !  -)))  -  ))minor in Omniscience. Garrow
```

```
       /~~~~~~~~~~~~~~~~~~~~~~~~~~~~~~~~~~~~~~\    /~~\
      /                                       \  /    \
      !           Christopher King            !__!
      !    Consultant - NCSU Computing Center  !
      !         208 Hillsborough Building       !
      !              (919)515-3035              !
      !          chris_king@ncsu.edu            !
      ! "Calm down. It's only ones and zeros."  !
      !          - Sam Kass -                    !
      \~~~~~~~~~~~~~~~~~~~~~~~~~~~~~~~~~~~~~~/    /
       /_____    \_/
        _____/
```

*you will have to know how to use UUDECODE and an "un-ZIP"
program to make the file readable once you download it from the
menu. (See the Glossbrenner's Choice appendix for the tools you will
need.)*

And finally, there's Finger

We can close this chapter with what, conceptually at least, is an
enhancement to garden variety Internet e-mail. This is the *Finger
utility*. Actually, we should say *utilities*, because not all
implementations of this feature work in exactly the same way.

Developed at the University of California at Berkeley by Earl T.
Cohen as part of that organization's UNIX project, the Finger
program was designed to let professors easily tell their students when
they would be holding office hours. It also let students tell everyone
else what they were working on. They did this by creating text files
called ".plan" and ".project" and storing them in their "home
directories."

The text file might look like an e-mail signature file of the sort we
talked about earlier. It might include a professor's name, office
location, office hours, phone number, and so on. If you needed that

kind of information about Professor Barbara Simon, you could key in a command like **finger bsimon**.

If you were not located at Berkeley yourself, but were on the Net from a location in some other state, for example, you could use a command like **finger bsimon@sysname.uscb.edu** and the same information would appear.

The key thing to know, however, is that you can put nearly anything into your .plan file. It could be directions to your vacation home or your latest poetry or an advertisement for your products or services. Whatever is in the .plan file is what people on the Net will see when they Finger you at your location.

⇨ Cautions & caveats

All of which sounds great. But before you get too excited about the possibilities Finger offers, you should know that Finger is not available at all locations. Your access provider may make it possible for you to record .project and .plan files (you need to use both) on the system. But don't count on it. You can't even count on the provider knowing what the Finger utility is or does.

There is also the fact that not all Finger features work alike. You can never be sure what you will get when you Finger someone. If you enter the command with both upper- and lowercase letters, it might not work. As we've mentioned before, sensitivity to whether a letter is in upper- or lowercase is yet another quirky characteristic of UNIX and the Internet. Sometimes it matters; sometimes it doesn't. (If you're not sure, your best bet with Finger is to use all lowercase. You'll probably be right more often than not.)

These complexities make Finger largely unsuitable as a marketing and business tool. Still, if your connection to the Internet includes a Finger option, you can have a lot of fun using it to Finger different locations. As you will see in the nearby sidebar, it is truly amazing the kind of information you'll get back. All of which is the perfect segue to a *real* business application—the auto-responders discussed in the next chapter.

Try your hand at Finger

Here are some sample Finger commands for you to try:

Baseball Scores/Standings:
finger jtchern@headcrash.berkeley.edu

Baseball and Football Scores/Standings:
finger robc@xmission.com

Earthquake Information for the United States:
finger quake@gldfs.cr.usgs.gov

Interesting Internet sites (How to get a list of):
finger yanoff@alpha2.csd.uwm.edu

International Hockey League Newsletter:
finger 074345@xavier.xu.edu

NASA Headline News (recent press releases from NASA):
finger nasanews@space.mit.edu

Products/services being sold on the Internet (How to get a list of):
finger taylor@netcom.com

Space News (weekly publication):
finger magliaco@pilot.njin.net

Tropical Storm Forecast for the Atlantic Ocean:
finger forecast@typhoon.atmos.colostate.edu

Weekly Trivia:
finger cyndiw@magnus1.com

Auto-responders

The best marketing tool of all!

I MAGINE being able to instantly bounce a description of your product or service to anyone who sends an e-mail message to an address you've put into one of your print ads. That's exactly what an Internet auto-responder does.

This kind of feature goes by many names. But, while *mail daemon* (pronounced "demon") may be the most poetic, *auto-responder* is the most descriptive, so that's the term we'll use. The nearest equivalent in the non-online world is a *fax on demand* (FOD) system. FOD can be implemented a number of ways, but in its simplest form, a customer dials the phone and requests a fax by talking to a human being or by using the keys on a TouchTone phone.

FOD is a wonderful marketing tool that can nicely complement your Internet auto-responder. But it also calls for an investment of several thousand dollars. An auto-responder, in contrast, can be set up for about $100 and run at a cost of $50 a month or less.

⇨ Geared to information distribution

The reason auto-responders are so exciting is that they perfectly mesh with the design of the Net. The Internet, after all, is not really a *transactional* medium. It's an *informational* medium. Yes, that sounds like a lot of technobabble. But think about it for just a minute. The Internet was established by the U.S. government to facilitate the flow of information among the Pentagon, defense contractors, and research labs at the nation's colleges and universities.

Once established, the Net was *developed* largely by people in the academic world. They're the one's, after all, who had the time to create and expand concepts like Finger, Archie, Gopher, and FTP. Good souls that they are, these people tend not to think in terms of capitalism and the transactions needed to make it work. Many are on record, in fact, as saying that all information should be free.

As a result, the Internet that has developed over the last 20 years is very much geared to information distribution. There are lists—and

lists of lists—of informational items. There are file collections and Campus Wide Information Servers (CWIS), and Veronica and Jughead and everything else, all of it designed to help you find and obtain *information*.

Not that transactional services and security measures cannot be overlaid onto the Net. But these things are really just at the discussion and preliminary trial stage today. In our opinion, it will be many years before these issues are resolved and a universally convenient solution has been implemented.

The "me" approach

Besides, as you know from previous chapters, the idea of easily and cheaply selling products online is a pipe dream born more of corporate fantasies than of reality and a passionate desire to serve the customer. In sales talk, online transactions are a good example of companies taking the "me" approach. (What works best for me? What's the least-cost way of handling a transaction?) And that orientation almost never works.

⇨ The "you" approach

That's why we're so excited about the concept of Internet e-mail auto-responders, for it lets a company say, "Tell us what *you* want to know, and we will provide the information you need—instantly!" The prospect need only send a blank message to an address like **books@infomat.com** to receive several pages of information about your product or service, including an order form, if you like.

⇨ In the LISTSERV tradition

You'll also hear this kind of feature called a *mailbot* (short for "mail robot"). As such, it is part of a long tradition on the Internet of letting computers do the work.

123

For example, when you want to be added to an electronic mailing list, you typically send a message to a *list server*. This is a computer running a program called LISTSERV (no final *E*). The trick is to include in the body of the message the word "subscribe" or "sub" followed by the name of the mailing list and your name.

Thus, if you were to send a message to **listserv@brownvm .brown.edu** containing the line subscribe MACIRC-L John Smith, the list server at Brown University would add you to a mailing list called MACIRC-L, a list that focuses on Macintosh Internet Relay Chat.

⇨ And mail servers, too

Similar programs called *mail servers* also exist. Their purpose is to automatically send one or more files to your electronic mail mailbox in response to your request. Sometimes, you must be sure to include some special word in the message's subject line. Sometimes you are supposed to leave that line blank and key in send followed by the directory path and exact name of the file you want.

Different mail servers support different commands, so it's important to pay attention to the specific instructions on how to use a given mail server to retrieve a particular file. (As an experiment, send a message to **mailserv@ds.internic.net**. Leave the subject line blank, and key in help as your message.)

⇨ Finally, something usable!

Mail servers like this are clever. And long-time Internet users don't mind the complexity. Frankly, many of them *thrive* on it.

But, clearly, complexity of this sort just won't play with the general public. Fortunately, in the fall of 1994, someone finally got it right. As a result, you and other businesspeople can now put a line like this in your ads: "To learn more, send a blank e-mail message to **Ajax@infomat.com**."

That's it. No detailed instructions, case-sensitive e-mail addresses, or special "magic" words. Just a blank letter to an Internet e-mail address. The instructions are so simple that you can even include them in your radio and print ads.

And what will your prospects see? Often within *seconds* they will get a message back from your auto-responder containing whatever information you want them to have. The response from QuoteCom Data Service shown in Fig. 7-1 is a good example.

Figure 7-1

```
This is an automatic response to your request for information about
QuoteCom.  More extensive information may be found using:

    ftp.quote.com                in the directory /pub/info
    email to services@quote.com  with Subject of "help"
    http://www.quote.com/
.........................................................
                    QuoteCom Data Service

QuoteCom supplies financial market data to Internet Users.  There are
four primary aspects to the QuoteCom service:

    1)  Intraday price quotes (15 minute typical delay from exchange)
        Available on demand for stocks, commodities, mutual funds,
        and other financial instruments.  Includes simple balance
        sheet data for stocks.

    2)  Portfolio tracking and reporting via email.
        Users can receive an email message at the close of each
        trading day detailing the performance of a portfolio.
        Limit alarms may be set which, when triggered, will generate
        an email message advising the user.

    3)  News and analysis.
        QuoteCom has licensed trading-oriented business news from
```

Here's part of the first page of an auto-responder message from QuoteCom Data Service. To receive a copy yourself, send a blank message to info@quote.com.

It could be a corporate "backgrounder" or press release. It could be your price list, plus a ready-to-print order form. Just ask yourself: If I could instantly send, say, three pages of text to any prospective customer, anywhere in the world, what would I say? (We'll share some ideas with you in a moment.)

And the cost? How does $50 a month sound? That's $600 a *year*, plus a one-time set-up fee of $150, for a total of $750 the first year and $600 each year thereafter.

 # But more than a little hard to find

Once again, the truly new development in this area is the opportunity to deliver information to your prospects instantly in response to a simple, blank message sent to your auto-responder address.

It's entirely possible that your Internet access provider can set you up with this option. But those we've contacted do not include it on their rate cards. And when you call, the person you speak to will typically promise to check and call you back. Sometimes they do; sometimes they don't.

One such provider did call back with the news that their charges for setting up a mail server would be $50, plus $50 a month, with a limit of two megabytes of storage space on the system. This is not at all unreasonable. But clearly, no one at the company had thought through the process of offering a mail server as a feature for business. Their handling of the query simply did not inspire confidence.

 # Marc Hyman's Internet Automat

Then we encountered Marc Hyman, and we knew once again the refreshing feeling of dealing with a specialist who really knows what he's talking about. Mr. Hyman is the creator of the Internet Automat, a state-of-the-art auto-responder system whose motto is "Information Served Fresh, 24 Hours-a-Day!"

You can get Mr. Hyman's latest information via auto-responder, of course. Send a blank message to **infomat@infomat.com**, wait about 30 seconds, and then check your mailbox for new mail. Barring some problem on the Net, you'll find a nicely formatted four-page message from the Internet Automat. Mr. Hyman's regular e-mail address is

msh@rain.org, and his company is BBR Media in Santa Barbara, California, voice phone: 805-568-8076.

You will definitely want to send a blank message to **infomat@infomat.com**, but here is a quick run-down of the service and its costs. The basic rate is a one-time set-up charge of $150 and then $50 a month. For this you get to send a message as large as 20,000 bytes (20K)—equivalent to about 10 double-spaced typewritten pages. And you can change your message twice a month at no additional charge.

If you're a small business, which is to say the typical one-person shop billing about $100,000 a year, the set-up charge is just $75, and the monthly rate is $25. The maximum message size available under this plan is 10K (about five double-spaced pages), and you are entitled to one free message change per month.

If you would like your own domain name, which is to say, if you want prospects to be able to send mail to **info@ajax.com** instead of **ajax@infomat.com**, the company charges a one-time fee of $50 to register the name with InterNIC.

 # No need for "metering" charges

That's it. We asked Mr. Hyman if there was any per-message charge or other cost pegged to the number of responses his auto-responder issued. "There is no reason for anyone to pay a metering charge," he said.

"The cost of sending out a single e-mail response is tiny," Mr. Hyman continued. "Message volume really only begins to be a factor when you're sending out large documents to thousands of people a day. But if you're sending out a 10,000-byte response to 100 to 200 people a day—which is about what we're running for many of our clients—there's no need for a per-message charge."

 # How to pick an auto-responder vendor

This is such a new area and the terminology is so fluid that you'll need to exercise more than the normal amount of caution when picking an auto-responder vendor. Here are some of the questions you should ask:

➤ Do I have to subscribe to your system?

➤ What's the set-up fee?

➤ What's the maximum size message I can send?

➤ Is there a per-message charge?

➤ Is there a total volume charge?

➤ Do you charge for storage space on your system?

➤ How many changes can I make per month, and at what cost?

➤ Do you operate in *immediate* or *batch* mode?

You may find that some vendors will require you to open an account with them in order to use their auto-responder feature. Information Access Technologies, Inc., for example, offers a service called HoloMailer, "automated mail information service for businesses." But to use it, you've got to first subscribe to the HoloNet system. There's no initial fee for this, but the minimum cost is $6 per month, which is applied to your usage of the system. (For automatic information, send a blank message to **info@holonet.net**.)

That may be fine with you, since you will be able to use the system's other features as well. But it may also add to your monthly expense if you are already getting Internet access elsewhere.

As for one-time auto-responder set-up fees, HoloNet charges $100, while Marc Hyman's Internet Automat charges between $75 or $150, depending on the size of your business. Thus, at this early stage, $75 to $150 would seem to be the range for setting up an auto-responder.

Auto-responders to try

Listed here are a number of auto-responders you may want to try. Just send a blank e-mail message to any of these addresses. As you review the responses, think about how you might be able to use a service like this. Also, notice that some responses contain additional auto-responder addresses you can use to obtain more specific information on some product or service.

books@infomat.com	Books written by Alfred and Emily Glossbrenner (catalog and order form)
demo@cexpress.com	Demonstration programs available from Computer Express
hitech-catalog@infomat.com	Hi-Tech Component Distributors (discount hard disk drives)
info@awa.com	AnyWare Associates FAXiNET (send and receive faxes via the Internet)
info@cexpress.com	Computer Express hardware/software catalog
info@commerce.net	CommerceNet (non-profit consortium, created with the help of the U.S. government, whose charter is to build the infrastructure needed for doing business on the Internet).
info@digital.com	Digital Equipment Corporation (DEC)
info@holonet.net	Information on HoloNet's HoloMailer auto-responder service
infomat@infomat.com	Information on the Internet Automat, BBR Media/Marc Hyman's auto-responder service
info@quote.com	QuoteCom Data Service (investment and financial news service)
info@telebase.com	EasyNet Service (access to 250 databases)

Message size & metering

The maximum message size may be less important than it first appears. Assume 65-character lines and 28 lines per double-spaced page. At one byte per character, including spaces, that works out to 1,820 bytes per page. So you will need between 9,000 bytes (9K) and 10,000 bytes (10K) for messages equivalent to five double-spaced pages.

That may well be enough. You don't want to overwhelm your recipient, after all. In any case, a 10K maximum on message size is quite workable.

Your vendor may charge you for each response sent. And on top of that there may be a charge for the total volume sent. HoloNet places no limit on message size. But it charges five cents per message and $1 for each megabyte of data sent.

So, suppose your responder ends up sending out 50 messages a day (or about 1,500 a month), each containing 10K of data. At a nickel a message and $1 per megabyte of data sent, that amounts to $75 plus $15, for a total of $90. Add to this the $6 monthly minimum that HoloNet charges, and you're at $96—substantially more than the $25 or $50 you would be charged under the Internet Automat's flat-rate billing.

Obviously, if you advertise your auto-responder aggressively and it ends up sending out 200 or so messages a day (which is not uncommon for well-advertised services), the difference between the Internet Automat's flat-rate billing and HoloNet's message-volume billing is even greater.

We like the folks at HoloNet, but we know from their literature that HoloMailer is only one of many Internet-related services they offer. Whereas, offering an auto-responder is the single focus of the Internet Automat.

Changes & storage charges

Unfortunately, at this writing, neither the auto-responder information provided by HoloNet or the Internet Automat even mentions making changes in your message. Clearly, though, this is something worth investigating since you may want to change your message to feature certain products, special offers, or whatever from one month to the next.

Nor does the question of charges for storage on a system come up. Yet the vendor we spoke of earlier that charges $50 per month for a mail server feature limits storage to two megabytes. That's plenty of space, but it is a charge neither HoloNet nor the Internet Automat even refer to—yet another indication of how immature this market really is.

Most important: Immediate or batch?

It's a debatable point, but, in our opinion, an auto-responder ought to respond *instantly*. And by that we mean within 30 seconds or less. Your prospects and customers ought to be able to sign onto Delphi or AOL or any of the other Big Five—or onto their SLIP/PPP connections—and send a blank message to your auto-responder address. In the time it takes them to click on the right icons or menu choices or otherwise enter the commands needed to check for new mail—your response should *be* there!

Some online systems actually announce the fact that you have new mail the moment it arrives. It doesn't matter what you happen to be doing on the system at the time, the announcement will still be made. Other systems remain silent when mail arrives. The only way you'll learn about new mail is to sign off and then sign on again, or to check your mailbox. Thus, you may want to say in your ads: "For more information, send a blank message to books@infomat.com, wait 30 seconds, then check your mailbox for new mail."

What you need to know is that the speed of your auto-responder's response depends on your vendor. That's because there are two ways

vendors send such responses: They may respond to each message as soon as it comes in, or they may place messages in a holding area for an hour or more and respond to an entire batch at one time.

You may or may not agree with us about how "sexy" it is to offer an instantaneous response. But you should definitely ask your prospective auto-responder service vendor about the typical response time, and whether responses are sent *immediately* or in *batch mode*.

FireCrystal tips on preparing your message

Through FireCrystal Communications, your co-authors offer a consulting service to businesses interested in making money on the Internet. You may think you can prepare and format an effective auto-responder message on your own, and of course, you can.

That is exactly what most current auto-responder users have done— and it shows. As more people discover this technique, the competition for a customer's attention will grow. After all, an auto-responder can easily deliver your message—the trick is in getting the recipient to read it.

This is something we're pretty good at. Over the years, we've helped clients ranging from Michelin to Merrill Lynch. If you think we may be of help, write to us at Alfred@Delphi.com, or fax us at 215-736-1031, or phone us at 215-736-1213. We will be delighted to explore the possibilities with you.

Meantime, here's our advice for creating a truly effective auto-responder piece:

❶ *Make your message visually appealing. Good copywriting is important, but visual appeal in this medium is even more so.*

We recommend keeping your text to no more than five pages. Indent the copy 10 spaces on each side, with margins set at 10 and 75. Use the business-letter style of single-spaced paragraphs separated by a single blank line. (See Fig. 7-1 for an example; the folks at QuoteCom Data Service do it right!)

Try to think in terms of points you can set off with bullets (lowercase o), and indent and align for attractiveness.

❷ *If you haven't already done so, get yourself a really good advertising copywriter. Take the time to meet with the writer. Present your current print materials (brochures, catalogues, press releases, etc.), and explain which products, features, and benefits you feel are most important.*

The copywriter may or may not agree with you. But that's okay since there is nothing like a disagreement to help you take a fresh look at something.

❸ *A fresh look is so important, we've made it Step 3. Don't make the mistake of simply transcribing your current print materials. As your copywriter will tell you, every medium is different.*

Long, detailed letters may work with direct mail, but they're not appropriate for e-mail responses. On the other hand, you're not laboring under the space constraints of a magazine ad. And you can assume that since the customers are coming to you, they really want some solid information.

❹ *Insist that your auto-responder text end with an order form. Include the traditional Internet "cut here" line, and make the form the kind of thing someone can easily print out, fill in, and then send to you via regular mail.*

And don't forget to include your land address, toll-free phone, regular phone, fax number, and regular Internet e-mail address.

❺ *Test it yourself. When you've got your message prepared, e-mail it to your auto-responder provider. Then, when you know for certain that your provider has activated your responder, sign on to a system—any system—and send a blank message to your auto-responder address.*

Take the "you" approach once again and pretend that you are a customer who has seen this address in one of your company's print ads. If you don't like what you see, make sure that corrections and modifications are made.

⇨ Conclusion: Tell the world

We think you will find an auto-responder to be the single most effective marketing tool on the Net. And, of course, you're not

limited to just one. The cost is so low that you can easily afford to set one up for each major product category.

But, whether you've got one auto-responder or a dozen, none of them will do you any good until you spread the word.

All of your print, radio, and TV ads should include a line telling people to hit your auto-responder. And if you don't currently do any advertising, maybe the introduction of your auto-responder would be an effective focus for an ad. You'll also want to take maximum advantage of the free listings available in various Internet directories. And you should plan on regularly posting discrete announcements in the appropriate Internet newsgroups and Big Five SIGs or forums.

As it happens, telling the world is precisely what we're going to show you how to do as we cover these and related topics in the next chapter.

Spreading the word

Advertising &
FREE directory listings

W E'VE all heard about those wildly successful businesses whose advertising and marketing expenditures are limited to placing a tiny ad in the back of some obscure monthly publication. No newspaper or radio ads, no direct mail, no coupon "paks"—nothing but this dumb, cheap little ad that somehow seems to pull like an industrial electromagnet.

Maybe the stories are true. But they don't track with the rough and tumble, highly competitive reality most of us know. And if there is one thing that reality teaches, it's that all of your advertising, marketing, and sales efforts *must work together*!

Now, we are not saying that you absolutely have to have an auto-responder address. There are many other ways to use the Internet for marketing and sales. It's just that an auto-responder makes everything else so much simpler and easier. What we *are* saying is that there is little point in setting up an auto-responder message if you don't tell people about it. And your efforts in this area should all be designed to work together.

Thus, in this chapter, we'll show you how an auto-responder can add tremendous leverage to conventional print and other ads and how to get yourself listed in free Internet directories. In the *next* chapter, we'll show you how an auto-responder can help you use Internet newsgroups to tell people about your product or service—without getting "flamed."

 # Uncommon common sense

We can start with conventional advertising and the need to have everything work together. Consider Procter & Gamble. If that company does not get its latest soap product onto store shelves *before* it begins a nationwide advertising campaign, the money spent on that campaign will be largely wasted. If McDonald's wants to offer major movies on videotape to promote some new addition to its menu and fails to have those tapes in the stores and ready to go when the ads hit, it will not only have wasted millions of advertising dollars, it will have millions of angry customers.

It's just common sense, right? Why are we making an issue of this, anyway? Two reasons. First, in our experience, sense of this sort is far less common than you might imagine. That means there's an opportunity for you to steal a march on your competitors. Second, the Internet is so vast and it offers so many ways for you to "cross-promote" that you're foolish if you do not do so.

A small-business example

You should start by taking a cold-eyed, critical look at your product or service and asking yourself whether using the Internet is really likely to be beneficial to you. Clearly, not every product is suitable for electronic marketing.

Why? Because, by definition, Internet users must also be computer users. There may be a couple hundred million DOS/Windows and Macintosh computers installed worldwide, but we are a long way from a computer in every home.

This is also one of the main reasons that much of the Net-based marketing you see at this stage is from companies selling computer hardware and software. It stands to reason that Internet users would be interested in that kind of stuff.

Selling noncomputer merchandise

But here's the key point: Computer ownership and use also connotes *above-average* income. There are thus all kinds of other goods and services many Net users are interested in that have nothing at all to do with computers.

So let's suppose you're a really small business. Just for a moment, put yourself in the shoes of one of the many highly skilled cabinetmakers we're so fortunate to have here in Bucks County, Pennsylvania.

You're the guy who takes a pile of seasoned bare wood and transforms it into a wonderful canopy bed or Chippendale chair or richly polished, multi-drawered highboy with a deep, hand-polished honey finish that is simply to die for.

How can the Internet work for you?

It's an interesting question, because most of the cabinetmakers we know don't even own a computer. And none of them has much money for advertising.

Yet each has a collection of wonderful "signature" pieces they specialize in making that can be customized to a person's special needs. There are woods and stains and finishes; fabrics and designs and custom work to discuss. Most can effortlessly duplicate any piece of furniture you see pictured in a magazine.

More bang for your advertising buck

As a cabinetmaker with a highly unique line of products and services, you have a lot of information to convey, not to mention the possible need to offer a little customer education. But you can't possibly do it in a print ad. Like most businesses, you can only hope that your print ad stirs enough interest to generate an inquiry.

And who handles that inquiry when it comes in? Do you send out a four-color brochure or a stapled packet of photocopied pages? How many queries come from mere "tire-kickers," people who really have no intention of buying? The answers to each of these questions involve time and money—and the possibility that a good deal of both are being wasted.

An ad in the *New Yorker*?

Now look at the leverage the Internet can provide!

Start by taking a look at where your competitors advertise. But don't look at only one or two issues of a publication. Look at six months' to

a year's worth. If the same competitors appear in each issue over a year's time, it is a sure sign that the publication is working for them.

Let's assume that you notice all the ads for cabinetmakers and related professions in the *New Yorker*. Readers of the *New Yorker* are definitely upscale, the kinds of people who are likely to be interested in fine cabinetmaking (as the ads show) and to also own or have easy access to computers and modems.

At this writing, the *New Yorker*'s rate base is 700,000 readers. And for a cabinetmaker, a one-inch black and white ad would cost $640 per insertion. That's enough space for a picture of one of your creations, a few descriptive words, and the necessary contact information. Which, in addition to your name, address, and phone number, includes the line, "or send a blank message to info@furniture.com."

There will come a time when an Internet auto-responder address like this will be as common as an "800" number. But for the next couple of years, it will be seen as sexy and unique. You just know that any *New Yorker* reader with even a passing interest in reproduction furniture is going to hit your auto-responder.

One ad, one time, won't do it

The only real mistake you can make is being too cheap to commit to something other than a one-time-only insertion. If you're offering U.S. government-certified, one-ounce, 24k gold nuggets for $5, plus shipping and handling, you might get an overwhelming response from a single ad.

But if you're featuring a reproduction Federal mirror or a pencil-post bed and suggesting that readers contact you for more information, the response for any given ad will probably be less than you hope for or expect. If you can't afford to be there every *week*, see if you can manage every *other* week for two or three months. Six insertions over 12 weeks will cost you $3,840. Not insignificant, but you can probably make that back if you sell just one or two pieces.

 # Adding up the benefits

Advertising is yet another one of those businesses in which no one really knows what works. You make your best guess and make the commitment needed to run the ad several times. Who can say what the response will be?

But let's assume that 200 people hit your auto-responder each time your *New Yorker* ad runs. Some of them surely would have contacted you by phone or by land mail. So your auto-responder has just saved you all the time, trouble, and expense of replying by mail.

Some of them surely would never have taken the trouble to mail you a query or even to pick up the phone. But they're on the Internet at least once a day, and your auto-responder made it so easy for them to send you a request for more information. These are people you wouldn't get to "talk to" any other way.

 # Only qualified customers

Will you make any sales directly from your auto-responder? As a cabinetmaker, probably not. But here's what you *can* do. Plan to feature, say, five of your pieces in your auto-responder copy. Give each a specific name and a paragraph or two of description.

Then offer to send readers a color photograph of the specific item or items they are interested in. (Make it easy for them by including a ready-to-print form with a series of check boxes.)

This approach has at least two obvious benefits. First, you don't have to go to the expense of producing a color brochure. Just take a couple of good pictures, and have 50 prints made of each. Second, while time and effort will be required to mail out the photos, at least you'll know that you probably are not dealing with a tire-kicker. Your auto-responder has thus "qualified" your prospective customers.

Needless to say, a similarly synergistic approach can be applied to any product line. Just make sure that you think through the process:

People see your ad and hit your auto-responder; they read your auto-responder copy, which gives them information *and* makes it easy to get still more information about the items they're interested in—in this case, by requesting a color photo by regular mail.

 # Internet directory listings

Advertising by conventional means—newspapers, radio, and magazines—may or may not work for you. But there's one thing you can say for sure: The companies selling you the space or air time know a heck of a lot more about their readers, listeners, or viewers than do companies selling space on the Internet.

Electronic advertising is so new that the superstructures of rate bases, circulation audits, Nielsen ratings, and the like have not yet developed. Not that conventional tools of this sort are necessarily all that accurate to begin with. But at least they offer some indication that you are getting what you're paying for in terms of exposure.

On the Net, no one really knows. So companies tend to charge what the market will bear. We are a long way away from the day when an Internet ad can be priced in cost per thousand.

Still, there is a way to get your feet wet without spending a dime. And that is with a *free listing* in one of the many Internet directory services that now exist.

It's not the information, it's *finding* it

As we wrote in our 1987 book, *How to Look it Up Online: Get the Information Edge with Your Personal Computer*, the problem with online information is not one of quantity or availability. With very few exceptions, you can learn everything you want to know by going online. The problem is *finding* the information you want—even on commercial systems like Nexis and Dialog that publish tons of information on each database they offer.

Internet users have the same problem. But to a degree that is all but unimaginable. That's because the Net is so disorganized. The Net may link 30,000 or more separate networks, but each might as well be an independent planet spinning off into space.

Hence the need for lists, lists of lists, and directories. As you will see in our books *Internet 101* and *Internet Slick Tricks*, scores of dedicated individuals have devoted themselves to preparing and maintaining lists of Internet resources of every sort. In so doing, they have made a name for themselves. That's why you'll hear about lists like the "December List" created by John December, the "Yanoff List" by internaut Scott Yanoff, and the "Unofficial Internet Book List" by author Kevin Savetz.

Making money instead of making a name

Precise dates are not important, but sometime in the latter half of 1994, online Internet directories became all the rage. At that point, instead of trying to make a name for themselves, longtime Internet users began trying to make some money. And more power to them!

As a result, there are now a number of services offering directory listings to businesses. We're about to profile some of the leading companies in this field and tell you how to get listed in their directories. There are three things you should know, however.

First, it is quite typical for a company to offer you a free, basic listing but to charge for a more elaborate entry. This makes perfect sense. Just as the usefulness of a single telephone can be measured by the total number of other telephones you can reach with it, the more entries a given directory has, the more attractive it is likely to be to Internet users. And the more people who use it, the more you can charge for your expanded directory entries.

Second, everyone in these early days has his or her own idea about the most successful format or approach to take. In looking at the various alternatives people have created, you almost feel like you're

watching Darwinian evolution in progress. At this stage, Life has rolled out its initial entries. The adaptation stage has not yet begun.

Third, it is painfully obvious that we are still at a very early stage. In our opinion, none of the directories we're about to discuss has got it right. It sounds harsh, but none of them is really ready for prime time.

 # Directories to consider

All of which may have changed as you read this. But our sense is that most directories have been designed by people who know the Internet inside and out but who have no concept at all of the right way to present information to nontechnical people.

In any event, the Internet directories you should consider at this writing include:

➢ The InterNIC's Directory of Directories

➢ Dave Taylor's Internet Mall

➢ Msen's Internet Business Pages

➢ AT&T's 800 Directory

➢ Susan Estrada's NetPages

Keep track of those directories!

These days, nothing is as certain as death, taxes, and the advent of still more Internet directory services. Without a doubt, you will encounter any number of directory services not cited here. Sample them all. Then put yourself in the shoes of your typical customer and sample them again from that perspective.

If you like what you see, by all means get yourself or your business listed. But, whether you get listed with one of the directories discussed in this chapter or somewhere else, keep track of your listings!

We all know what a chore changing to and from Standard and Daylight Savings Time is—all the clocks, wristwatches, computers, VCRs, microwave ovens, and so on. Imagine the nuisance of changing

> *your company's phone or address entry in a dozen different Internet directories—when you have no record of where you're listed in the first place.*

→ The InterNIC Directory of Directories

As you may recall from Chapter 5, the InterNIC (Internet Network Information Center) is the nonprofit organization responsible for, among other things, registering domain names. But, working with AT&T, which has always been a major sponsor of the InterNIC, the organization has produced what they call the Directory of Directories. This should definitely be your first stop. Try the directory yourself, and then read the instructions you will find there for adding your own listing.

The InterNIC Directory of Directories is available in many forms (Gopher, Telnet, WWW, FTP, etc.). The way we recommend using it is to find the item on the menus offered by your local access provider or online system that lets you search "All the Gophers in the world." Then specify that you want to connect to the InterNIC Directory Gopher at this address: **rs.internic.net**. (The "rs" stands for "reference services.")

The first Gopher menu that appears will include an item labelled "InterNIC Directory of Directories." Select that—it was item 4 when we were there recently—and you will be shown a list of nearly 40 different options. Here's a sample of the first few items:

```
InterNIC Directory of Directories
Page 1 of 1

1   Information about the Directory of Directories         Text
2   Directory-Level Table of Contents                     Text
3   Entire Table of Contents                              Text
4   How to list a resource in the Direc. of Direc. (Standard)   Text
5   How to list a resource in the Direc. of Direc. (Expanded)   Text
6   Search by keyword                                     Search
7   Recent Additions to the InterNIC Directory of Directories   Menu
8   Agriculture                                           Menu
9   Bulletin Board Systems                                Menu
```

```
10   Businesses on the Internet                           Menu
11   Computing Centers                                    Menu
12   Databases                                            Menu
13   Dictionaries                                         Menu
14   Directories                                          Menu
15   Education                                            Menu
(etc.)
```

Entries labelled "Text" in the far right column are text entries. The ones labelled "Menu" are either part of the InterNIC Gopher or are designed to connect you to someone else's Gopher.

→ Searching by keyword

Probably the most important entry on this menu is item 6, "Search by keyword." Select it, and respond to the prompt with a keyword likely to be associated with the kind of business or topic you want to find.

The next most important entry is item 3, "Entire Table of Contents." Open your comm program's capture buffer so you will be sure of recording the incoming text in a file. The text will look like this excerpt from the Businesses on the Internet section of the Table of Contents:

```
   Entry Name                                   Entry File Name
   ----------                                   --------------
3k-Gopher - 3k Associates Gopher Server ............. 3k-gopher.b
AA-COmp-MStrs. AA Computer masters .................. aa-comp-mstrs.b
Adjunct Resources ................................... adjunct-resources.b
AMORE - Womens and Mens Exotic Lingerie ............. amore.b
ANSWERS-INC ......................................... answers-inc.b
Apollo Advertising - Advertising service ........... apollo.b
AT&T 800 Directory - AT&T 800 Directory on the
        Internet ................................... att-800-directory.b
AT&T Automotive Services ........................... att-auto-service.e
AT&T-TEC - AT&T Technical Education Center .......... att-tec.b
Auction - Electronic Auction ....................... auction.b
Automatrix-WWW - Automatrix World-Wide Web server ... automatrix-www.b
BRANCH-MALL - Branch Information Services Electronic
        Mall ....................................... branch-mall.b
(etc.)
```

The Table of Contents gives you a very quick way of finding out what companies are in each section of the directory—without the need to work your way through a series of menus.

 # An actual example

The complete Table of Contents is important for another reason. It will give you a better idea of things to search for by keyword.

The Table of Contents for all sections of the directory easily runs 150K or more. It would print out to nearly 50 single-spaced pages. So don't print it. Once you're offline, bring the file into your word processor and use the program's search function to look for words of interest.

Here's what we did, for example. We looked through the Table of Contents file offline and noticed an entry for the Nautical Bookshelf. Sounded interesting, so we signed on again, and opted to search by keyword, specifying *nautical*, of course. The system found a hit, which we knew it would:

```
1  Nautical Bookshelf - Nautical Bookshelf On-Line Resource Center   Text

Enter Item Number, SAVE, ?, or BACK: 1
```

We selected the item, and here is what we saw:

```
Nautical Bookshelf - Nautical Bookshelf On-Line Resource Center
Page 1 of 1

Nautical Bookshelf - Nautical Bookshelf On-Line Resource Center
Resource Type:  Commercial
Keywords:  Directory, information server, archive, introductory material,
           nautical books, nautical bulletin board, boating tips, publishing
           information, book search
========================================================================
Description:  The Nautical Bookshelf gopher provides Internet end users
              with information about nautical resources for instruction
              in powerboating, sailing, and racing. End users can find
              information on appropriate books and purchase the books via
              the Internet.
Access:       Nautical Bookshelf's gopher server can be accessed through
              the Internet via any gopher pathway leading to nautical.com.
Services:     - Internet Guide to Nautical Books
              - Top 20 Best Selling Titles
              - Automated Mailer to retrieve index, full catalog, boating
                tips, and purchasing information
              - Mail interface to all services:  Inquiries and orders to
                staff@nautical.com. Download information via info@nautical.com.
              - An on-line nautical bulletin board open to anyone interested
```

```
             permits Internet users to interact with boaters and staff.
             Send subscribe message to staff@nautical.com.
=========================================================================
Last Verified [mm/dd/yyyy]:07/05/1994    Last Updated
[mm/dd/yyyy]:07/05/1994
=========================================================================
Address: Nautical Bookshelf
         1344 Broadway/ Suite 123
         Hewlett, NY 11557
E-Mail:  staff@nautical.com
Phone:   1-800-249-9446
```

 # Getting your own FREE listing

Wow! What a splendid directory entry. And you know what? It was FREE. The InterNIC offers two kinds of directory entries: *standard* and *expanded*. Expanded entries cost $100 a month and require a minimum commitment of three months. Standard entries are free, but they are limited to 1,264 *characters* (not words) in the "Keywords" and "Description" sections. As it happens, that is almost exactly the number you'll find in the Nautical Bookshelf listing.

For instructions on how to submit a directory entry like this yourself, return to the first menu in the Directory of Directories and notice item 4, "How to list a resource in the Direc. of Direc. (Standard)." Open your capture buffer and record this item to disk.

Each directory entry is a text file, so that's what you will create. Use the Nautical Bookshelf entry as your model. And notice that you will have ample space to tell people that you have an auto-responder and where they should send a blank e-mail message. (Nautical Bookshelf even has its own Gopher!)

As you pick your keywords, put yourself into the minds of your prime prospects: What words would *they* search for? Remember, you're probably way too close to the trees to see the forest, so back up and pretend you don't know all you know about your business. (Once again, FireCrystal Communications would be happy to help you prepare and submit your listing as part of our consulting service.)

 # Dave Taylor's Internet Mall

Dave Taylor, with Rosalind Resnick, is the author of *The Internet Business Guide: Riding the Information Superhighway to Profit*, $25 from Sams Publishing. Unlike some other books on the topic, this one is *not* 30 pages of really useful information packed into 300 pages of fluff. If you can only buy one book, we're certainly glad you chose ours—the one you are now holding. But if you can afford an additional $25, you should certainly consider the Taylor/Resnick book.

We know Ms. Resnick only through her writing, which is really quite good. But we've met Mr. Taylor online—when we were doing a live conference/interview on CompuServe to promote our Random House book *Internet Slick Tricks*. We've learned that he is the author of the Elm mail program and have exchanged e-mail with him since. We've always found him to be thoughtful, considerate, and a pleasure to deal with.

Mr. Taylor has created a presence known as The Internet Mall: Shopping on the Information Highway. It is sponsored in part by Ceram, Inc., Internet Distribution Services, Mecklermedia Corporation, and Netcom Communications Services. Entries are organized using the conceptual framework of the typical shopping mall.

Practically speaking, the Internet Mall consists of a large text file which you can download or capture and then bring into your word processing program to search on the basis of a keyword. None of which sounds too glamorous, does it? But it really makes a lot of sense because it's so quick, easy, and efficient.

For example, when we searched the file on the word "coffee," our word processor took us to the following text (the plus signs indicate an item that is new or has been modified since the last issue):

```
+ TOP FLOOR: The Food Court+
Popcorn is much more than just something you put in the microwave
oven and to prove it Myers' Gourmet Popcorn of Colorado Springs
is now on the Internet! Receive a catalog of their many products
```

```
by sending email to the company: "mgp@aol.com"
+
+ Capulin Coffee from Ash Creek Orchards has hit the Web with the
+ same "kick" felt in each wonderful bean. Capulin coffee has
+ never been touched by water so it retains its full flavor and
+ potency. The sales from Capulin Coffee support a grass roots
+ conservation project on the Pacific coast of Mexico. Capulin
+ Coffee can be reached on the WWW at http://eMall.com/

(etc.)
```

 # How to get listed on the Internet Mall

There is no charge for a listing on Dave Taylor's Internet Mall. But to qualify for inclusion, you must offer products for sale on the Internet, and your customers must be able to order your products through the Net *directly*—either by Gopher, WAIS, WWW, or e-mail. Excluded from this list are Internet service providers, contract technical support from companies, or other similar marketing and sales schemes.

As explained in the "Notes on the Internet Mall" provided at the end of the file, Mr. Taylor takes responsibility for all the prose in each listing, but he does not "guarantee the legitimacy of any service listed." To get listed in the Internet Mall, send a query to **taylor@netcom.com**.

 # Where to get your copy

You can Finger Dave Taylor (finger taylor@netcom.com) to get the latest information from Mr. Taylor himself on how to obtain a copy of the Internet Mall. Here are the various ways it is offered as of this writing:

➢ Send a message to **taylor@netcom.com** with the words "send mall" as the SUBJECT.

➢ FTP to **ftp.netcom.com** and look in the directory /pub/Guides. Both compressed and uncompressed versions are available there.

➢ Check the newsgroup **alt.internet.services**.

➢ For a World Wide Web version, check **http://www.mecklerweb.comlimall.**

➢ Join the IMALL-L mailing list, and you'll automatically get the latest Mall file every two weeks. To add your name to the list, send e-mail to **listserv@netcom.com** with the words "subscribe IMALL-L" in the *body* of the message.

⇨ The Internet Business Pages

The Internet Business Pages (IBP) is a service of Msen, Inc. (pronounced "em-sen"). You can access it by using the Gopher at **garnet.msen.com**.

Listings are free. To get the IBP registration form for your company, send e-mail to **ibp-info@msen.com** and put "send form" in the SUBJECT line or in the text of the letter. The form includes name, address, and voice, sales, and fax phone. Plus e-mail address, general description, and a series of keywords describing your business or service.

This appears to be a very good feature, and Msen is certainly a major player in the business-on-the-Net field. But apparently if your prospective customers want to search the IBP database, they will need some special client software. The IBP literature suggests that you FTP to **ftp.msen.com** and look in the directory /pub/msen/ibp for the necessary files.

We decided not to go to that trouble, so we cannot report on how searchable the IBP database is. If you've got the time to put up with all this rigamarole, let us know how easily you can search the IBP database, once you have downloaded, installed, and learned to use the appropriate "client" software. (And keep in mind as you're doing it that this is the process your customers will have to go through as well.) You can reach *us* quite easily at Alfred@Delphi.com.

⇨ The AT&T 800 Directory

We have no hard data to back this up, but you just know that phone directories are enormously profitable to whichever phone company or publisher issues them. Like *TV Guide*, it is something all of us need (except for our 73-year-old friend, Albert, who, Scotsman that he is, hits us up each week for the TV section of the Sunday paper, which he also refuses to buy).

So it is not surprising that AT&T has not only long been a player on the Internet and in the InterNIC, it has also introduced at least one directory—a directory of businesses who have toll-free 800 numbers. (See Fig. 8-1 for a sample page.) This is how AT&T describes the directory:

> The AT&T 800 Directory on the Internet contains the 800 number listings which appear in the printed versions of the AT&T 800 Consumer and AT&T 800 Business Directories.
>
> It contains approximately 150,000 listings and will be updated on a monthly basis. The current version allows users to browse through the listings alphabetically by category, and by company name. Search capability will be incorporated in the near future.
>
> In addition, we plan to incorporate company advertisements and home pages in future versions of the offering. Please refer to the AT&T 800 Directory frequently asked questions (FAQ) section which is referenced on the AT&T 800 Directory Home Page for further information.

Here is how to get access to AT&T's World Wide Web (WWW) site where the directory is located:

http://att.net/dir800	AT&T 800 Directory on the Internet
http://att.net/dir800/FAQ.html	800 Directory FAQ section
http://www.att.com	AT&T Internet Home Page, which allows users to link with the AT&T 800 Directory on the Internet

Figure 8-1

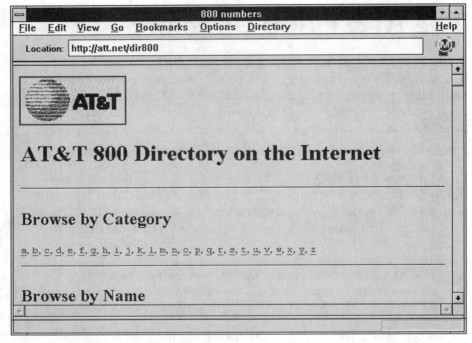

Here's a sample from the AT&T 800 Directory on the World Wide Web. It looks great!

⇨ How to enter your listing

How do you include your listing or advertisement on the AT&T 800 Directory on the Internet? The answer, according to AT&T, is to call 800-562-2255, assuming you are a current AT&T 800 service customer.

If you are *not* a current AT&T 800 service customer, you must first call 800-222-0400 to order AT&T 800 service. Upon becoming an AT&T 800 service customer, you will automatically qualify for a free listing in the AT&T 800 print and Internet directories.

If you have any questions about the directory, you may call James Chow, Product Manager, AT&T 800 Directories, at 201-631-3964, or contact him via e-mail: **jchow@attmail.com**.

⇨ Susan Estrada's NetPages

We liked Susan Estrada the first moment we talked to her. You may know her from her book, *Connecting to the Internet*, published by O'Reilly & Associates. And from her involvement in issues concerning the intersection of the Internet and business.

Well, Ms. Estrada and her company, Aldea Communications, Inc., have come up with a crackerjack idea: Why not do a *real* Yellow Pages of Internet resources? And why not make the publication available in every form imaginable? Aldea has done just that, and they call the product NetPages.

This is very much an electronic analog to the White and Yellow Pages of the typical phone book. White Page listings (name, address, phone, etc.) are free. Yellow Page listings include display ads and are billed on the basis of space occupied. Prices for Yellow Page listings range from a low of $9 to a high of $4,000 for a full-page color ad.

When we asked Ms. Estrada what made her directory unique, she pointed out that no other directory is currently available in so many different forms. You can get NetPages in printed form, on CD-ROM, or as a downloadable file. Or you can access a World Wide Web site.

⇨ All about NetPages

NetPages is published twice a year. The White Pages, where listings are free, is sorted into two sections, Business and Individual. To enter your free listing, send the following form to **np-add@aldea.com**. Make sure that you include the entire form and put your answers after the colons. (This allows automatic entry and verification of your listing.):

Your first name (Max 30 chars):

Your last name (Max 40 chars):

Your e-mail address (Max 210 chars):

Your company name (Max 70 chars):

Your title (Max 70 chars):

City (Max 35 chars):

State (Max 10 chars):

Country (Max 25 chars):

Listing Section (Choose Business or Individual):

⇨ Get the paper version!

This is all to the good. But if you are interested in seeing what NetPages is all about, our advice is to order the paper version. Send a self-addressed mailing label or a 10×13-inch envelope, plus stamps or a check for $2.90 to cover postage ($8.75 for shipping outside the U.S.) to:

Aldea Communications, Inc.
Shipping Department
2380 Camino Vida Roble, Suite A
Carlsbad, CA 92009

⇨ Making the most of NetPages

In our never-ending effort to bring you the best solutions and information, we used our online skills to locate and download not only the NetPages Yellow Pages file, but also the special software needed to view it.

Special software? Yup. NetPages is available online in three formats: Adobe Acrobat, Farallon Replica, and ready-to-print PostScript. But not plain text. (At least not at this writing.)

The reason is *graphics*. A NetPages Yellow Pages advertiser who is paying for graphics probably wouldn't be tickled about seeing his or her listing in plain text. But graphic images force the NetPages Yellow Pages file to balloon to nearly one megabyte. So figure on about eight minutes of CompuServe time at 14.4 kbps, the highest speed connection that system offers. (On CompuServe, the NetPages files are in Library 4 of the INETFORUM.)

⇨ Getting the "viewer" software

You will spend more time locating and downloading the software you will need to *view* the NetPages file on your computer.

As the authors of a book about CompuServe, we *know* how to discover if there is a free Acrobat or Replica "viewer" program on that system. What we found was a Replica viewer that required over 12 minutes to download at 14.4 kbps. The program required another five minutes to install into Windows. Add the eight minutes needed to download the Replica version of the NetPages Yellow Pages, and you're at 25 minutes, not including all the time spent searching for an Acrobat or Replica viewer program.

It is our understanding that, as you read this, you will be able to find a copy of the Replica software in Library 4 of the CompuServe INETFORUM. A free Acrobat reader has also recently become available, so you may find that software there as well. (Ms. Estrada recommends the Acrobat version of the directory because "the graphics are better and they do a pretty good job of compression.")

⇨ Was this trip worth it?

We love the concept, we like Susan Estrada, and we can see what the NetPages is getting at. But we are sorry to report that even after you've done all this, the results are less than thrilling.

We were running on a 386DX at 25 MHz with 8 megs of RAM and one meg of memory on our video card. This system is no longer state-of-the-art, but it's a long way from being ready for the junk

Figure 8-2

The NetPages greeting screen as seen via Replica.

heap. Farallon's free Replica viewer program was working just fine, but images like the one shown in Fig. 8-2 took forever to appear.

As for using Replica's built-in search function—forget it! Set the thing working, go out to lunch, and maybe, if you've stumbled on the right keyword, you'll have something of interest on your screen when you get back. Otherwise—who has time for this? It was *terrible*!

⇨ The graphics conundrum

The conundrum so many people on the Internet seem unable to get away from is the fact that *advertisers want graphics*. But graphics are simply not workable. At least not over a 14.4 or 28.8 connection, and not with the systems people have bought in the past five or six years.

But even if you could wave a magic wand and instantly turn everyone's system into the hottest, fastest Pentium or Power PC box on the market today, there is still the "knowledge factor."

Think of yourself as a consumer. Even if you have a moderate level of knowledge, would you have any idea what to do with a file called NPYPRF.RPL? Could you have found it in the first place? Would you have known how to locate and download the necessary free Replica reader program?

Of course not! It has taken your co-authors over a decade to fill our heads with such nonsense. And nonsense it is, even though it is the only thing that could bring you the image shown in Fig. 8-2 and Fig. 8-3.

Figure 8-3

Here's a typical graphical listing in the NetPages Yellow Pages directory, brought to you by Replica.

But how many of your customers or prospects are likely to have misspent the last 12 years of their lives in this fashion? So how useful is your paid ad in this directory likely to be? In our opinion, today it is as useful as the number of *printed* paper copies of the NetPages that are distributed. Tomorrow, CD-ROM-based copies may fill the bill.

For additional information about NetPages, contact Aldea Communications:

Aldea Communications, Inc.
2380 Camino Vida Roble
Carlsbad, CA 92009
800-862-5332
619-929-1100
619-929-0580 (fax)
General e-mail: info@aldea.com
Advertising info: ads@aldea.com

Bottom line on directories

The Internet is such a fast-moving target that it is all but impossible to make any definitive statement about it. Anything you say is sure to be proved wrong two months, two weeks, or even two *hours* from now. Thus, we would be the last to suggest that the directories discussed here are the last word. (Among other things, we haven't covered directories devoted to companies with World Wide Web sites.)

They are more like the opening salvo. We strongly suggest you get yourself listed here, but you cannot let it go at that. You or someone you trust has got to check the Net regularly for new directories or directory services you may want to investigate.

In any event, our advice is to set up your auto-responder and then get your company listed in as many free directories as you can, always trying to work the e-mail address of your auto-responder into your listing.

Every situation is unique. But, in our humble opinion, the most satisfying responses are likely to come from people who see your auto-responder address in your print ads. Yet it is foolish to leave any stone unturned. So if directory services are offering free listings, you should definitely take the time and effort needed to get your company listed.

Making the most of newsgroups & mailing lists

I F electronic mail is the most used Internet feature, *newsgroups*—and to a lesser extent mailing lists—are certainly the most popular. Both can provide you with an incredible amount of truly incredible information. But, unlike setting up an auto-responder, making the most of newsgroups and mailing lists requires a sincere investment of time.

Is it likely to be worth it? We honestly cannot say. The one thing we can most definitely tell you is that it would be foolish to ignore these two features of the Net. At the very least, you've got to know what they are, what they cover, and how to use them. If only for informational purposes.

⇨ Finding out what people are saying

For example, newsgroups and mailing lists make it easy to discover what people think of your products or the products produced by your competitors. All you have to do is read the "postings" to the relevant newsgroups or add your name to the relevant mailing lists.

According to the *Wall Street Journal* (September 15, 1994), Dell Computer Corp., Packard Bell Electronics, Compaq Computer Corp., and numerous other companies made a special effort to monitor Internet newsgroups—and their SIG (Special Interest Group) equivalents on such systems as CompuServe, Prodigy, and America Online—for any mention of their products.

Dell has even created an Internet SWAT Team to "peruse traffic for any mention of Dell products, ready to swoop into 'threads' of conversations to help solve customer problems, change negative perceptions, and protect the company's reputation."

⇨ Taking the time

The information aspects of newsgroups and mailing lists may or may not make sense for your particular business. But it is certainly

significant that major companies take these communications forums very, very seriously.

These two features can also be extremely helpful to anyone who wants to turn a profit on the Net. But like anything else of value, to reap the benefits, you've got to be willing to spend time and energy. And, in the case of Internet newsgroups, you've got to proceed with *extreme* caution.

In this chapter, we'll show you exactly what to do. And, as you will see, having an auto-responder service set up before you begin dabbling in newsgroups can be a major benefit.

Why are they called "news" groups?

Internet newsgroups—or netnews as they are sometimes called—are transmitted among sites by a program called Usenet, *which is a contraction of the words "USENIX" (the name of the large UNIX user group) and "network." The program was designed by Jim Ellis, Tom Truscott, and Steve Bellovin in 1979 at the University of North Carolina. Its original purpose was to automatically transmit news about various aspects of the UNIX world, hence the name "newsgroups."*

But, of course, things have grown far beyond that. Of some 10,000 groups available today, only about 30 are devoted to discussing matters related to the Unix operating system.

Today, there are newsgroups devoted to every imaginable subject. Everything from the TV shows Beavis and Butt-Head *and* The Rockford Files *to tips on brewing your own beer.*

Newsgroup essentials

Internet newsgroups are such a major factor on the Net that we could easily write a book about them alone. But here are the bare facts every businessperson must know:

> ➤ Conceptually, newsgroups are merely "player piano rolls" of messages, or *articles* in Netspeak. Each group is devoted to

some topic. The comments Internet users may want to make about that topic are posted one after the other into a long piano roll.

➤ No one controls the newsgroups on the Net. The notes people post circulate like bits of dust in the jet stream. The flow of messages among Internet sites is constant, and that stream encompasses the entire world.

➤ The only filtering that takes place is when a given site administrator decides not to accept or make available to users the contents of certain groups. And frankly, there are newsgroups devoted to topics that will curl your hair. Absolutely *anything* goes! As a result, not all systems carry all groups.

➤ Millions of people read the netnews daily. But no one reads every group. The software used to read netnews keeps track of the groups you have chosen to read regularly and which messages in those groups you have not yet read.

➤ Anyone can post a new article or a reply to an article on almost any group. Taken together, a new article and the replies (and replies to replies) it generates form a *message thread*. The only limitations are that the postings be appropriate to the group, that no single posting be longer than the equivalent of about 15 single-spaced pages of text, and that you use plain, 7-bit ASCII text.

⇨ Crucial points

The single most important thing you must know about Internet newsgroups is this: You are not to do any advertising, marketing, promotion, or selling—except in those newsgroups that were created for that purpose.

You might get away with doing it on other groups, if you do so in the right way. If you don't, you'll get *flamed* by group participants. That is, you will receive many a nasty message and word will be spread that you are not a good person, your products stink, and your company should be boycotted.

Flame messages—or just *flames*—should reassure anyone who might be concerned about the death of passionate discourse in this country. For the essence of a flame is *passion*. And without for a moment condoning the crude and obscene flames that are inevitable, one can certainly sympathize with a longtime Net user's desire to keep advertising from intruding into yet another aspect of life.

Besides, the Internet makes it easy to talk back to an advertiser— something most of us would love to be able to do the next time a wonderful movie is interrupted at a crucial point by a commercial for deodorant or floor wax. Truth to be told, many of us *do* talk back to the TV set to no avail. But on the Internet, an advertiser can hear you. And so can everyone else who reads the newsgroup.

 # How to get a comprehensive list

One thing you will quickly learn about the Net is that there is a FAQ (Frequently Asked Questions) file or a list for nearly everything. In the case of newsgroups, the FAQ is called Answers to Frequently Asked Questions about Usenet, and it is posted regularly to the newsgroups **news.announce.newusers** and **news.answers**.

The original list of newsgroups was created by Gene Spafford and then taken on by David C. Lawrence. The list comes in several parts: two parts for the alternative (ALT) groups and two for everything else. As a convenience, all of these files are available on the Newsgroup Essentials disk (Internet 4) from Glossbrenner's Choice. Or, you can get them via FTP or newsgroup postings:

➢ FTP to **ftp.uu.net**
   Path: /usenet/news.answers/alt-hierarchies/
   Path: /usenet/news.answers/active-newsgroups/

➢ Check these newsgroups:
   news.lists
   news.groups
   news.announce.newgroups
   news.answers

 # Searching offline

Once you've got the comprehensive list of newsgroups on your disk, the next step is to identify the ones most likely to be of interest. That way, you will be able to tell your newsreader program exactly which group to go to.

So, with your list of newsgroups on disk, it just makes sense to use your computer's power to search it. The program we like for this purpose is Vernon Buerg's famous shareware LIST program, but any word processing program with a "search" function will do. Just key in any topic that occurs to you, and activate the search function.

For example, we searched the Lawrence newsgroup list for the word *business* and found all of the groups shown here. Check the nearby sidebar for a description of the various newsgroup categories (alt, bit, clari, etc.).

alt.business.import-export	Business aspects of international trade.
alt.business.internal-audit	Discussion of internal auditing.
alt.business.misc	All aspects of commerce.
alt.business.multi-level	Multi-level (network) marketing businesses.
alt.computer.consultants	The business of consulting about computers.
bit.listserv.buslib-l	Business Libraries List.
bit.listserv.e-europe	Eastern Europe Business Network. (Moderated)

bit.listserv.japan	Japanese Business and Economics Network. (Moderated)
clari.apbl.biz.briefs	Hourly business newsbrief from the AP. (Moderated)
clari.apbl.biz.headlines	Headlines of top business stories. (Moderated)
clari.biz.briefs	Business newsbriefs. (Moderated)
clari.biz.earnings	Businesses' earnings, profits, losses. (Moderated)
clari.biz.features	Business feature stories. (Moderated)
clari.biz.industry.health	The health care business. (Moderated)
clari.biz.misc	Other business news. (Moderated)
clari.biz.review	Daily review of business news. (Moderated)
clari.biz.top	Top business news. (Moderated)
clari.biz.urgent	Breaking business news. (Moderated)
clari.nb.business	Newsbytes business & industry news. (Moderated)
k12.ed.business	Business education curricula in grades K-12.
misc.entrepreneurs	Discussion on operating a business.
soc.college.org.aiesec	The Int'l Assoc. of Business and Commerce Students.

Newsgroup hierarchies

To make it easier for people to find what they're looking for, Usenet newsgroups are divided into topics. Each main topic is further divided, and the result is often divided again and again, as areas are created for discussions of ever greater specificity.

*For example, a group called **alt.music** might be formed to discuss music in general. But as people really get into the swing of things, some may decide that they really want to focus on baroque or jazz or hip-hop. So **alt.music.baroque** might be formed, along with **alt.music.jazz** and **alt.music.hip-hop**. And so on.*

Here are the main topic categories of Usenet newsgroups:

- *alt*   *Alternative newsgroups. Basically, topics that don't fit neatly anywhere else. Many Usenet sites don't carry these groups.*

- *bionet*   *Biology, of course.*

- *bit*   *Topics from Bitnet LISTSERV mailing lists.*

- *biz*   *The accepted place for advertisements, marketing, and other commercial postings. Product announcements, product reviews, demo software, and so forth.*

- *clari*   *ClariNet is a commercial service run by Brad Templeton. For a subscription fee paid by the site that carries its feed, Clarinet provides UPI wire news, newspaper columns, and lots of other goodies.*

- *comp*   *Topics of interest to both computer professionals and hobbyists, including computer science, software source code, and information on hardware and software systems.*

- *ddn*   *Defense Data Network.*

- *gnu*   *As in "gnu is not UNIX." The Free Software Foundation and the GNU project.*

- *ieee*   *Institute of Electrical and Electronic Engineers.*

- **k12**   *Topics of interest to teachers of kindergarten through grade 12, including curriculum, language exchanges with native speakers, and classroom-to-classroom projects designed by teachers.*

- **misc**   *Groups addressing themes not easily classified under any of the other headings or which incorporate themes from multiple categories.*

- **news**   *Groups concerned with the Usenet network and software.*

- **rec**   *Groups oriented towards the arts, hobbies, and recreational activities.*

- **sci**   *Discussions relating to research in or application of the established sciences.*

- **soc**   *Groups primarily addressing social issues and socializing.*

- **talk**   *Groups largely debate-oriented and tending to feature long discussions without resolution and without appreciable amounts of generally useful information.*

⇨ Get your feet wet!

We've introduced you to the Internet newsgroup concept, told you how it works, and warned you not to risk getting flamed. We've also shown you how to get a comprehensive list of all the newsgroups currently on the Net.

Now we must ask something of you. Before you read any further, take the time to go online and experience what it's like to read one or more newsgroups. This is very, very easy to do. As you read this, all of the Big Five consumer systems will offer access to newsgroups. And, of course, all Internet access providers do so as well.

On many systems, you will be able to choose one or more "news readers" to use in actually reading articles. Our advice is to stay away

from newsreader programs with names like "nn" or "trn" and opt instead for the Delphi newsreader or the AOL newsreader or the CompuServe newsreader, or whatever.

Select a newsreader and then select the option that lets you specify a given newsgroup by name. Try one of the business groups like **misc.entrepreneurs** or **alt.business.misc**. Set your communications software to capture incoming text to disk and just explore!

Now for the payoff!

We're going to assume at this point that you have indeed followed our advice and spent an evening or two exploring Internet newsgroups. If that's the case, you are probably feeling overwhelmed by the breadth, depth, and diversity of this part of the Net. At least we hope so. That way you won't underestimate your task.

We hope, too, that you have started to get a sense of the extent to which each newsgroup constitutes a community. As such, each group has certain unwritten "community standards" on what is acceptable behavior and what is not.

In one group it might be considered bad form to ever reveal which company you work for, and it might be considered rude for one person to even ask such a question of someone else. Another group might be more like an industry trade show, where everyone wants you to know his or her corporate affiliation.

How can you tell what a given group's standards, mores, and concept of "acceptable behavior" is? There is only one way—you have *got* to spend time reading the postings in the group. That's why we noted earlier that working the newsgroups can be very time-consuming indeed.

The *best* way to proceed

There is absolutely no way to know whether your participation in a newsgroup will lead to additional sales. There is no way to know whether your efforts will be worthwhile. What we do know is this: Newsgroups are among the most popular features on the Net, and, with proper care, sensitivity, and an auto-responder you can use them to help get your story out. Here are the steps we recommend.

Get the Lawrence list

Get the Lawrence list of newsgroups described earlier in this chapter. Put it on your hard disk and search it for words that pertain to your product or business. That will give you a "starter list" of newsgroups likely to deal with or discuss your product or service.

Then take a day—yes, a full day—to explore all of these groups. Capture all of the messages to a disk file and then, once you are offline, read or print out that file. Try your best to get a sense of the group. If an issue is raised or a comment made to which you would like to respond, circle it in red.

You can always broaden the scope later, but you should probably start with just the one or two newsgroups that seem to bear most closely on your product, service, industry, or whatever.

Think "town meeting"

Think of each group as a town meeting of a very small town, held in Town Hall, of course. This is the most crucial step of all, for just think about what this mind set means.

Among other things, it means that everybody knows everybody else. (Or almost.) Mr. A knows what Ms. B has had to say in years past on a given issue, and Mr. C can always be counted on to make a curmudgeonly comment on anything. Ms. D is a natural leader who does a pretty good job of keeping the discussion on course, while Mr.

E is the proverbial clown who has never met a bon mot he didn't like—or utter.

It sounds like Norman Rockwell, and it is probably equally reflective of reality. But that's not the point.

The point is to see yourself as someone entering a town meeting of this sort. If it were a real town meeting and you had any sense at all, you would sit quietly and listen for a while before even thinking about making a comment of your own.

And you would be furious if some boor were to pound on the door, force it open, and toss a flurry of advertising flyers into the room. It would make you so mad that you would absolutely sputter with rage.

How dare they! Yet intrusions of that sort are exactly what some people, in misguided, stupid attempts to somehow make a fortune on the Internet have attempted. We can only hope that cooler, more sensitive heads will prevail in the future at companies, ad agencies, law firms, and the like.

Take it slow

Again, think of yourself in a town meeting. Some longtime resident rises to complain about the requirement that sidewalks in front of private homes be shovelled clean within 12 hours of a one-inch snowfall. "What if I'm sick? What if someone is crippled? What if someone is on vacation?"

If you happen to operate a snow removal service in that particular town—even if it's just a pick-up truck with snow tires and a blade and maybe a snowblower in back—no one's going to flame you for standing up and saying, "Gee, my company can help. We offer really good service at excellent rates. If you'd like to know more details, send a blank e-mail message to our auto-responder at **snow@infomat.com**."

A response like that is absolutely excellent. But notice how the fact that you have already set up an auto-responder is the key. If you didn't have an auto-responder, you would be tempted to present all of

your services and their prices as part of your newsgroup posting. That would be seen for exactly what it is—a bold-faced ad for your services. And, quite rightly in our opinion, that would not go down well with many members of the newsgroup/town meeting.

⇨ The best approach of all

At the risk of pushing the town meeting analogy too far, put yourself once again in the bleachers at the high school gymnasium or on a plastic chair in the basement of the township building. The same long-time resident raises the same questions about the ordinance requiring homeowners to clear their walks after a snowfall.

You stand up and say:

> We'd be happy to help. We will give seniors a 20 percent discount and do the sidewalks of disabled citizens for free. Plus, we have a booklet created by the National Library of Medicine about snow shovelling and heart attacks which we will be pleased to send to anyone who's interested.
>
> For details, just send a blank e-mail message to our auto-responder at snow@infomat.com.

⇨ The way to market on the Net

Ladies and gentlemen, *that* is the way to market on the Internet. Set up an auto-responder so that only those users who want your information will see it—which is to say, you will not be forcing your information on someone via e-mail or newsgroup. Even to a Net "newbie," sending mail to an auto-responder is quicker than calling an 800 number, though you may want to set up an 800 number as well.

Make the effort to identify the names of groups that might attract people interested in your product. Spend a lot of time exploring and winnowing the number down to a few key groups.

Then spend more time getting to know the "community" that each of these groups represents. Don't be bold. Be meek and mild and timid. At first. Get a sense of the group, just as you would get a sense of the house at a community town meeting.

Try to become a part of the community. Everyone is welcome, but you have got to participate. That means you will probably have to spend some time *every* week to keep up.

Leave your ego behind

As part of your offer, think in terms of *giving something back*. So many businesses are like car dealers. They plaster their names all over the place and insist that people come in—when in reality no one cares who owns the dealership or who the guy or gal is in the first place.

When you go online to offer your products or services, leave your ego behind. Take a genuine interest in the "community" and do not pull any punches. If you are honest, if you are sincere, and if you can think of some way to "give back to the Net"— whether it is a senior citizen discount or some useful or funny or otherwise interesting text file—Internet users will *want* to do business with you. And they will tell their friends, which is incredibly easy to do on the Net.

Of course your co-authors, operating as FireCrystal Communications, will be happy to help you *every* step of the way. We can identify key newsgroups, work with you to develop an appropriate "giving back to the Net" offer, and guide you in posting appropriate messages. For more on these services, see the FireCrystal Communications appendix at the back of this book.

Hand-crafted selling

In advertising parlance, the men and women who are actively involved in the Internet are the "opinion leaders" and the "early adopters" for a certain general line of products and services. They are very, very bright, and they have easy access to more information than "Joe and Jane Sixpack" can even imagine exists.

So be honest, be forthright, and be generous in the extra information you offer. Provide genuine value and absolutely superb customer service, and you will have an excellent chance of becoming a vendor of choice in the Internet newsgroup community.

The worst mistake you can make is to allow yourself to become bedazzled by the vision of the pot of gold at the end of the online rainbow. The Internet and the online world are *not* like radio and television. You cannot simply blast your ad to millions of sets and expect a boost in sales.

It's ironic, but online selling is a lot more like going door-to-door than it is like buying an ad on some top-rated TV or radio program. Yet many a fortune has been made by personal, door-to-door selling.

If you've got a truly good product or service to offer, if you're willing to work, and if you care about your customer, you can make a fortune and put every dollar in the bank with pride.

The Big Five systems, too

Among the Big Five consumer systems, the equivalent of an Internet newsgroup is a Special Interest Group (SIG). That's the generic name everyone uses. But, to be precise, CompuServe calls them "forums," GEnie calls them "RoundTables," Prodigy and AOL call them "clubs" or "bulletin boards," and Delphi calls them "SIGs."

Regardless of the name they go by, the SIGs on the Big Five systems are also worthy of your attention. Since all of these systems support Internet e-mail, citing your auto-responder in a discussion thread is very worthwhile. (The one problem at this point is that, alone among the Big Five, CompuServe charges its users at least 15 cents for each Internet e-mail message received.)

You may want to consider contributing some files to a given SIG's library. Press releases, product descriptions, price lists—and especially, truly cool, free programs—are always appreciated. Just remember that whether you're focused on the Big Five or on the Internet, you must never forget the concept of "community."

Regardless of the system you use, your Internet auto-responder will make it easy for you to present your product line or tell your story. So you won't be in the position of "advertising" where it is not appropriate.

 # Details, details: Three crucial pieces

It would be nice if we could call this section "Three *Easy* Pieces," but that would not be truthful. The fact is that there are three things you should know about Internet newsgroups that do indeed require some effort.

 ## Internet "Happenings"

First, you should know about a newsgroup called **comp.internet. net-happenings**. This is a group that will actually welcome your announcement of the opening of a Gopher or World Wide Web site, or the fact that you have set up an auto-responder. There is no way of knowing how many people are likely to read your posting to this group. But, since it doesn't cost anything, why leave this particular stone unturned?

The only caveat is to limit yourself to about 100 lines of text. As you will see when you visit the group before preparing your own posting, the articles put up by some companies are far too long. Keep yours short and sweet. After all, anyone who wants more information can request it via e-mail or hit your auto-responder.

Converting binary files to text and back

Second, there is the matter of *binary* files. Internet newsgroups, like Internet mail, can handle only plain, pure, standard, 7-bit ASCII text. Graphic images or computer programs, however, exist as collections of 8-bit, nontext bytes.

Don't worry about the details right now. The fact is that a graphic image or computer program cannot be sent as an e-mail or newsgroup posting until it has first been converted into 7-bit ASCII text. The most widely used conversion technique—binary to text and back—is called UUENCODE/UUDECODE. Versions of the UUCODE program exist for almost every kind of computer. See the Glossbrenner's Choice appendix for selection of programs for DOS and Windows users.

⇨ Starting your own newsgroup

Simply trolling relevant newsgroups for hot-button topics takes a lot of time. So much time that some companies have been known to pay people to do nothing but look at Net newsgroups.

But suppose you want to create a newsgroup of your own. Suppose your company's big enough, and widespread enough, and—doggone it, people like you! What do you do then? The answer is simple.

Anyone can create an ALT (alternative) newsgroup devoted to any topic you can imagine. Establishing groups in the other areas requires more effort and patience. Among other things, you must first consult the Net to see if there is sufficient interest in the kind of group you propose. But these strictures do not apply to groups in the ALT area.

If your company is a node on the Net, ask the person who is responsible for networking about setting up a newsgroup. If you're not big enough yet to be a node on the Net, ask your local Internet access provider. (All the FAQs you need to learn about creating newsgroups are available from Glossbrenner's Choice.)

The one caveat we would offer here is that if you decide to create your own newsgroup, you had better be prepared to appoint someone to monitor it. And, of course, you will want to mention your newsgroup in your auto-responder message.

How do ALT groups get created?

*Here is an excerpt from the file **alt-creation-guide** that is posted periodically to the newsgroups **alt.config**, **alt.answers**, and **news.answers**. The entire file is available from Glossbrenner's Choice:*

> *Like any group in Usenet, a group gets created (typically) when someone sends out a special "control" message to "newgroup" it. This is injected into the news system mostly like any other article that you read, except it has special syntax. Different sites on the net behave differently when one of these messages arrives. The news software has various ways of acting automatically on the message based on who sent it, and what hierarchy the group to be created is in (alt in our case).*

> *With respect to alt, some sites will automatically honor any "newgroup" control message it sees, and some will mail the message to the news admin who will make the decision to carry the group or not.*

> *Read on in the section "Some Positive Suggestions." Do not ask me how to send a control message, because I won't answer you. I don't have the hours it takes to go back and forth finding out what kind of news system you have, what kind of access you have to the system, and if you've followed the other guidelines as specified in this document.*

Clearly, creating an ALT newsgroup is a tad more involved than it would at first appear. This may be the reason why we have yet to find a book offering specific, hands-on instructions for preparing a control message.

*Or it may be that there is something of a Code of Silence among Internauts in this regard. After all, if everyone and his neighbor began creating ALT newsgroups, the system would quickly be overwhelmed. One consultant we know of who may be able to help you create a group is Matthew Fusfield. You can reach him at **mattfusf@omni.voicenet.com**.*

Mailing lists

Now let's consider Internet *mailing lists*.

These work just like a conventional paper-mail mailing list in that, once your name has been added to a list, messages relevant to the list will begin to appear in your electronic mailbox automatically.

As a businessperson, this can work for you in two ways. First, mailing lists can be a wonderful source of information on a given subject. If you are interested in some technical or theoretical aspect of your industry, for example, you may discover that joining the right mailing list is like becoming a member of a perpetual symposium.

Second, once you've really gotten to know the Net, you may decide that starting your *own* mailing list would be a good idea. But just as not *every* product or service is well suited for marketing on the Internet, not *every* company should have a mailing list.

Just for the fun of it

Let's have some fun and invent a completely fictitious (as far as we know)—yet workable—example. Let's assume your company specializes in reproductions of the world's greatest sculptures, scaled down to sizes appropriate to a suburban garden. Michelangelo, Brancusi, Moore, and many others are well represented in your collection.

Imagine how easy it would be to create a two-page article on each of the pieces by Michelangelo alone. How the master came to sculpt it, what critics have said about it over the ages, why your reproductions are so meticulous, and so on.

Now imagine that you have created those pieces and that you have set up a free Internet-based mailing list that will automatically send out one of your write-ups to everyone on the list once a month. Your transmissions will simply appear in their e-mail mailboxes. (Along with an order form, of course!)

No cost. No obligation. Anyone on the Internet or on one of the Big Five systems can subscribe or cancel at any time. And everything is automated by a computer running LISTSERV software.

All you have to do is keep the articles and information coming. No small task, of course, for someone trying to run a business. But talk about establishing a personal, interactive relationship with your customers! Your mailing list is like a magazine (without the pictures). If you like, you can set things up so that subscribers can contribute their own articles and comments. With you serving as "moderator," of course.

⇨ Thinking about mailing lists

Setting up your own automated Internet mailing list is not difficult to do. When you feel you're ready, contact your local Internet access provider and ask about the cost for creating a List Server or LISTSERV that will automatically add people to your mailing list and automatically send out the files you want them to have. And, by all means, provide instructions in your auto-responder telling people how to get on your list. (Again, you must make everything work *together!*)

One provider we know, for example, charges $50 to set up a list of 50 names, with a monthly maintenance fee of $25. But there is no message-based charge. You can send members of such a list as many articles as you want. Probably, you can negotiate an even better deal with your local access provider.

⇨ Essential facts

For more details on mailing lists, see our book, *Internet 101* from Windcrest/McGraw-Hill. Here, however, are the key things a businessperson needs to know.

✳ Getting a list of lists
Two of the most comprehensive lists of mailing lists are the SRI List of Lists by Vivian Neou and PAML (Publicly Accessible Mailing Lists)

by Stephanie Da Silva. To get the SRI List, send an e-mail message to **mail-server@sri.com**. Include the line "send interest-groups" in the body of the message. For PAML, check the newsgroups **news.lists**, **news.answers**, or **news.announce.newusers** where it is posted periodically.

As a convenience, both of these lists are also available from Glossbrenner's Choice on a disk called Mailing List Essentials (Internet 5). This disk also includes DOS search software to make it easy to find mailing lists of interest. See the Glossbrenner's Choice appendix at the back of the book for details.

✳ Moderated & unmoderated

Some mailing lists are *moderated*, meaning all contributions go to a single individual who then determines what gets sent to the list as a whole. On an *unmoderated* list, in contrast, whatever any subscriber sends to the list server computer gets sent automatically to everyone.

✳ How to subscribe

Subscribing to a mailing list is easy. In most cases, you simply send a request to a *subscription address*, where a human being or a computer reads it and adds you to the list. From then on, you read and respond to messages from the list's *main address*. Be careful not to send your subscription request to the main address. The SRI and PAML lists of mailing lists include subscription instructions for each list.

A "list of lists" example

Here's an example of the kinds of entries you will find in the SRI List of mailing lists maintained by Vivian Neou. We found this entry by simply searching the SRI List for the word "marketing." This is a particularly appropriate example for two reasons. First, this is a list you may want to subscribe to. Second, the list owner's company, Point of Presence, is in the business of helping companies set up Web sites and otherwise establish themselves on the Net.

INET-MARKETING@EINET.NET
  Subscription Address: LISTPROC@EINET.NET
  Owner: Glenn Fleishman <fleglei@connected.com>
  Last Update: 7/31/94 Description:

The INET-MARKETING list is devoted to the discussion of marketing goods and services in an appropriate way on the Internet. To join, send a mail message to the subscription address containing "SUBSCRIBE INET-MARKETING Your Name of Your Organization" (please put your name, such as Glenn Fleishman of Point of Presence Co. instead of Your Name . . .; do not put your e-mail address: the list processor automatically determines that from your reply address. If that is not your desired mail address, you can change it later).

The topics of this list are limitless, but should be focused around: how to reach consumers/end-users/purchasers; how to advertise and market appropriately; forums for marketing; CommerceNet's attempts to unify the business of doing business on the Net; commercial Internet "publishers" and "shopping malls"; ordering and credit card purchasing.

This list is moderated. The list owner recommends that after you subscribe, you send the command "SET INET-MARKETING MAIL DIGEST" to the subscription address. This option will send you one <32K digest of posts per day or so (sometimes more often if there are many posts) rather than each post as an individual piece of mail.

Conclusion

Clearly, newsgroups and mailing lists are a wonderful source of information. They are two key Internet features that you will not want to miss. The e-mail addresses we've given you here and the files you will find on the Internet disks you can order from Glossbrenner's Choice will help you get plugged in quickly.

Newsgroups and mailing lists can be used for marketing as well. But as we have emphasized repeatedly, doing so requires time and effort. Above all, it requires sensitivity. Unfortunately, there is really no way to know whether such efforts will pay off for you. But if you do decide to give it a try, make sure you set up your auto-responder first.

Gopher-based storefronts

CHAPTER 10

AFTER you've established your auto-responder and gotten into newsgroups and mailing lists, the next step up on the Internet marketing ladder is to rent space on a Gopher. A Gopher, as you may recall from Chapter 4, is a menu system. There are any number of legends about how this piece of software got its name, but we think we know the real answer.

Go for this, go for that

On a Hollywood movie set, the gopher is the guy or gal whom the stars or the higher ups tell to "go for coffee" or "go for a jelly doughnut." On the Internet, the Gopher software is designed to go quite literally for whatever resource you request by selecting a particular menu item.

It's a brilliantly simple and effective concept. Every item on every Gopher menu has two parts. There is the text of the menu item that you see, and there are the "hidden" Internet commands needed to go out and bring you whatever that menu item promises.

To reveal these hidden commands, try keying in info followed by the number of the Gopher menu item you're interested in. Or, if the system you're using displays a pointer next to the column of menu item numbers, move the pointer to the target item and hit your equals (=) key.

A Gopher example

We'll go into the details in a moment, but right now, imagine that you have keyed in or clicked on some command that resulted in the following Gopher menu appearing on your screen:

```
Page 1 of 1

1    Bosley's Flowers on the Internet                       Menu
2    Forest Hill Vineyard - Chardonnay                      Menu
3    Toucan Chocolates - Fine Chocolates                    Menu
4    Muscovy Imports - Contemporary Russian Fine Art        Text
5    Sweeps Vacuum & Repair Center, Inc.                    Text
6    Buy Fuller Brush Products at Distributor Discount       Text
```

```
7    Videos - WGBH Presents 3 Exciting NOVA Videos        Menu
8    Unique Concepts - Treat of the Month for Cats and Dogs Text
9    Talk 'N Toss Prepaid Telephone Calling Cards         Text
10   Travel Gems - 5-10% Off All Airline Tickets          Menu
11   Career Resumes - Resume Writing Service              Text
12   Stop Smoking in 5 Days - Stop Smoking Center         Menu
13   St. Lucia Vacation Rental                            Text
14   Seventeen State Street - Manhattan Office Space      Text
15   Janet L. Stimach, Real Estate in the Greater Seattle Menu
```

Notice that some of the listings are identified as "Text," meaning that if you select those items, you will be presented with a simple text file of information about the product or service being offered. Others are identified as "Menu" items. If you select any of these, you will be taken to a submenu offering additional choices.

But these are details. The main thing to consider is that you and your company could be on a Gopher like this. If someone were to choose, say, "Bosley's Flowers on the Internet," that would lead to a submenu listing five or six standard arrangements, each of which includes a text description of the arrangement and ordering instructions.

On the other hand, if someone were to select "Buy Fuller Brush Products at Distributor Discount," they would get a text file that included an order form for people to fill out and send in using regular mail service. By so doing, users would be able to buy Fuller Brush products at the "Independent Distributor" discount.

Where does the information come from?

When you select an item from a Gopher, you may be presented with either a submenu or a text file. Naturally, it does not matter to you where either of these items comes from. But it's important to point out that, while the menu items *you see come from a computer at your "Gopher site,"* the text files *that appear might actually come from halfway around the world!*

It is very, very important for you to grasp this concept. On the Internet, all points are the same. Distance does not matter. Information travels so fast that the hundreds or thousands of miles separating two computers simply do not signify. So the computer presenting you with a Gopher menu and the computer delivering the

text file that appears when you select an item might as well be one, as far as we human beings can tell.

The reason we're hitting this so hard here is to prepare you for the World Wide Web, the focus of the next chapter. When you use a Gopher, you select an item from a menu that may trigger an FTP file transfer, a WAIS database search, a Telnet logon to a distant computer, or some other action.

World Wide Web pages may include menus as well. But what you will usually find are hypertext "hot link" words that you can double click on. Much of the time your double click causes the Web site to do exactly what Gopher does—namely, reach out and pick up a file or take some other action involving a distant computer.

The main difference is that Gopher makes users pick an item off a menu, while the Web lets users double click on highlighted words. The results, however, are often the same. Identical, even. At least in terms of the information delivered to the prospective buyer. It's true that the Web offers graphics, but, as you know from our previous vituperations, World Wide Web graphics are useless to most people.

Exploring Gopherspace

In our opinion, Gophers are the best information retrieval feature on the Internet. We can easily send e-mail using one of the Big Five consumer systems. And each of those systems offers a wide array of newsgroup-like SIGs. But nobody can match a really good Gopher.

You will simply have to try this for yourself. If you're a DOS user, we recommend Delphi. Sign on, key in internet gopher at the Main Menu and just explore. If you need a graphical interface, we recommend America Online. Sign on to that system and key in Ctrl-K to generate a prompt for a "keyword." When the prompt appears, key in Internet Center. Double click on the Gopher icon, and have a ball! (As you read this, it is likely that CompuServe, GEnie, and Prodigy will have begun offering Gopher access as well.)

Is Gopher right for you?

Before you can decide whether a Gopher approach is right for you and your business, you have got to go experience a lot of Gophers that are oriented to sales and marketing. You will find lots of examples later in this chapter. Right now, though, we need to talk about *concepts*.

The first thing you've got to do is to think about your product line or the range of services you offer. As a *menu* system, Gophers are ideal for companies that have a large line to sell. If Panasonic or Sony were to maintain Gophers, for example, just think of the items you would find on the menus and submenus and sub-submenus of such a Gopher. Radios, televisions, VCRs, breadmakers, CD Players, computer disk drives—the list of products is seemingly endless.

For companies like that, with many different product lines and many different products to sell, the menu-style presentation Gopher provides makes a huge amount of sense. Properly done, Gopher menus can make it very easy for prospects to zero in on just those items they want to know about.

But what if you're, say, a maker of down-filled pillows? Or what if you're a CPA offering tax preparation and a range of other services? Do you really need a Gopher-style menu system to help prospects better understand your products and services?

A simple auto-responder may be better

Probably not. If you were to rent space on the Branch Information Services Gopher (branch.com), your bill would be about $960 for the year. (That includes a home page on the World Wide Web and an automated e-mail responder, so it's not a bad deal.) Your main menu item would probably lead to a text file, not to a submenu of some sort. Whether you're a pillow maker or a CPA, the range of products

and services you offer probably does not require a menu system to explain.

A single, well-worded text file would probably do the job. Just be sure to include an order form at the end of your Gopher file to make it easy for customers to place an order or request more information. Gophers, unlike World Wide Web sites, are not really designed to interact with customers and accept orders on the spot.

For all of these reasons, if you've got a relatively simple story to tell, you might be better off setting up an auto-responder and spending your time and money spreading the word about how people can access it. After all, like the typical bricks-and-mortar shopping mall they are modeled after, Internet "malls" do advertise in a general way. They want to attract people. But they don't advertise specific shops.

Sample lots of storefronts

At this early stage of development, most Internet "shopping malls" will rent Gopher-based storefronts to anyone whose check doesn't bounce. That means that if you sell, say, flowers, fine chocolates, or audio CDs, you could very easily be cheek-by-jowl with half a dozen other merchants selling the exact same merchandise. And who needs that!

This entire field is evolving at a breathtaking pace. But good old, practical common sense will triumph in the end. We have some really good Gopher-based storefronts to show you—every one of which will eagerly rent you space.

But before you send anybody a check, check them out. Put yourself in the shoes of a prospective customer and sign on to a given Gopher-based "mall." Play around with it. Then see if you can get some information on what it will cost you to get your firm listed at a given site.

Don't make a commitment to anyone until you've tried several Gopher sites. (A nice collection of sites follows.) Then make up your

own mind. Do you really need a Gopher-based service to tell your story? What does the "mall" company say about the steps it will take to advertise its existence and bring in customers? What's their policy on competitors—are you guaranteed to be the only gourmet coffee store, for example, or will there be others? Does the mall connect to the Net via at least a T1 line (1.544 megabits per second) so it can send and receive Internet information at high speeds?

The Branch Mall

Jon Zeeff's Branch Information Services certainly has one of the more impressive offerings for companies seeking to do business on the Net as part of a "shopping mall." But the company's Gopher may be its least appealing feature. And the reason is revealed by the very last item on the Branch Mall Gopher menu:

59 The real Branch Mall uses WWW/Mosaic at htpp://branch.com:10

The policy at Branch Information Services is to give all customers an auto-responder, a listing on their Gopher, and a home page on the World Wide Web—all for one price. But clearly they've devoted most of their attention to their Web site.

The Branch Gopher, at this writing, blasts about 60 menu items up your screen. That's because most of the items on the main menu lead to simple text files instead of submenus. As a result, it is nearly impossible to find anything.

This may have changed as you read this, so be sure to check them out by using your access provider's Gopher option to Gopher to **branch.com**. Then use your provider's Web browser (Mosaic, NetCruiser, NetScape, etc.) to experience the Web version of the Branch Mall at **http://branch.com:10** or **htpp://branch.com: 1080**.

Rates start at $960 per year for a single Web page (plus a Gopher listing and an auto-responder). You supply a photo or graphics file and ad copy, and Branch Information Services will prepare your page for you. If you want visitors to your Web site to be able to enter their

orders interactively online, the cost is an additional $500 per year. Lots of other options, including custom services and putting entire product catalogs online, are available. All prices are subject to change, but the ones we've quoted here will give you a starting point.

You can reach Branch Information Services by voice phone at 313-741-4442.

 # The Internet Information Mall

Still another impressive offering is the Internet Information Mall offered by Andrew Currie's Colorado-based Cyberspace Development, Inc. At this writing, two main options are available—the Internet Brochure and the Internet Storefront. Note that Cyberspace quotes their prices for an initial six-month period, and advises potential vendors that renewal fees will be "negotiated on an individual case basis."

The Internet Brochure is basically a text file describing your company, products, etc. Cyberspace Development charges you on the basis of how you want to *distribute* your text file. An e-mail-based auto-responder is $250 for six months. An auto-responder, plus a Gopher menu listing is $1,750 for six months. A Web page, plus a Gopher listing, plus an auto-responder is $2,000 for the initial six months, plus $50 an hour for set-up services.

Those prices sound high compared to Branch Information Services. But before you reject Cyberspace Development out of hand, consider that all of these fees include two hours of consulting services to help you select and prepare your materials, 10 megabytes of storage space, one free update of your file per month, an e-mail alias, and a monthly report on the number of hits you've had on the system.

The second offering is the Internet Store. This includes everything described for the Internet Brochure, but adds the capability of accepting orders and credit card information via your own credit card merchant account. The cost for a Gopher and auto-responder under this option is $2,500 for the initial six months. The cost for a

Gopher, auto-responder, and WWW page is $3,000 for six months, plus $50 for Web page set-up services.

Since this is a chapter about Gophers, we should also point out that the Cyberspace Development Marketplace Gopher is quite well organized. Admittedly, this company has some 13 stores, compared to Branch's 60, but they seem to have paid much more attention to their Gopher offerings, as this first-level menu makes obvious:

```
1    NEW RELEASE! The Internet Adapter (tm) : SLIP on your shell Menu
2    Online Bookstore                                           Menu
3    The Maloff Company (Internet Reseller Market Report)       Menu
4    Opposite Field - Mixing Business with Pleasure             Menu
5    UNIROM - CD-ROMS World Wide                                Menu
6    Trendwatch - Your Highway to the World                     Menu
7    Mastermind Mall                                            Telnet
8    Information Law Alert                                       Menu
9    Interactive Publishing Alert                               Menu
10   *Alternative-X*                                            Menu
11   Essential Data, Inc.                                       Menu
12   INFOMARK - International Telecom Information                Menu
13   Digital Future Newsletter                                  Menu
14   About MarketPlace.com - The Internet Information Mall (tm) Text
15   More Information on Cyberspace Development, Inc.            Menu

Enter Item Number, SAVE, ?, or BACK:
```

Here is how to check out Cyberspace's Marketplace: Use Gopher to reach their Gopher menu at **marketplace.com**. Then use Mosaic or your favorite Web browser to look at their Web site at **http://marketplace.com**.

For the latest information on their prices and service offerings, send a blank e-mail message to each of the following addresses:

➤ info@marketplace.com

➤ prices@marketplace.com

➤ faq@marketplace.com

The company's address for regular e-mail is **office@marketplace .com**. The voice phone is 303-938-8684.

 # The Merchandise Mart

The Merchandise Mart is still another offering that deserves your consideration. It's a product of the Electronic Newsstand, one of the better known locations on the Net. (The company claims that the newsstand location, of which the Merchandise Mart is a part, is accessed over 60,000 times a day.)

To reach the Electronic Newsstand and hence the Merchandise Mart, Gopher to **internet.com**. (The Electronic Newsstand is a marketing partner with Robert Raisch's The Internet Company, hence the nifty "internet.com" domain name.) Here's the menu you will see, followed by the submenu displayed when you choose "The Merchandise Mart" from the main menu:

```
Page 1 of 1

1    Introduction to The Electronic Newsstand              Menu
2    Notice of Copyright and General Disclaimer — Please Read   Text
3    Magazines, Periodicals, and Journals (all titles)     Menu
4    Business Publications and Resources                   Menu
5    Electronic Bookstore                                  Menu
6    Music! (8 magazines and 80,000 CD titles)             Menu
7    Travel, Trade Shows etc./ Lufthansa Takes Off         Menu
8    The Electronic Car Showroom(tm)                       Menu
9    News Services                                         Menu
10   The Merchandise Mart                                  Menu
11   WIN A TRIP TO EUROPE SWEEPSTAKES                      Menu
12   Search All Electronic Newsstand Articles by Keyword   Menu

Enter Item Number, SAVE, ?, or BACK: 10

The Merchandise MartPage 1 of 1

1    Using The Merchandise Mart      Text
2    How marketers can participate   Text
3    Products and Services           Menu

Enter Item Number, SAVE, ?, or BACK:
```

You'll find much more information when you select the first two items of the "Merchandise Mart" menu. But basically, you can have a Gopher listing running up to six full pages (about 30,000 characters) for $200 a month, with a minimum commitment of three months, payable in advance.

The Merchandise Mart also has the ability to set you up with a customized interactive ordering program—which it calls a "door," a term more common in the BBS world. You will be charged a one-time fee of $40 an hour to have this feature configured for your business.

At this writing, the Merchandise Mart has only about seven merchants, but, like the other two firms profiled here, they really do seem to know what they're doing. So, check them out. Send e-mail queries to **mart@enews.com**, or call them at 202-331-1601.

 Still more alternatives!

So many Gophers, so little time. The three companies we've told you about here are far from the only ones offering Gopher-based storefronts and related services. We picked them because they give a good general sampling of what's available and what it's likely to cost. But you will also want to take a look at the following:

> Msen, Inc. (pronounced "em-sen"). Gopher to **garnet.msen .com**. You'll find lots of information abut Msen, Inc., and the Msen Marketplace, which currently offers listings from companies like Ameritech Cellular Services, the Detroit Free Press, and White Rabbit Toys. For a price list, send e-mail to **info@mail.msen.com**. Or call them at 313-998-4562.

> The World. Gopher to **world.std.com**. The World system is a product of Software Tool & Die. It offers a full range of Internet access features, primarily to customers in Massachusetts. But it also offers its Vendor Archive, a service that lets World customers distribute their information via Gopher, FTP, and other popular Internet utilities.

> You'll find booksellers, consultants, non-profit organizations, and more on the main Gopher menu. But you will also find "Shops on The World." This is definitely something you should see, since "Shops" offers such a variety of merchandise and uses the Gopher menu system to good effect. For more information, send e-mail to **info@world.std.com** or call them at 617-739-0202.

➤ Telerama's Shopping Plaza. A Pittsburgh-based company and Internet access provider called Luce McQuillin has created a service it calls the "Shopping Plaza at Telerama." To reach it, Gopher to **gopher.lm.com**. The notion here is to give companies a chance to put up their electronic catalogues. Again, this is a service worth a look. For more information, send e-mail to **sysop@telerama.lm.com**, or call them at 412-481-8566.

⇨ Conclusion

Should you go with a Gopher or simply set up an auto-responder? Or should you contract with a service that offers you both, and a Web home page besides? It is hard to know what to do. But, then again, life, business, politics—they're all nothing but gambles based on our best guesses. And, boy is that *ever* true on the Internet.

We like the auto-responder concept because it's cheap and because it puts you in control. But if an auto-responder is to do you any good, you've got to advertise, whether using conventional print and electronic means or using newsgroups and mailing lists. We also love the fact that there are no competitors to worry about.

That's definitely *not* the case with one of the Internet "malls." In their eagerness and enthusiasm, the companies that offer Gopher storefronts and World Wide Web sites will take almost anyone. So imagine that you're committed to a one-year contract with such a company at a cost of nearly $1,000. And two months after you "open your store on the Net," the Internet "mall" you're dealing with accepts a direct competitor of yours.

Adding insult to injury, the Internet "mall" company organizes its menus so that all sellers of sports equipment are grouped together on one submenu, and all bookstores are grouped into another menu, and all florists are grouped into yet another menu, and so on.

This is great for shoppers because it makes it much easier to locate the kind of stores they want.

But what about you?

If you were Sears and you were at a real mall, you would know very well that your kitchen department and the kitchen department at Macy's were pretty much identical. But you're at one end of the mall, and Macy's is at the other. Any shopper who wants to compare prices will have to take a hike from one store to the other.

Depending on the size of the mall, the customer's stroll could take 10 to 15 minutes or more in one direction. But on an Internet shopping mall, the customer can move from one store to its competitor in seconds! That makes it incredibly easy to compare prices on brand-name goods.

Our advice is try the Gopher sites we have suggested here. Again, put yourself in your customers' shoes. Which site do you feel is likely to do the best job for you and your product line? When a company tells you that they promote their "malls," ask them for specific details: Which newsgroups? How often do they post? Do they have a conventional advertising or public relations agency to get their name into the print media?

At this stage, there is no way to know what to do. If you have one or two thousand dollars to risk and are willing to help promote your Gopher-based storefront on the Net, then it is certainly worth a try.

Just don't make the mistake of assuming that your customers will come to you. Whether you use an auto-responder, a Gopher storefront, or a World Wide Web site (the topic of the next chapter), you've still got to go out and tell prospective customers that you're there.

11

World Wide Web storefronts

IN terms of expense and complexity, the ultimate tool available to a business interested in making money on the Internet is a home page on the World Wide Web—with all its possibilities for graphics, sound, multiple fonts, and hypertext hot words.

But in terms of effectiveness in generating sales, well, who knows? Things may have changed as you read this. But right now, all of the articles in newspapers and magazines tend to feature the fact that the XYZ Company is entering the Information Age by putting up a World Wide Web home page. O frabjous day! Callooh! Callay!

There are no articles about how much money the XYZ Company is making as a result of being on the Web or how successful their "presence" has been. After more than a year of Internet and Web hype, news reports of this sort are conspicuous by their absence.

Has anyone managed to make a fortune on the Web? Has anyone even generated enough business to pay for the cost of creating and maintaining a Web home page? At this point, the rest is silence.

Loud & ludicrous claims

Or almost. In what *Boardwatch Magazine* editor Jack Rickard terms "Internet Math," the usage claims made by firms involved in selling Web sites and software have been both loud and ludicrous. Here's what Mr. Rickard had to say in the December 1994 issue, page 43–44:

> This has reached comic proportions—apparently everyone on the planet is both using Mosaic and running a Web server—at the same time. The methodology is a bit cute. You subdivide anything into micro parts, state it as a huge number with a qualifier, and then drop the qualifier kind of innocently.

> Web sites are a good example. Some of the sites are reporting as many as 10,000 "hits" per day. This implies some 10,000 individuals contacting the server. Actually, each reference to any page or image within a document is a hit—and we may actually be talking about 100 people here.

Similarly, we are seeing reports of 10,000 Web servers out there. This is erroneously derived from the reported 10,000 "pages"—also probably a wag.

⇨ The wisdom of Rob Raisch

One of the most articulate and perceptive contributors to the debate over the best way to market on the Internet is Rob Raisch of The Internet Company (**raisch@internet.com**). In a wonderful posting to the INET-MARKETING mailing list with the subject "How the Web beat the Media," he writes:

I should also preface this by mentioning that I would love it if what I talk about below was wrong.

Hell, I sell expertly managed, exceptionally well connected information services on the global Internet for a living and the more data I ship the closer I get to that Jaguar I have my eye on. (Not so subtle plug for The Internet Company—remember, I'm tired and cannot be held accountable. <wicked grin>)

Folks, I think we have a real problem here.

If MecklerWeb, GNN [Global Network Navigator] and projects like it continue to sell Mosaic as the easy way to market to over 25 million willing Internet consumers, we are heading for a "marketing crash" of immense proportions.

It's a question of managing the expectations of the advertiser. We have raised the stakes in online marketing to a point where we cannot provide that which we have promised: the consumer.

How many of the Fortune 1000 will it take do you think, yelling blue murder to the media that they have been cheated by Internet marketing projects to make the Internet look like the technological boondoggle of the next century?

Anyone remember videotex?

Mr. Raisch closes with what he calls "The Mosaic Challenge" to all the current marketing projects on the Net which deliver sexy graphics via Mosaic. He offers real money to anyone who can "show me that there are more than 50,000 users of Mosaic—used as a browser and retriever of graphical content on the global Internet on a regular basis."

These comments were excerpted from a July 1994 posting to the INET-MARKETING mailing list. To get a copy of the entire file, FTP to **ftp.einet.net** and check the path pub/INET-MARKETING/. There you will find each month's postings to the INET-MARKETING list in a separate file.

⇨ Graphics are "sexy"

The attraction—the "sexiness"—of the World Wide Web is easy to understand. After all, who wouldn't prefer a screen like the one shown in Fig. 11-1 to the text-based material found in an auto-responder or Gopher? It doesn't communicate a great deal of information—certainly not as much as a text file occupying the same screen space—but it projects a wonderful image.

⇨ You gotta be crazy to use a catalogue—right?

Why would you pick up a Lands' End, L.L. Bean, or Eddie Bauer catalogue, page through all the color photos and descriptions, select what you want, and then dial a toll-free 800 number to talk to a human being who will take your order?

Not when you can boot up your computer, wait for the software to load, wait again while your modem dials out at a "blazing" 28.8 kbps, and then key in a long, complicated series of letters and numbers to get to your Web site. No sir-ree!

And when you finally get there, you will, of course, be happy to wait two or three minutes for each of the photo-filled "pages" in your Web

Figure 11-1

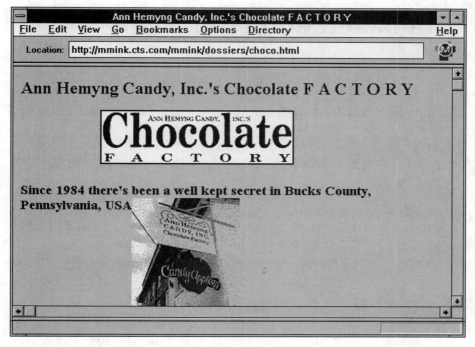

The chocolate factory.

catalogue to appear. And neither you nor your customers will mind that only a limited number of items are offered. It's not as though one can put the entire Williams Sonoma catalogue on the Web. (You could, actually, but it would be prohibitively expensive.)

And you just know that your customers will eagerly opt for your interactive online order form—untouched by human hands. Sure, they'll take it on faith that the gift they want is in stock and will get to Aunt Jane in plenty of time. Wait a minute—you *did* click on the "okay" button to approve the order, didn't you? Are you really sure your order was registered and that the product will be shipped? And who do you call if you are not sure?

199

 # The naked emperor, again

Folks, listen to us. The World Wide Web is a wonderful concept: photos, graphics, sound, multimedia, everything!

But it doesn't work. At least not now. At least not for selling goods and services. Not when the speed of data transmission is 28.8 kbps. As we've said before, that's the top speed currently available to the mass market, and only a small percentage of the mass market has moved beyond 9.6 kbps (9600 bps).

The Web will never work until the vast majority of households are able to tap it through their television cable systems or through fiber-optic connections put into place by the phone companies. And you can imagine how long we will have to wait for that to happen.

 # A painful experience

At 28.8 kbps, using the World Wide Web is a *painful* experience. If you put up a Web site, you can expect some of your prime prospects to try it once or twice for the novelty. But, unless they've got more time and money than sense, they won't be back.

Life is too short to spend much of it waiting for a color photo of your product to be pumped to computer over standard phone lines at 28.8 kbps. Most of your hits are likely to come from college students who have free access to high-speed connections and who generally never buy anything.

 # The "learning experience"

Okay, so what about the learning experience? What about all the insight you will gain that will put you miles ahead when the nation finally does get cabled for high-speed fiber-optics?

If you're a big company, the cost of gaining experience on the Net is so low it doesn't amount to a rounding error. Yet, whatever insight

you gain is likely to be filed away. By the time the company really needs it, it will have been lost or the point person on the project will have changed jobs or companies.

If you're a small company, you probably have no business even thinking about putting up a Web home page at this time. When the time comes that Web pages look like they will be truly effective, you can buy "experience" by the hour by simply hiring a consultant.

With all the railing we've done against graphics and the World Wide Web, you're going to think that we have some special animus against it. We do not. It's just that we see the cliff, and we see an industry motivated by self-interest and aided by an ignorant news media. And they're urging the lemmings onward, ever onward.

All we are saying is "Give common sense a chance!" Put yourself in the shoes of your customer—which should fit you pretty well by now, considering all the times we have urged this step—and try the World Wide Web sites cited here. The only caveat is that you do so using a 14.4 or 28.8 kbps modem, not some super high-speed connection you may have at the office.

 # Definition of terms

The quantity of information available concerning the ins and outs of the Web is staggering. So you should be relieved that you don't have to read much of it, unless you want to. We'll give you the basics here. If you want more, take a look at the two-part World Wide Web FAQ. You can get the latest copy by FTP-ing to **rtfm.mit.edu** and checking the path /pub/usenet/news.answers/www/faq, or you can get it on disk from Glossbrenner's Choice.

The WWW FAQ is very well done, and we highly recommend it—though it does veer into "byteheadedness" at times. In any event, there are really just a few key terms and concepts you need to know to have a basic understanding of the World Wide Web.

 # HTML, Mosaic, & URLs

At the heart of the World Wide Web is a page-description language called Hypertext Markup Language (HTML). HTML uses an approach similar in concept to PostScript. This is what's responsible for those gorgeous screens you see featured in newspaper and magazine articles about the Internet—the ones with full-color photos, snazzy fonts, and Mac/Windows-style sculpted buttons and controls. But these photos can be misleading.

Those screens are usually produced by the Web browser, Mosaic or NetScape, the latest version of Mosaic. Mosaic software is available for free, but it requires a SLIP/PPP connection. Ditto for Cello, Lynx, Viola, Midas, NetCruiser, Chimera, and the other Web browsers you may have heard of.

Another key term is URL, short for Uniform Resource Locator. This is a draft standard for specifying an object on the Internet. The object can be anything—a file, a newsgroup, a Web site, and so forth.

URLs are thus informative addresses that, in a single expression, tell you the kind of object and where it can be found. Here's an example:

```
file://wuarchive.wustl.edu/mirrors/msdos/graphics/gifkit.zip
```

This URL tells you that the file gifkit.zip can be found at the **wuarchive.wustl.edu** site, along the specified path. The two slashes after the colon indicate that a machine name follows. (Note: URLs are case-sensitive.)

The URL **http://info.cern.ch:80/default.html** specifies a World Wide Web site and HTML hypertext file. The "http" stands for Hypertext Transport Protocol. That's the tip-off that it's a Web site. And, as mentioned earlier, "html" stands for Hypertext Markup Language, the page-description language used to prepare Web-accessible documents.

Page preparation fees

There are two reasons why the "Internet industry" is so enthusiastic about WWW pages. First, the end results are pretty. Fonts and photos or graphics—it's great! Second, once you have supplied the images and the advertising copy, someone must code, convert, and otherwise transform your material into a Web page, at rates running from $40 to $100 an hour or more.

Talk about charging what the traffic will bear! Let's assume that you provide all the text and all the images necessary. The amount of work required to put your text file on a Gopher is minimal. It's about equal to the work required to prepare the script file needed to put up a conventional Web page.

 # Do it yourself?

We are great believers that you should "Do what you do best and hire the rest," a motto we stole from Sue Rugge, co-author of *The Information Broker's Handbook* from McGraw-Hill. On the other hand, it's important to have some idea of what you're buying.

As it happens, if you have some feeling for computer programming, creating your own Web page is not terribly difficult. The WWW FAQ cited earlier will help, as will an article by Angela Gunn in the November 1994 issue of *Computer Shopper* called "Power in Pictures—a Web-page primer." (The Gunn article is available on the Ziff-Davis Computer Select CD-ROM you may find at your local library, or in Computer Library Plus, which you'll find on CompuServe.)

As Ms. Gunn notes, "Embedded formatting codes direct Mosaic [or any other Web browser program] to display text in the various typefaces and sizes. Links to other files and sites are set off by additional coding, called anchors. . . The entire page is stored as a file with a .html extension."

Figure 11-2

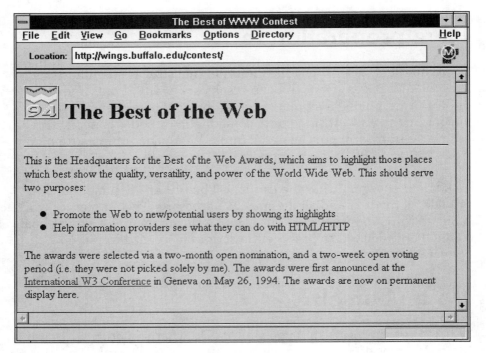

The Best of the Web contest.

For example, here is the HTML file that produced the screen shot shown in Fig. 11-2. You may not want to prepare such a file yourself, but you must admit, it doesn't look too tough:

```
<TITLE>The Best of WWW Contest</TITLE>
<H1><IMG SRC="/contest/logo1.gif"> The Best of the Web</H1>
<HR>

This is the Headquarters for the Best of the Web Awards, which
aims to highlight those places which best show the quality,
versatility, and power of the World Wide Web. This should serve
two purposes:

<UL>
<LI>Promote the Web to new/potential users by showing its highlights
<LI>Help information providers see what they can do with HTML/HTTP
</UL>

The awards were selected via a two-month open nomination, and a
two-week open voting period (i.e. they were not picked solely by
me). The awards were first announced at the <A
HREF="http://www1.cern.ch/WWW94/Welcome.html">International W3
```

Conference</A> in Geneva on May 26, 1994. The awards are now on permanent display here.

Directories & other Web goodies

One may not be able to rely on the numbers reported by various Internet companies, but there is no question but that the number of World Wide Web sites exploded in 1994. And there is no denying that this phenomenon has thrown into high relief a problem that Web users have always had—namely, *finding* things.

It's hard to say whether this problem will *ever* be solved. After all, can you imagine the size of an *international* business phone book listing all the companies you can reach via your handy telephone? As we have said repeatedly, on the Net, geographical location does not matter. So there is no natural division for creating "phone books."

On the other hand, the Internet has attracted some of the world's best minds, and it does place some remarkable tools in their hands. Thus, at this writing, we can recommend at least three sites or services designed to help you locate things on the Web.

Commercial Service Directory

The first is the Commercial Service Directory created by Open Market, Inc. You can contact them at **editors@directory.net**. At this writing, the Directory covers nearly 1,300 companies with Web sites.

You can submit your own listing by using Mosaic or some other Web browser to go to **http://www.directory.net/dir/submit.cgi**. And you can get the latest information by simply sending a blank e-mail message to **info@directory.net**.

This is a free service. There is no charge for listings. But listings are limited to companies, institutions, or organizations with a presence on the World Wide Web, *not* individual products or services.

Figure 11-3

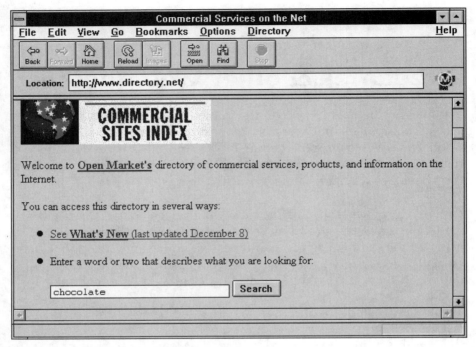

Searching commercial services.

The really neat thing about the Commercial Service Directory is that it is *searchable*. Thus, when you access its site with your Web browser, you will see a screen like the one shown in Fig. 11-3, where you can enter a word like "chocolate" and come up with the hits shown in Fig. 11-4. When you double click on the first bullet, "Ann Hemying Candy," you will be taken to the screen shown in Fig. 11-1.

⇨ What's New & "The Best"

Once you get your Web page up and running, be sure to submit it to the NCSA "What's New Page" at **http://www.ncsa.uiuc.edu/SDG /Software/Mosaic/Docs/whats-new.html**.

This site carries announcements of new servers on the Web and new Web-related tools. You can also check out the newsgroup **comp.internet.net-happenings**, which carries WWW

Figure 11-4

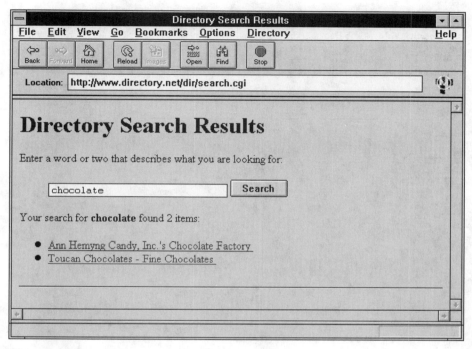

The results are in.

announcements and many other Internet-related announcements. As you read this, the group **comp.infosystems.www.announce** may also have popped into existence. See Fig. 11-5 for a sample. (Each week the opening page is sponsored by a different company.)

Finally, you should also use your Web browser to explore a feature called "The Best of the Web." Go to the site at **http://wings .buffalo.edu/contest/**. That will take you to a screen like the one shown in Fig. 11-6, which will lead you to a screen like the one in Fig. 11-7. This is a very well done feature, and you will enjoy exploring it on your own, we are sure.

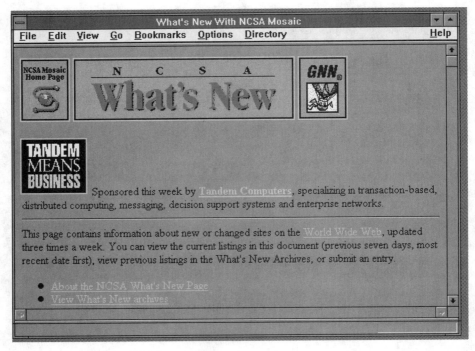

Figure 11-5

What's new on the Web?

Interesting Business Sites

Bob O'Keefe at Rensselaer Polytechnic Institute's School of Management in Troy, New York, maintains a unique list called "Interesting Business Sites on the Net." This is a short (about 50 items), highly selective list and is well worth checking out. To do so, you can use Veronica to look for "Interesting Business Sites on the Web" and thus find the Gophers that carry this feature.

*A better alternative, however, is to use Mosaic, Netscape, NetCruiser, or your favorite Web browser to go to **http://www.rpi.edu/~okeefe /business.html**. (Yes, that's a "tilde" or "squiggle" just before "okeefe"!)*

Figure 11-6

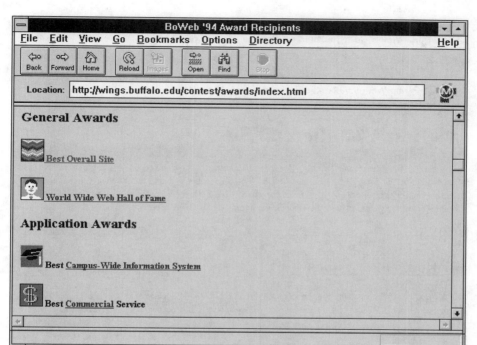

"The Best of the Web" general awards screen.

Two

⇨ Two top Internet magazines

If you want an easy way to keep up with the Net, get a subscription to *Internet World*. This magazine is published by MecklerMedia, a company whose books, magazines, and newsletters have been tracking the online world for over a decade, long before the Internet became publicly available. At this writing, charter one-year subscriptions (12 issues) are available for $19.97. Call 800-573-3062.

For in-depth coverage of the Internet as well as BBSs and commercial systems, we recommend Jack Rickard's *Boardwatch Magazine*. You will find articles that could benefit from severe pruning, but you will also find truly excellent information. Subscriptions are $36 a year (12 issues). Call 800-933-6038.

Figure 11-7

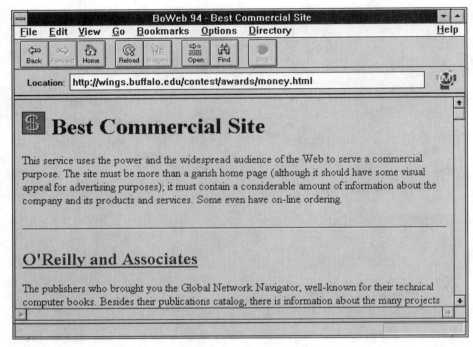

Best commercial site from "The Best of the Web."

Newsletter for businesses on the Net

Another publication worth checking out is *Internet Business Advantage (IBA)*, published by Wentworth Worldwide Media. *IBA* is a 20-page newsletter aimed specifically at businesses—particularly *small* businesses—using the Internet to market their products and services. The articles are short and nontechnical, and each issue is packed with practical advice on how to use the Net most effectively. You'll also find lots of "pointers" to interesting commercial sites on the Internet, business resources, brief company profiles, and so forth. Charter subscriptions are currently being offered at a special rate of $67 a year (12 issues). Call 800-638-1639.

⇨ More Web goodies

There are literally hundreds—if not thousands—of World Wide Web sites you can access. And many of them are devoted to marketing and selling products on the Net. By way of research, we think you will find accessing the sites listed below worthwhile:

➤ Branch Mall. See the discussion of the Branch Mall in Chapter 10. Access: **http://branch.com:1080** or **http://branch.com:10**.

➤ CommerceNet. This is an Internet-based home shopping network, that, as of October 1994, was funded with $12 million of seed money from the federal government and companies like Apple, Sun Microsystems, Lockheed, and the Bank of America. Participating companies are expected to pay $25,000 a year for a high-level membership, though lower-priced memberships will also be offered. Access: **http://logic.stanford.edu/cit/commercenet.html**.

➤ Cyberspace Development. See the discussion of Andrew Currie's Internet Information Mall in Chapter 10. Access: **http://marketplace.com**.

➤ Digital Equipment Corporation (DEC) Emall. DEC's Electronic Shopping Mall can be accessed at **http://www.service.digital.com/html/emall.html**.

➤ Global City. Books, hardware, software, and a variety of services. Access: **http://kaleidoscope.bga.com/km/KM_top.html**.

➤ Global Network Navigator (GNN) Marketplace. GNN is one of the major sites on the Net. It offers reference resources and information, special interest publications, netnews, special Internet-oriented publications, and much more. You must subscribe to gain access, but subscriptions are free. Access: **http://gnn.com/gnn.html** or **http://nearnet.gnn.com/gnn/mkt/mkt.intro.html**.

➤ Internet Distribution Services. Electronic publishing and distribution of catalogs and product information. Access: **http://www.service.com/home.html**.

> ➤ Internet Mall. Dave Taylor's "Shopping on the Information Highway," a frequently updated list of commercial services available via the Internet. See the discussion in Chapters 8 and 12. Access: send e-mail to **taylor@netcom.com** with the SUBJECT line "send mall."

> ➤ Internet Plaza. Internet services for companies that would like to sell products online or provide information about products online. Access: **http://xor.com/plaza/index.html**.

> ➤ Internet Shopping Network. From the Home Shopping Network (HSN) and Viacom, Inc. (owner of MTV, among other things). Products from hundreds of vendors, along with a query interface. Access: **http://shop.internet.net**.

> ➤ MecklerWeb. A communication and marketing system. Access: **http://www.mecklerweb.com**.

> ➤ Telerama's Shopping Plaza. See the discussion of Telerama's Shopping Plaza in Chapter 10. Access: **http://www.lm.com/**.

> ➤ Yahoo Marketplaces List. Some Internauts consider this the definitive list of the very best WWW sites. Log onto this location and you can get almost anywhere on the Web. The system's 20,000 pages can be searched by keyword. Access: **http://akebono.stanford.edu/yahoo/** or **http://akebono .stanford.edu/yahoo/Economy/Business/Corporations/ markets/**.

⇨ Payment concerns

In Chapter 12 you will find lots of information on how a variety of specific companies are actually using the Internet to market their products and services. It is our hope that you will be able to learn from their successes and from their mistakes as you find your own niche on the Internet.

We cannot leave the business of business, however, without saying a word or two about the fog that seems to surround payment, credit card, and ordering issues on the Internet. It's a subtle point, but the concern that has been raised about whether it's safe for a customer to

key in credit card information when ordering a product is very similar to the enthusiasm you hear about the World Wide Web.

Forget about the conventional news media. Whether from laziness or stupidity, they have only the vaguest idea of what is being discussed. With a few notable exceptions, most high-tech and science reporters are mere conduits.

The sky is falling, the sky is falling

So when some Internet nerd who has been spending way too much time in front of a CRT suggests that keying in your credit card number is potentially risky because he or she or some other equally knowledgeable nerd could just possibly extract such numbers from the millions of e-mail messages sent every day, well, reporters react like iron filings in the presence of a magnet.

No one bothers to look into how much effort and expertise are required to do this. The alarm is raised. And reporters who, in our experience, exhibit a persistent and unreasoning bias against anything having to do with computers, science, technology, or advertising (even though advertising dollars pay their salaries), eagerly misinform the public about the dangers of using a credit card to buy products on the Internet.

It's a situation ripe for a Jerry Seinfeld monologue:

> Using your credit card number on the Net? Hellooo? Like this is somehow different from calling a number you've seen in a newspaper or mail-order catalogue and giving that same number to a total stranger over the phone?

> Or writing your number on an order form and entrusting it to the U.S. Postal Service. Right. Or giving your card—your card itself!—to a waiter at some restaurant who can run off as many charge slips as he wants while you're having your last cup of espresso.

 # Get real, get serious!

In all seriousness, you are far more likely to have your purse or wallet stolen or to be the victim of some kind of credit card number-stealing ring working out of an airport car rental counter (they know you're out of town!) than to have it intercepted on the Internet. And as more and more people become Net users, the traffic and the difficulties of intercepting a credit card number just increase.

Sure, it's technically possible for a very dedicated, very knowledgeable individual to find a way to intercept and use un-encrypted credit card numbers. But why would anyone who really was that smart go to all that trouble? If you're a crook at heart, just get a minimum wage job as a server at a restaurant and keep a record of every credit card number and name you process.

You will hear about DigiCash, NetCash, and encryption of credit card numbers. All of which are interesting solutions. But none of which may be necessary. At this stage, no one really knows.

In our opinion, having customers send you credit card numbers and expiration dates via e-mail or some kind of Web-based interactive order form is at least as safe as having them dial your toll-free number and place orders verbally.

If your Internet-based customers and prospects are concerned, all you need do is make it clear that they can order by fax, phone, or conventional paper mail. Just as they would if they were ordering out of a normal mail-order catalogue.

Now let's turn to the last chapter and see how a number of companies are using Internet resources to market their products.

12

"Interpreneurs" in action

I goes without saying, but we have to say it anyway: Marketing on the Internet is anything but a mature industry. The forms, the conventions, the received wisdom about what works and what doesn't are still evolving. And, this being a computer medium, they're evolving with breathtaking speed.

It can all be nerve-wracking at times. But it can also be very, very exciting. There are certain restrictions rooted in Net culture regarding the places where overt advertising is acceptable and where it isn't. But that leaves a virtually limitless horizon of possibilities bounded only by your own creativity.

That's the common theme running through the activities of the "Interpreneurs" we want to tell you about in this chapter. Each of them has found some way to use the various features of the Internet to promote their businesses or otherwise turn a profit. Not a huge profit, to be sure, but apparently, enough to make it worth staying in the game.

Nautical Bookshelf

Alfred learned that *leeward* is pronounced "looward" at the Culver Summer Naval School, and he parlayed that knowledge and his skills in sailing everything from Sunfish to square-riggers into teaching gigs during college. The best of which was serving as Sailing Master at the Seal Harbor Yacht Club in Seal Harbor, Maine one summer. He's also read all of C. S. Forester and Alexander Kent and has just discovered Patrick O'Brian.

So you might think that we would be predisposed to list in the direction of the Nautical Bookshelf on purely subjective grounds. But wait until you see what this company has done. We know them only from their Internet presence, but boy, someone at their home office in Hewlett, New York—or a savvy consultant they've hired to help them—knows how to market on the Net!

 # Seven synergistic steps

First, Nautical Bookshelf has set up an auto-responder. To get free information, all you need to do is send a message to **info@nautical .com**. Leave the subject line blank and make sure that you include in the message the word INDEX in uppercase, framed by angle brackets, like this: <INDEX>.

Second, they have a Gopher. It's physically located at the University of Minnesota, but you can reach it by pointing your nearest Gopher to the address **gopher.nautical.com**.

As you will discover, Nautical Bookshelf uses its Gopher exceedingly well. Remember, Gophers are designed to present information as a series of menus or submenus. Thus, you may find an initial, top-level line for Nautical Bookshelf, but when you select it, you will see menus like these:

```
Nautical Bookshelf - Nautical Bookshelf On-Line Resource Center Gopher
Page 1 of 1

1    About the Nautical Bookshelf Resource Center        Text
2    An On-Line Guide to Nautical Books                  Menu
3    Getting Your Free Nautical Book Guide               Menu
4    How to Order Nautical Books                         Menu
5    How to Get a 20% Discount                           Text
6    Frequently Asked Questions (FAQ) About Nautical Books Text
7    Boating Tips                                        Menu
8    Join the Nautical Bulletin Board  (It's Free!)      Text
9    How to Join the Mailing List (It's Free!)           Text
10   Scavenger Hunt                                      Text
11   What's New?                                         Text

Enter Item Number, SAVE, ?, or BACK: 7

Boating Tips
Page 1 of 1

1    Adding a New Circuit             Text
2    Aluminum Spreaders               Text
3    Checking Hoses                   Text
4    Crew Overboard                   Text
5    Diesel Engines                   Text
6    For Wheel-steered Boats          Text
7    Have I Done All The Simple Things? Text
8    Making Your Zincs Work           Text
```

```
9   On Sea Sickness...                    Text
10  Should the Propeller Be Locked?       Text
11  Showing the Boat                      Text
12  Spotting Navaids                      Text
13  Tapped Sheave                         Text
14  Tarp Tie-Down                         Text
15  Teak Tips                             Text
16  The Getaway                           Text
17  Troubleshooting Alternators           Text
18  Winter Storage                        Text

Enter Item Number, SAVE, ?, or BACK:
```

All of the "Text" items contain good, useful, nonsales information that prospective customers can benefit from without spending a dime.

But notice item 10, "Scavenger Hunt," on the first menu. This leads to a list of 20 questions, the first of which is "According to Plutarch, what is the best antidote for sea sickness?" Item 16 asks, "'Keeping a civil tongue' on board is required by which prolific nautical author?"

The kicker is this: The answers to all 20 questions can be found somewhere on the Nautical Bookshelf Gopher. What a great way to get customers to explore! And the reward for answering all of them? You get your name added to the Nautical Gopher Hall of Fame.

This is one heck of a lot of fun for everyone. The image it projects is delightful—who wouldn't make a special effort to order a given nautical book from such a joy-filled company? And the dollar cost for user and company is next to nothing. The crucial factors are imagination, creativity, and a dedication to maintaining the online commitment.

You can just tell. Someone at Nautical Bookshelf knows how to use the Internet and has made the commitment to care for this particular online garden every day. The results, in our opinion, are spectacular!

⇨ Points three through seven

But this only takes us to point three, which is that the company has established and published an e-mail address, **staff@nautical.com**,

and promises that messages sent there will be read and responded to by a human being.

Fourth, there's a Nautical Bookshelf mailing list, which you can subscribe to merely by sending an e-mail message to **staff@nautical .com**. Make sure that you include in the body of the message a line like "subscribe bookshelf Jean Smith," where "Jean Smith" is your name.

Fifth, there's a discussion group, which you can join by sending a message to **staff@nautical.com** containing a line reading "subscribe nautical Jean Smith," assuming, once again that "Jean Smith" is your name.

Sixth, a private Nautical Bookshelf bulletin board has been set up. For dial-up information, send a letter to **staff@nautical.com**.

Seventh—yes, *seventh!*—someone at the firm has seen to it that it is listed in the InterNIC Directory of Directories. And, as we showed you in Chapter 8, the listing they've put up is neat, clean, easy-to-read, and effective. And, it includes Nautical Bookshelf's land address, e-mail address, and toll-free phone number.

What can you learn?

We're no more brilliant than anyone else. The truth is we *stumbled* upon Nautical Bookshelf in the InterNIC Directory of Directories. But we know a well-done presentation when we see it and can now say that if Nautical Bookshelf did not already exist, we would have been forced to invent it.

It is quite simply the paradigm of everything we've been saying in this book. The essence of which is that you've got to first make the commitment to tending your online garden every day, and then you've got to do your damnedest to use every available tool and to make everything work synergistically.

Your auto-responder text should not only present your land address and phone number, it should include your e-mail address and

instructions for tapping your Gopher, subscribing to your mailing list, plugging into your BBS, and so on.

You don't have to offer everything that Nautical Bookshelf offers—indeed we have no idea whether that company has found all its interrelated efforts to be worthwhile—but you should certainly use every tool you can. And you should spend the time and effort and care to make sure that each tool includes pointers to every other tool. And notice that, at least at this writing, there is no big, elaborate World Wide Web home page for Nautical Bookshelf.

Bottom line: Nautical Bookshelf is sharp, and it has a lot to teach you about how to effectively use the Internet, regardless of the products or services you sell. To get the full picture, the best place to start is probably with their InterNIC Directory of Directories listing. To do that, select the "All the Gophers in the World" item from your Gopher menu and then specify **rs.internic.net** as discussed in Chapter 8. That will put you into position to find the Nautical Bookshelf Gopher that branches off the InterNIC menu.

 # Moon Travel Handbooks

Moon Publications, publisher of the Travel Handbook series, also uses the Internet to good advantage. The company has set up a Gopher that looks like this:

```
Moon Travel Handbooks
Page 1 of 1

1    About Moon Travel Handbooks                                  Text
2    Search all the file & menu titles in the Moon Travel Server  Search
3    Road Trip USA                                                Menu
4    Trans-Cultural Study Guide                                   Menu
5    Asia Travel Booklists                                        Menu
6    Travel Health: Staying Healthy in Asia, Africa, and Latin Am Menu
7    Travel Matters Newsletter                                    Menu
8    Catalog of Moon Travel Handbooks                             Menu
9    Ordering Information                                         Menu
10   Tibet Handbook Author Tour                                   Text

Enter Item Number, SAVE, ?, or BACK:
```

Notice that the first item leads to a text file that tells you about the company and its books, while the second item lets you search the Gopher for book titles and descriptions. All but one of the remaining items lead to submenus, which is the way Gopher should be used.

When you visit this site, check item 8, "Catalog of Moon Travel Handbooks." This leads to a submenu offering text write-ups on each book the company publishes. You will want to do that, but you will also want to select item 9, "Ordering Information."

This will take you to a menu that makes it easy for customers to find the name, address, and phone number of bookstores that carry Moon Travel Handbooks. The list is searchable by ZIP code. Once again, *that's* the right way to use this technology!

Moon Publications also offers an interactive version of its *Big Island of Hawaii Handbook* on a Web server that includes audio clips of the author (Joe Bisignani) on where to go and what to see. And it has begun a project called *Road Trip U.S.A.* that encourages Internet users to make suggestions and offer input as the book develops. It is also expected to help build advance publicity for the book.

Finally, Moon offers free subscriptions to its "Travel Matters" newsletter. (Users of its Gopher will find this is an item on the Ordering Information menu.) We also like the fact that every text file you view concludes with this:

```
-------------------------------------------------------------
This file is from the Moon Publications gopher/www server:
                   gopher.moon.com 7000
                http://www.moon.com:7000
      Comments and suggestions to   gopher@moon.com
```

With all the information you obtain and print out from the Internet, it is very easy to forget exactly where each file or piece of paper came from. By incorporating this information right into the file, Moon Publications makes sure that you always know how to return to its locations. It is one more indication that these folks really know what they're doing. But it is also an indication of how much care, thought, and attention to detail is required to create such an impressive Net presence.

Moon Publications is based in Chico, California. Voice phone: 800-345-5473; fax: 916-345-6751; e-mail: **travel@moon.com**.

The Capitol Steps

The Capitol Steps, a Washington, D.C.-based comedy troupe made up of former Congressional staffers, aides, and other self-described layabouts is a sheer delight. You may have seen them on C-SPAN or PBS, or heard them on National Public Radio—not that there's anything wrong with that. But the last place you would expect to see them selling their albums and tapes is on the Internet.

On reflection, though, setting up a Web site at **http://het.brown .edu/people/mende/steps** (note that it's "het," not "net") was an absolutely brilliant move. (See Figs. 12-1 and 12-2.) The general

Figure 12-1

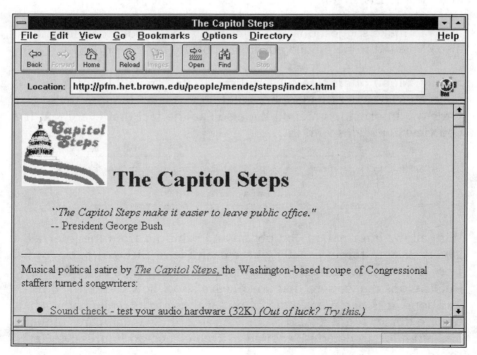

The Capitol Steps home page.

Figure 12-2

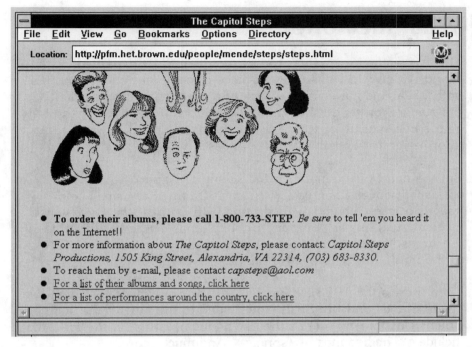

Line art appears fast!

demographics of today's Internet users make them ideal prospects for highly political, completely nonpartisan, side-splitting humor. And, in theory, the Web makes it easy to listen to sample cuts from their albums.

The home page was created by Paul Mende at Brown University. But Mike Tilford is the evil genius behind the Capitol Steps point of presence on the Net. At least, he's the guy who answers (delightfully) when you send a message to **CapSteps@aol.com**. When he inadvertently sent us some faulty information, he wrote back: "Sorry for the misdirection. That's what you get for hanging around with politicians—the urge to answer even if you don't know what you're talking about . . ."

⇨ What they offer

This is exactly the kind of product that *should* be marketed on the World Wide Web. Unlike, say, a piece of computer equipment, it's both visual and aural. With a click of a mouse you can see sketches of the players, or get a list of the radio stations that will carry the New Year's Eve special, or view a list of the dates, locations, and contact information for upcoming appearances.

But the heart of the matter is the selling of Capitol Steps albums. As you will discover when you go to this site, there are small color images of each album cover, starting with *Lord of the Fries* which includes such hits as "Snippity Bobbitt" and "There is Nothin' Like the Ames," a song about the mole planted by the Soviets at CIA sung to the music for "There is Nothin' Like a Dame."

Then there's the 1993 album, *The Joy of Sax*, which includes "I've Taken Stands on Both Sides Now," sung to the tune of the Judy Collins classic. And there's the 1992 album, *Fools on the Hill*, that includes "The Tsounds of Tsongas." And much more.

⇨ Trouble with sound

It's all great stuff, and the Capitol Steps generously include at least one sample cut from each album. Wow! What a neat idea. Click on the sound icon and hear a sample song. (See Fig. 12-3.) We've got a SoundBlaster and speakers and can't wait to try it!

Unfortunately, this process did not work. We double clicked on a sound icon and spent the next 10 minutes waiting for nearly one megabyte of data to be transmitted to our machine at 28.8 kbps. Finally, the download was over. Oh, boy, here we go! Then Netscape, the latest Web browser program from the creators of Mosaic, informed us that the necessary "helper" program was not available. Huh?

Our software then proceeded to hide or erase or otherwise make disappear the file we had just spent 10 minutes getting.

Figure 12-3

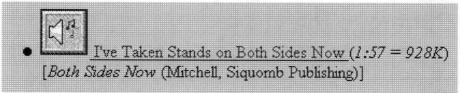

Click here for sound samples.

⇨ A sad, sorry tale

If we had not been writing a book, we would have said "file it" or words to that effect and gone on to something else. As it is, we ended up spending the better part of two hours trying to make it work.

The first stop was the Netscape "Help" function. Which, it turns out, is online. Literally. No on-disk manuals for them, no sir. Everything you need is on the Net. Great. So after a lot of time and frustration we finally discovered that you have to tell Netscape which programs to load to deal with files that end in certain extensions.

Trouble is, when you're at a Web site in Netscape and you click on an icon to bring you sound, Netscape doesn't tell you that it is downloading a file called, say, SQUAK.WAV. So you have no idea what the filename or file extension is.

To his credit, Paul Mende, creator of the Capitol Steps home page, includes a short "Sound Check" option that downloads a few seconds worth of "Yankee Doodle" into your machine. More importantly, he includes the technical information that the sound files are in the Sun Microsystems "audio" format and that such files end with the extension ".AU."

Huh? Doesn't look like any file extension we've ever seen. Why on earth wouldn't this site use the ".WAV" sound file format that is standard with Microsoft Windows, or the ".VOC" format that is native to the industry-leading SoundBlaster sound card?

⇨ Cutting to the chase

To make a long, sad story short, we used our account on Netcom and that company's NetCruiser software to return to the Capitol Steps home page on the Web. Maybe, we thought, NetCruiser would be smart enough to play sound files of any sort. Wrong.

Indeed, NetCruiser has the very bad flaw of making you wait until all the images and text on a given Web home page—however long and involved said home page may be—have been transmitted to your computer. (Mosaic had the same flaw, but Netscape corrects it by letting you click on "Stop.") At 28.8 kbps, we had to wait nearly five minutes for all the album cover art and text on the Capitol Steps page to be transmitted through NetCruiser before we could do anything.

In the end, NetCruiser did not play the sample. But it did report the name of the file, in this case, YANKEE.AU. Once we finally persuaded NetCruiser to let us out and we had exited from Windows, we had this ".AU" file on disk. What do to?

As the authors of several books about how to find shareware software online and elsewhere, we had some ideas. In the end, we found a little program on CompuServe that converts ".AU" Sun Microsystem sound files into ".VOC" SoundBlaster files. After investing close to two hours, we were rewarded by hearing the first few bars of "Yankee Doodle" come out of our speakers.

We have no idea whether the good folks at the Capitol Steps are aware of how difficult it is to use their Web site. And it is not as if we were using some obscure Web browsing program. This is one of the best Web sites you will find, and we tried it with two of the best browsers you will find, Netscape and NetCruiser.

And it doesn't work!

You can see what they have in mind. And this particular page is so good, it makes you long for a personal T1 line or ISDN connection. But if, as the *New York Times* reports (15 December 1994), less than 10 percent of Internet users—somewhere between two and

three million—have access to the kind of connections that let them display graphical Web pages, how many of those are likely to have the knowledge, skills, experience, and motivation to get the strains of "Yankee Doodle" coming out of their speakers?

Again, this is a wonderful site. Well planned and well thought out. As for converting ".AU" files to ".VOC" files, we've made the necessary program available through Glossbrenner's Choice. And our complaints should in no way detract from the Capitol Steps themselves. (Though if they were FireCrystal Consulting clients, we would advise them to create a sound-sampler package and plant it on CompuServe, America Online, and the rest, while making it available on the Internet via FTP.)

Finally, let us all remember the advice Capitol Steps member Mike Tilford personally gave us: "Remember in 1996 to vote the Capitol Steps ticket—Perot/Quayle. (Our motto: 'What's good for us is not necessarily good for the country.')"

Dave Taylor's Internet Mall

Dave Taylor, co-author of *The Internet Business Guide*, has established a nifty *free* service called The Internet Mall. This is a fast-growing, regularly updated listing of companies selling products and services on the Internet.

We talked about the Internet Mall in Chapter 8 as a way for companies to spread the word about products and services they are selling on the Net. What we want to focus on here is how Interpreneur Dave Taylor himself is using Internet features to good effect.

The Mall is the direct result of research Mr. Taylor did for an article in the July/August 1994 issue of *Internet World*. It started in early 1994 as a 200-line text file listing 34 companies. By year's end it had grown to over 3,500 lines and nearly 1,000 companies, shops, travel agencies, professional service establishments, and the like.

The Internet Mall is, in effect, a large text file. A concept that is so simple, it's brilliant. Anybody with any kind of access to the Internet can get a copy:

➤ Send a blank e-mail message to **taylor@netcom.com** with "Send Mall" as the subject.

➤ Sign up for the IMALL-L mailing list by sending an e-mail message to **listserv@netcom.com** containing the line "subscribe IMALL-L" in the message area.

➤ Use Finger to **finger taylor@netcom.com** to instantly retrieve information on all the various ways to obtain a copy of the Internet Mall.

Talk about using the Net! But that's not all. Mr. Taylor also distributes copies of the Internet Mall to the relevant SIGs, forums, and clubs of the Big Five consumer online systems.

⇨ Follow the money

But, if listings are free, how does Mr. Taylor earn his money? That's what we asked. He replied, "I seek to earn the cost of the project through corporate sponsorships and distribution of the compilation on various media (e.g., printed publication) . . . I've sold print rights, book rights, and now online Web rights to companies for a percentage of profits.

"At this juncture I receive approximately 50 requests to be added to the Mall each week, and that number is growing. I don't accept them all: Excluded from the list are multi-level marketing schemes . . ., Internet access providers, and computer consultants."

Dave Taylor is responsible for all the text you read on the Internet Mall. "I proofread, edit as needed, remove any annoying hyperbole, and generally ensure a consistency of tone, voice, and style throughout the entire Internet Mall listing. A typical entry is four lines of text total, specifying what company, what's for sale, and how to contact them for more information. As I am trying to help promote Internet-based commerce, I don't list postal addresses, phone

numbers, FAX numbers, or any other non-electronic contact
information."

For your convenience, sample listings from Dave Taylor's Internet
Mall are available from Glossbrenner's Choice. But you can also get
the file by FTP-ing to **ftp.netcom.com** and looking in the directory
/pub/Guides/. Usenet newsgroup readers will find that it shows up
on the first and fifteenth of each month in the newsgroup
alt.internet.services.

Dave Taylor has also created two mailing lists that help promote the
Internet Mall and keep it in the public eye. Subscribers to IMALL-L
receive the Mall every two weeks automatically. IMALL-CHAT, on the
other hand, provides a forum for discussing commerce on the
Internet—and specific vendors—with other businesspeople. Joining
either list is as easy as sending e-mail to **listserv@netcom.com** with
a message containing the phrase "subscribe IMALL-L" or "subscribe
IMALL-CHAT."

⇨ How companies get listed

Dave Taylor's company is Intuitive Systems. You can reach him at
317-497-2400 or **taylor@netcom.com**. Here's what he had to say
when we asked him how companies get listed on the Internet Mall:

> Send me a succinct three- or four-line description including your
> company name, what you have to offer, and how customers can
> get more information. Pointers can include e-mail addresses,
> Gopher hosts, FTP sites, Web URLs, and whatever else you'd
> like. Note that I don't include phone numbers or FAX numbers. If
> your listing is more than five lines, I'll reject it!
>
> Once received—and once I have the time—I will edit your listing
> for length and clarity and then mail that back to you for
> confirmation and an accuracy check. If you like it, I'll add it and
> we're all done. If not, we can dance around to get it to be
> something mutually acceptable.
>
> Remember that since I list over 1,000 companies, I can't offer
> you more than a few lines of space, so please don't ask for a

paragraph or two about your company. Also, I can only list one business per person. If you're spread across multiple firms, please pick the one that is most apropos.

Judging the traffic

Dave Taylor is a neat guy with a neat product. He is also generous with his insights and advice. Here, for example, is his take on the best way to gauge traffic on your Internet site:

> *Many of the stores here [on the Internet Mall] are learning to measure their traffic rate differently too. In a regular retail outlet, roughly 20 percent or so of the people who walk into a store buy something. (This varies based on the cost of the items, of course.) On the Net, however, 1 or 2 percent is a more realistic figure, which means that companies excited by 20 to 40 visitors a day are only going to see a sale or two each week.*
>
> *That's why automation is so important, so visitors can get the information they seek without any human intervention (imagine answering 500 or more e-mail messages a day by hand!). With 500 visitors per day, a 2 percent sales ratio, and a typical product cost of $25, companies can realize $91,000 per year in sales, minus, say, $50 per month online time. A profit of about $90,000 per year (plus word of mouth, plus media coverage, etc.). Best of all, it's all customers that wouldn't have visited the stores otherwise.*
>
> *I can go on talking about this stuff. It's a whole new business model evolving before our eyes.*
>
> *Think about it. Change the numbers slightly so we have 1,000 per day visiting, improve the sales rate to 5 percent with bargains, competitive online advertising, etc., and up our monthly cost to $250 per month. Now we're looking at over $450,000 net per year!*

The Company Corporation

"You can form your own corporation, by phone, in any state, in as little as 8 minutes, as low as $45." That's what the headline of a rather substantial ad in a November 1994 issue of the *Wall Street Journal* read. There was a photo of a David McAllister, Incorporation Specialist, and no land address was given. Instead, the ad included the following:

1-800-542-2677 Ext. 5460

CompuServe: GO CORP

Internet: www http://incorporate.com/tcc/home.html

The unique selling proposition here is that The Company Corporation can create a corporation for you for a total fee of about $120, when your local, friend-of-the-family attorney might charge you as much as $3,000 to do the same thing.

"Tell me more!" you say. Perfect. Just key in go corp on CompuServe or check our Web site. Or, though it is not advertised in the *Journal*, check our Gopher at **server1.service.com**. (You could also do a Veronica search on "Company Corporation" to come up with all the menu items in Gopherspace that contain that phrase.)

The Company Corporation can be reached via e-mail at **corp@incorporate.com** or by voice phone at 800-542-2677, extension IDS. They've got an interesting and potentially valuable service to offer. But explaining the features and benefits, and the reasons why it is often best to incorporate in the state of Delaware, takes time and space.

Thus, they are perfectly suited to using expensive print advertising to point prospects to *inexpensive* online resources. Certainly, the *Wall Street Journal* is the right publication for this firm.

And it has covered all bases. Those who are not technically savvy enough to be on the Net or on CompuServe have a toll-free number

to call, while those who are on the Net get the instructions they need to tap into the firm's Web site. Our only complaint is that the company did not cite its Gopher address.

But that's a quibble. Our point here is that The Company Corporation has the need to explain the features and benefits it offers in far more detail than would be affordable in a standard print ad. So it uses a standard print ad to direct interested parties to CompuServe and Internet locations that can instantly provide the necessary information at little or no cost.

In our opinion, that's the way to do it! We're well aware that not every reader will have the funds to put an ad in the *Wall Street Journal*, but this same concept can be applied to any kind of print media. Provided, of course, that your customers are the type of folks who not only read the publication but who would also recognize a CompuServe or Internet address.

Let them communicate!

Personal computers and modems of every stripe have penetrated a huge proportion of upper-income American homes. So if your business or store serves a suburb or bedroom community of a major city, you should definitely think about including your auto-responder or e-mail address in the ads you place in the local "shopper" or town newspaper. More of your customers may be online than you have any idea of.

Yes, advertising space in print publications is limited. But even the smallest ad has space to include an e-mail or auto-responder address somewhere. You must mind your product or service, of course. But, while one should never say never, the online approach is likely to be much more successful if you offer products priced below $100 than if you are trying to sell cars or home remodeling services priced in the thousands of dollars.

Our point is that an awful lot of your local customers may very well be online and have the capability of tapping your auto-responder or Gopher. So it is worth thinking about including your Internet particulars in a local ad.

Still more great companies

No one knows how many companies are marketing their products on the Internet. And probably no one ever will know. As this chapter has shown, however, there are many companies that are doing a superb job of using Internet features for all they're worth. Probably, we could write a book on "the good, the bad, and the ugly" of World Wide Web sites alone.

In any case, as you use the tools and skills we have given you to explore the Net, you will definitely want to check in on Computer Express, Walnut Creek, and QuoteCom.

Computer Express

Started in 1985 by the husband and wife team of Philip and Lesley Schier, Computer Express had one of the first storefronts on the Net. Since that time, the firm claims to have had over 200,000 satisfied customers for its computer hardware and software products.

That's a big number, but then again, Computer Express is *everywhere* online—Prodigy, CompuServe, AOL, Delphi, and the Internet. Here's how to reach them:

➤ Voice: 800-228-7449, Ext. 159 (within the Continental U.S. only); or 508-443-6125 Ext. 159 (all other callers). Hours are 8 a.m. to 10 p.m. Monday through Friday, and 10 a.m. to 5 p.m. Saturday and Sunday (Eastern time). The company is "open on evenings and weekends to provide the best service possible."

➤ Electronic newsletter: To subscribe or unsubscribe to the Computer Express newsletter, send e-mail to **list@ cexpress.com**.

➤ Gopher: **cexpress.com 2600**

➤ Web: **http://cexpress.com:2700/**

➤ Demo programs via FTP: **ftp.std.com**. For a list of currently available demos, send e-mail to **demo@cexpress.com**.

➤ To request a price quote for a product, send e-mail to **quote @cexpress.com**. In the body of the message, use braces ({) and (}) to enclose the name of your product. For example, to request a quote for EXCEL, send a message like this:

```
From: Your E-mail Address
To: quote@cexpress.com
Subject: Quote Request

{EXCEL}
```

➤ You can also request a copy of the company's electronic mail order form by sending the following message to **info@ cexpress.com**:

```
From: Your E-mail Address
To: info@cexpress.com
Subject: Information Request

<orderform>
```

➤ For all other questions and comments, send e-mail to **service @cexpress.com**.

We have never ordered anything from Computer Express. But after seeing how hard they work to spread the word electronically, we would be inclined to do so. At the very least, the next time we need a piece of hardware or software, we will definitely check their prices. We hope you will do likewise, if only to see how thoroughly one company can use the Net.

 # Walnut Creek CDROM

Walnut Creek CDROM, located in Walnut Creek, California, is one of the leading creators and purveyors of CD-ROM-based shareware, text files, and Internet information. You can call 800-786-9907 for voice information. But Walnut Creek has set things up such that all you need to do to get an instant copy of its current catalog is Finger them at **info@cdrom.com**.

Or you can FTP to **ftp.cdrom.com** and look in the directory /pub/cdrom/catalog. Or you can send a blank e-mail message to **info@cdrom.com** to hit their auto-responder. You will also find Walnut Creek on Dave Taylor's Internet Mall.

We like this company a lot. We like what they produce and are impressed with the way they have taken a low-key but thorough approach to making themselves known and to distributing their catalogue on the Net. Try one or more of the options listed here and see what you think.

 # QuoteCom Data Service

As you know from Chapter 7, QuoteCom Data Service uses an auto-responder to make it easy for customers to get quick information about what the firm offers.

These services include 15-minute-delayed price quotes on stocks, commodities, mutual funds, and other financial instruments; portfolio tracking and reporting via e-mail; news and analysis from Standard & Poor's, press releases from BusinessWire and PR Newswire, and company profiles from Reference Press; plus access to QuoteCom's historical database.

But an auto-responder is only the beginning. Here are the various ways this company has made itself accessible:

➤ By Telnet. Just Telnet to **quote.com** to access the custom quote server via simple pull-down menus to get current quotes, search for ticker symbols, view textual data and news, and modify your billing information.

➤ By E-mail. Send a blank e-mail message with the word "help" as the subject to **services@quote.com**. You may subscribe to QuoteCom by filling in a form and sending it to them as e-mail. Other services such as stock quotes and information requests are also available via e-mail.

➤ By FTP. If you FTP to **ftp.quote.com**, you will have access to historical data on stocks and other securities.

> ➤ On the Web. The address is **http://www.quote.com**/. (See
> Fig. 12-4 for the QuoteCom home page.)

In our opinion, QuoteCom is one of those companies that really
knows what it's doing on the Internet. You owe it to yourself to go
check them out. Indeed, you owe it to yourself to look at all of the
companies presented in this chapter, for this is anything but a random
selection. Our goal was to bring you the very best! Thus, it just makes
sense to use these firms as a yardstick for judging others who are
attempting to establish a "presence" and to use them as models,
should you eventually decide to establish a presence of your own.

Figure 12-4

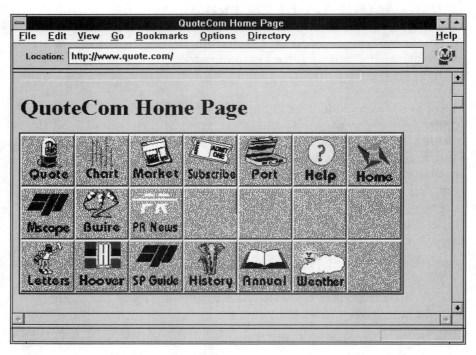

QuoteCom's Home Page on the Web.

 Conclusion: What's the rush?

We end as we began. Speculating on the pot of gold at the end of the Internet rainbow.

If it really does exist, which we doubt, no one has yet found it. But, rest assured, the minute someone does strike pay dirt, the word will spread, and "prospectors" the world over will show up to try to go the discoverer one better.

In the online world, things happen at "Net speed." Which means "instantaneously." Whatever you knew yesterday could be irrelevant by next Wednesday. That's why there is little reason to be concerned about getting in and "staking your claim" or "establishing your position" right now.

You're not dealing with real estate, after all.

Indeed, the two main truths about land and real estate simply do not apply here. The first truth is that "Land is a good investment because God isn't making any more of it." The second is the old chestnut, "Location, location, location."

Whether it's land or physical location, those two bits of conventional wisdom are based on *scarcity*. But the supply of Internet "land" is unlimited, and what value is there to "location" in a universe where all points are the same and can be reached with equal ease and speed?

Learn from others

Our advice is to take it easy and to definitely take the time to learn from what others have done. We tend to be skeptical of World Wide Web sites, but you may decide that a Web home page is just the thing for you. Or you may find that a Gopher is the perfect medium to tell your story to prospective customers. Or you may have a completely new idea.

There is definitely money to be made on the Internet, but you will have to apply yourself. We hope that in this book we have given you the knowledge, the tools, and the Net addresses you need to do just that!

FireCrystal Consulting

APPENDIX A

THIS appendix is designed to tell you about our company, FireCrystal Consulting, and how we can help you market your products or services on the Internet. If you have read and enjoyed this book, and if you are interested in having us help you establish a presence on the Net, skip the sales copy that follows and jump directly to the end of this appendix, where you will find information on how to contact us.

Otherwise, read on as we take our best shot at convincing you to pick up the phone or send us an e-mail query to arrange an appointment.

⇨ Taken at the flood

There is a tide in the affairs of the Internet. No doubt about that. In fact, as you read this, the first Internet tide will have just about reached its peak. That's the tide of *Time* and *Business Week* magazine covers—plus untold stories in newspapers and other magazines—that has served to raise awareness of terms like "online" and "Internet" in the minds of the American public.

It's a tide we expected to hit the beaches around 1982, the year that the first edition of *The Complete Handbook of Personal Computer Communications: Everything You Need to Go Online with the World* came out. We fondly remember our editor at St. Martin's Press, recounting the experience of seeing the 1983 movie *War Games*: "That's Alfred's book!" he said as he pounded his wife Nancy's knee.

Well, yes. But boy were we all wrong!

At the time, not even the online industry appreciated the amount of hardware and software that would have to be moved into American homes or how steep the learning curve would be.

No one, not even your authors, fully grasped the amount of spade work that had to be done. Families needed a good reason to buy a computer in the first place, and the price had to be right. Once purchased, they needed time to get familiar with the machine before

taking the next step into the brave new world of modems and online communications.

⇨ The gospel of the Electronic Universe

It took over a decade for the online tide to arrive. During which time we kept preaching the gospel of the "electronic universe" and its life-enhancing powers. Three editions of the *Complete Handbook*, plus one book devoted to CompuServe and another devoted to GEnie, as well as *How to Look It Up Online*, *Internet Slick Tricks*, *Internet 101*, and more. It has taken some time, but the total number of Glossbrenner books sold now tops 300,000 copies.

So we are a "presence" in the online field. Some might even say a "fixture." Whatever. The fact is that we bring some very special credentials to the table. (This is the sales part—the part where we wheel in the heavy artillery to persuade you to hire us.)

⇨ Who are your people?

Emily has close to two decades' experience in computing, marketing, and project management, including nine years with the IBM Corporation as a marketing representative and marketing manager for Fortune 500 accounts.

Alfred has written brochures, manuals, speeches, film scripts, booklets, press releases, and print ads for companies like Merrill Lynch, U.S. Trust, Dow Jones, Chase Manhattan, Sun Oil (Sunoco), Nissan, Monarch Life, Michelin, Berlitz, and others.

⇨ Saving you time & money

Bottom line: We know corporate America. We know sales, marketing, and advertising. We know the Internet and the rest of the electronic universe—in depth.

If you want to offer your goods or services electronically, we at FireCrystal Consulting have the skills, the experience, and the credentials to save you a lot of time and money, and to show you the best way to market your product on the Internet, the Big Five consumer systems, and bulletin board systems (BBSs).

A typical initial consultation runs $100 to $200. But before you make that commitment, we will be happy to spend five minutes on the phone with you to help you decide whether you should be on the Net or in the electronic universe at all. If you have read this book, you know we will tell you the truth.

If you feel it would be worthwhile to discuss things in detail, we will ask you to schedule a phone appointment—which you can charge to your Visa or MasterCard, or pay with a check mailed to us in advance of the call.

The next step

At the end of that initial consultation, you will have a very good idea of the best way to proceed. And, if you like, we can help you with any and all of the details—everything from creating and laying out the sales copy for your auto-responder message or messages to designing the Gopher menu system or World Wide Web pages that will present your products or services most effectively.

We will also show you which newsgroups and mailing lists to follow on the Internet, and which SIGs (Special Interest Groups) to check into on the Big Five consumer systems. We can help you avoid violating the online culture and getting flamed. We will advise you on ways you can "give back to the Net" by offering something free as a public service. If setting up your own on-site bulletin board system seems worthwhile, we can advise you on that as well.

What makes you special?

No two products, services, or companies are exactly alike. Our goal at FireCrystal Consulting is to work with you to discover what makes

your offerings special and to help you articulate those qualities on the Internet and in the electronic universe in the most effective, time- and cost-efficient way possible.

As for what makes *us* special—aside from being truly wonderful people who are fun to work with—no one else can offer the same combination of writing skills and in-depth knowledge of the online world. If you like this book, you'll love what FireCrystal Consulting can do for you. Please give us a call!

FireCrystal Consulting
699 River Road
Yardley, PA 19067-1965
Voice: 215-736-1213
Fax: 215-736-1031
E-mail: Alfred@Delphi.com

The Internet Toolkit &
Glossbrenner's Choice

C OMPUTERS, the Internet, and consumer online services aren't really all that difficult to use, provided you've got two things—the right information and the right software. We've done our best in this book to give you the right information. This appendix addresses the other need—the right software.

Through years of experience, your co-authors have become experts in public domain and shareware software for DOS/Windows machines. (We've even written several books on the subject, including *Glossbrenner's Guide to Shareware for Small Businesses* from Windcrest/McGraw-Hill.) We know exactly what utilities and tools you need to make it easier than you've ever imagined to go online, and as a convenience to readers, we have long made them available on disk as part of a collection called Glossbrenner's Choice.

In addition to the software, however, Glossbrenner's Choice also offers a series of disks called the Internet Toolkit. These disks contain the FAQ (Frequently Asked Questions) files, the best guides to resources, and other information you'll need if you want to make the most of the Internet. With just two exceptions (Internet Disks 3 and 6), the disks in the Internet Toolkit contain plain, pure ASCII text files. Which means that they can be used by *both* DOS/Windows users and Macintosh users.

If you have a Macintosh . . .

The PowerPC chip notwithstanding, it is likely to be a while before Macintoshes and PCs can share the same software. But the two systems have long been able to share text files, thanks to Apple's SuperDrive 3.5-inch disk-drive technology. If your Mac was manufactured after August 1989, it is almost certainly equipped with one or more SuperDrives and thus has the ability to read 1.44MB Mac- and DOS-formatted disks.

Check your reference manual for an appendix titled "Exchanging Disks and Files with MS-DOS Computers," or words to that effect. As you will discover, the necessary Apple File Exchange software is supplied on one of the utility disks provided with your Mac system software. If you are using System 7.5, check your disks for a program called PC Exchange.

Follow the Apple File Exchange or PC Exchange instructions, and you will be able to copy the files on the Internet Toolkit disks onto your hard drive. Since the files are all plain ASCII text files, you can read and search them with your favorite word processor as easily as if you had created them yourself. There is no need to worry with any of the "translator" modules supplied with the Apple File Exchange software.

Glossbrenner's Choice disks

Here's a list of the disks described in this appendix:

The Internet Toolkit

Internet 1 Internet Must-Have Files

Internet 2 FTP Essentials

Internet 3 Telnet Essentials (DOS/Windows only)

Internet 4 Newsgroup Essentials

Internet 5 Mailing List Essentials

Internet 6 Compression Tools (DOS/Windows only)

Internet 7 Just the FAQs

Internet 8 World Wide Web Essentials

Internet 9 Making Money on the Internet Companion Disk

DOS/Windows Tools and Utilities

Communicator's Toolchest

CommWin Communications Package

Encryption Tools

Idea Processing

Instant File Management: QFILER, QEDIT, & Associates

Qmodem Communications Program

System Configuration Tools

TAPCIS for CompuServe

Text Search

Text Treaters

 # The Internet Toolkit

The disks in the Internet Toolkit collection contain key FAQs, directories, guides, lists, and other information about using various features of the Internet. Any word processing program can be used to view, print, and search the files for keywords.

All of the disks are 3.5-inch, high-density (1.44MB). Most computer users today have at least one drive in their systems that can read high-density disks. If you don't, you really should consider getting one. A high-density drive sells for about $40 at local computer stores. The only reason not to upgrade is if you've got a very old system that's not worth putting more money into. In which case, it's probably time to get a new computer.

 ## Internet 1—Internet Must-Have Files (Mac-readable)

This disk includes the latest versions of the key text files which every Internet user should have. All of these files are available on the Net, but you may find it more convenient to get them in one neat package:

> ➤ *The Internet Services FAQ* by Kevin Savetz

> ➤ *Special Internet Connections* by Scott Yanoff

> ➤ *The Unofficial Internet Book List* by Kevin Savetz

> ➤ The List of Subject-Oriented Internet Resource Guides

> ➤ John December's *Internet-CMC List*

> ➤ John December's *Internet Tools Summary*

The disk also includes *The Beginner's Guide to the Internet*, an excellent tutorial for DOS and Windows users by Patrick J. Suarez.

✳ *The Internet Services FAQ*

Kevin Savetz is not only one of the most knowledgeable Internauts you are ever likely to find, he is also one of the best writers you are likely to encounter on the Net or in real life. His Frequently Asked Questions (FAQ) file on Internet basics is must reading for everyone. It includes sections like "I'm new to the Internet—Where do I start?", "What kind of information is on the Internet?", and "Are there any magazines about the Internet?"

Mr. Savetz has written a book based on his file. Look for *Your Internet Consultant: The FAQs of Life Online* by Kevin Savetz. Or call Sams Publishing at 800-428-5331 for more information.

✳ *Special Internet Connections*

This is the famous Yanoff List you are sure to hear about. It tells you about what Scott Yanoff feels are the best resources available on the Net for specific topics. Those topics range from Agriculture to Weather, Atmospheric, and Oceanic information. The Yanoff List calls on you to use all your fundamental Internet skills to get the information or goodies you want. So you will have to learn how to FTP a file.

If you want to get the list online and need to know where to look, use the Internet Finger utility. Finger **yanoff@csd4.csd.uwm.edu** for a list of locations where you can find the current version.

✳ *The Unofficial Internet Book List*

This is another super list prepared and maintained by Kevin Savetz. The reviews are only two or three sentences long, and Mr. Savetz makes no claim at comprehensiveness. (That's probably what the "Unofficial" is all about.) But in our opinion, he is right on target.

We were especially pleased to get a letter from Mr. Savetz after he read our *Internet Slick Tricks*. "I just wanted to let you know that I think it's great. I mean really great. I haven't seen a book this honest, readable, and fun since, well, mine :-) or *Internet Starter Kit for the Mac*. Congratulations on a fine job!"

✳ **The List of Subject-Oriented Internet Resource Guides**

Prepared by the Clearinghouse for Subject-Oriented Internet Resource Guides at the University of Michigan, this file is probably the single most important file for anyone who is truly interested in mining the deep information resources of the Net.

The file itself is a directory—a list of *other* files and where to get them. These other files have been prepared by professors and students and others, and each one pulls together and presents in one neat package information on the main resources available via the Internet on a particular subject.

At this writing, the subjects for which there are corresponding resource files (over 160 in all) include topics like aerospace engineering; animals; astronomy; business; cable TV; environmentalism; theater, film and television—to name just a few. In each case the subject file shows you the newsgroup names, Telnet and Gopher locations, mailing lists and list servers, electronic newsletters and journals, key e-mail addresses, and FTP sites that are relevant to that subject.

✳ **John December's** *Internet-CMC List*

The full title of this incredible resource is *Information Sources: The Internet and Computer-Mediated Communication* by John December. This list is essentially a wonderfully detailed table. It organizes and categorizes resources by topic and gives you the Internet feature to use (FTP, Gopher, etc.), the address to target, and the path to follow once you get there.

There are so many wonderful things to say about Mr. December's continually updated publication that, instead of saying anything, we will say the one thing that matters: Get the list!

✳ **John December's** *Internet Tools Summary*

Ditto for this John December file as well. Among the Internet Information Retrieval Tools this file discusses are Finger, Netfind, Nslookup, Ping, WHOIS, X.500, Archie, FTP, Jughead, Knowbot, Maltshop, Trickle, and Veronica.

In each case, Mr. December gives you a quick handle on the tool and then tells you where to get more information on how to use it, tips, demos, and so on. As a word of caution: You must have some idea of what Telnet and FTP mean and how to use these features to be able to understand and benefit from either December list. (See Disk 2 for Telnet information and Disk 3 for FTP information.)

 ## Internet 2—FTP Essentials (Mac-readable)

As you know from Chapter 4, FTP stands for "File Transfer Protocol." Although one can use FTP to offer files to customers and prospects, the complexities involved place what we feel is an unacceptable burden on them. As a businessperson, you have to make it as easy as possible for a prospect to request and receive information about what you offer. And FTP, quite frankly, is a pain to all but the world's UNIX nerds.

On the other hand, knowing how to use FTP is an important Internet skill for anyone who wants to tap the Net's in-depth information and shareware software resources. You will find a complete, Glossbrenner-written, step-by-step tutorial for using "anonymous FTP" on this disk.

In addition, you will find an excellent FAQ by Perry Rovers on the subject, including a list of FTP sites that's about as comprehensive as one can imagine.

 ## Internet 3—Telnet Essentials

For DOS and Windows users only, this disk contains Peter Scott's remarkable Hytelnet package. This package contains a gigantic database of Telnet locations that includes at least one screen per location describing what you'll find there. It is, in effect, a gigantic, computerized directory of Telnet sites.

For ease of use, the entire thing is organized as a hypertext-style menu system. Also on this disk is Bruce Clouette's optional Subject Guide for the main Hytelnet menu, as well as a Windows front-end program, WINHytelnet.

Internet 4—Newsgroup Essentials (Mac-readable)

Internet newsgroups are important sources of information. But they are also the ideal spots to place a short, simple message alerting people to your auto-responder site.

Here you'll find two lists of Internet newsgroups, organized by newsgroup category (alternative, computer, recreation, science, etc.). The best way to use these files is to put them on your hard disk and then bring them into your word processing program, where you can use a "search" feature to locate keywords on the lists. The lists include:

➤ The List of Active Newsgroups (Parts 1 and 2)—This list includes newsgroups for all categories except ALT (alternative), which has its own list.

➤ The List of Alternative Newsgroups (Parts 1 and 2)—This list includes *only* newsgroups in the ALT category. Alternative groups can be focused on absolutely anything. The most popular, however, are those in the ALT.SEX hierarchy.

We've also included the DOS program ROT13.EXE, a utility you will need to encode and decode off-color jokes and the like found in some of the humor-oriented groups. The ROT13 approach rotates each letter in a message 13 characters down in the alphabet, which turns readable text into gibberish that can only be "unencrypted" by running the ROT13.EXE (or Mac equivalent) against it. The idea is to protect sensitive souls who might inadvertently stumble upon readable text they might find offensive.

Should you want to create your own newsgroup, you will find two valuable information files here as well. One outlines the procedure for creating an ALT newsgroup; the other does the same for the other kinds of newsgroups. Note that you will still have to find someone

capable of sending the proper "control" message to get a group created, as discussed in Chapter 9.

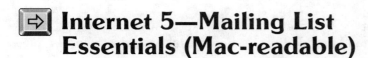

Internet 5—Mailing List Essentials (Mac-readable)

This disk contains two gigantic lists of Internet and Bitnet mailing list: The SRI List of Lists and Publicly Accessible Mailing Lists (PAML). Nearly every existing mailing list gets a meaty paragraph-long write-up, usually prepared by the list's creator. These write-ups offer lots of keywords for you to find when you bring the following files into your word processing program and apply its "search" function:

Internet 6—Compression Tools

This disk is for DOS and Windows users only. It contains all of the programs you will need to uncompress or unarchive the various files you will find at FTP sites around the Net. File compression and archiving (bundling several files into a single file for easier downloading) have long been popular in the world of commercial online systems and bulletin boards. And fortunately, only a few main techniques and formats are used, principally ZIP and ARC in the DOS/Windows worlds and StuffIt in the Mac world.

Unfortunately, this kind of simplicity does not rule on the Net. Over the years Net users have developed any number of ways to compress and/or archive files. If you want to be able to uncompress and unarchive those files, you've got to have the correct utility program. That's what this disk provides. Among many others, it gives you the programs you need to deal with files that end in .ARC, .ARJ, .BTOA, .CPIO, .GZ or .Z, .HQX, .SIT, .TAR, .UUE, .Z, and more.

Internet 7—Just the FAQs (Mac-readable)

On this disk you will find two things. First, there is the gigantic 100-plus page FAQ Index listing all of the FAQ files currently available on

the Internet. The FAQ Index includes precise filenames to help you locate the files via Archie. Once you know where a file lives, you can log onto that site and get a copy via anonymous FTP.

Second, there are what we feel are some of the key FAQ files you may want to have on hand (in addition to the ones already described). Here's just a sampling:

➢ Addresses FAQ—How to find e-mail addresses and locate people on the Internet.

➢ Compression FAQ—All about compression programs. Where to find them, how to use them, troubleshooting, and more.

➢ Gopher FAQ—Questions and answers about using Internet Gophers.

➢ Pictures FAQ—Information on graphics images on the internet, newsgroups devoted to graphics, decoding and encoding images, image formats, and so forth.

➢ Veronica FAQ—Answers to frequently asked questions about using the Veronica search utility on the Internet.

⇨ Internet 8—World Wide Web Essentials (Mac-readable)

This disk contains a huge amount of information about the World Wide Web. From a business perspective, the Web is most interesting as a novelty and as the strongest argument yet for an updated edition of Charles Mackay's 1841 classic *Extraordinary Popular Delusions and the Madness of Crowds*. Tulipomania and the South-Sea Bubble are nothing compared to the blind rush to Web home pages!

Still, the Web, hypertext, hypermedia, and all that other good stuff is not going to go away. As a businessperson, it's something you need to know about. And there is no better place to start than with the files on this disk. These include:

➢ *Entering the World Wide Web: A Guide to Cyberspace* by Kevin Hughes

➤ *A Beginner's Guide to HTML* from the National Center for Supercomputing Applications (NCSA)

➤ *A Beginner's Guide to URLs* from NCSA

➤ *The URL FAQ* by Alan Coopersmith

➤ *The List of WWW Service Providers* by Mary E. S. Morris

➤ *Interesting Business Sites on the Web* by Bob O'Keefe

➤ *The World Wide Web FAQ* by Thomas Boutell

There simply isn't enough space to thoroughly explain these and the other files you will find on this disk. Suffice it to say that they are the *essence*. They've got all the information, all the samples, and the tons of pointers to Web sites you need to thoroughly understand the current state of the World Wide Web. And, should you feel that a Web home page is right for you, just check the Morris list of WWW Service Providers to locate a firm that can help you put up your page.

There are three items of special note, however. First, this disk contains at least two files in HTML format. These are plain text files, so anyone can read them, but they contain hypertext markup language text codes that let you read them with Mosaic or Mosaic Netscape, or some other Web browser.

This is a very, very interesting development, because the HTML files are like "scripts." You load Netscape or some other Web browser, go online with your Internet access provider, and then tell your browser software to read one of these files from your disk. The software responds exactly as if you had logged onto a distant Web page instead of telling it to read an HTML file on your disk.

The text in your local file appears in fonts on the screen, and when you double click on some highlighted word or phrase, you are taken to some Web site somewhere on the Net. Remember, you are connected to the Internet by virtue of activating Mosaic or some other Web browser.

Second, this disk includes a file called NETSCAPE.TXT that contains all of the Help information offered by Mosaic Netscape as a single large (140K+) text file. Perhaps it's an occupational hazard, but the talented individuals who create Internet-related facilities and programs are so deep into the Net that they frequently lose sight of reality. As far as they are concerned, everything should be on the Net, not on your local hard disk drive.

We won't tell you what we think of this. But we were not at all pleased to discover that when you click on Help while using Netscape, the software doesn't show you a text file drawn from your disk. Instead, it logs you onto some WWW site someplace, with all the delays that can entail, and asks you to click for your help there.

Admittedly, like everyone else at this writing, we're using a pre-release beta version of Netscape. So your situation may be different. But many readers will still be as tickled as we were to get their hands on a text file of Netscape help information.

Finally, this disk includes a DOS program called SUN2VOC that will convert sound files found on Web pages in the Sun Microsystems .AU (audio) format into .VOC files that can be played by your SoundBlaster sound card.

We found this to be essential when accessing the Capitol Steps Web home page with Netcom's NetCruiser, a program that has the good sense to record sound files on disk for processing later—something that, as far as we can tell, cannot be said of Netscape. In any case, given the number of Sun Microsystem-based nodes out there, SUN2VOC may come in handy when you want to listen to a sound file.

 # Internet 9—*Making Money on the Internet* Companion Disk (Mac-readable)

In the best of all possible worlds, what you would pay for when buying a book is not just information but the *right* information—information that's been selected, culled, interpreted, packaged, and

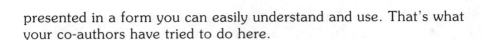

presented in a form you can easily understand and use. That's what your co-authors have tried to do here.

We have given you all of the tools and information you need to plug into the Internet and to begin using it to market your product or services. You do not absolutely, positively need this disk. On the other hand, it's got lots of really great stuff on it for those who want to know more about making money on the Internet. Among the text files on this disk are:

> *Advertising on the Internet FAQ* by Michael Strangelove

> *International Connectivity* by Larry Landweber

> *FAQ: International E-mail Accessibility* by Olivier M.J. Crepin-Leblond

> *The Internet Mall* by Dave Taylor (excerpts)

> *The Internet Press: A Guide to Electronic Journals about the Internet* by Kevin Savetz

> *Internet Pearls* by William Hogg of SoloTech Software

> *The POCIA (Providers of Commercial Internet Access) Directory* by the Celestin Company.

> *Guide to Network Resource Tools* by EARN Associates

> *A Primer on How to Work with the Usenet Community* by Chuq Von Rospach

Weighing in at over 240K, the EARN *Guide to Network Resource Tools* (Gopher, WWW, Archie, Veronica, WHOIS, WAIS, and much more) is a book in itself. The excerpts from Dave Taylor's Internet Mall are enormously instructive, and the POCIA Directory will made it easy to find an Internet service provider, regardless of your location.

Also on this disk, for DOS/Windows users, is a program called Internet Acronyms from William Hogg's SoloTech software. Searchable, viewable, printable, or accessible as a TSR, Internet Acronyms gives you close to 200 pages of Net acronyms and file extensions and their meanings. DOS and Windows users will also find a program called NetDemo from Rick Hower that serves as an interactive tutorial for using many of the Internet's main features.

Sure, it's "retro" of us to say so in an age when everything is supposed to be "on the Net," but when you think about the tons of information that can be delivered for $5 on a 3.5-inch disk, compared to the amount of time and money you would have to spend to locate, download, and decompress the same files, opting for the on-disk solution makes a lot of sense.

DOS/Windows tools & utilities

It's been our experience over the years that, whatever computing task you want to accomplish, there's almost always a program that can easily do it. In fact, there are often several programs that fill the bill. The trick is to find the programs and pick the very best ones. That's what our Glossbrenner's Choice collection of software for DOS/Windows users is all about.

All of the programs are fully functional, and most are extensively documented in ready-to-print manuals. The software itself is either *public domain* (PD) or *shareware*. Public domain programs are yours to do with as you please. But if you like and regularly use a *shareware* program, you are honor-bound to send the programmer the requested registration fee, typically $15 to $25. No one can force you to do this, of course. But when you see a really good piece of software, supporting its creator's efforts is something you will sincerely want to do.

Communicator's Toolchest

If the comm program you use doesn't have the ZMODEM protocol, you can use the tools provided on this disk to add it. ZMODEM is quite simply the best download protocol, and every online communicator should have access to it.

The disk also includes a program for adding support for CompuServe's QB (Quick B) protocol to virtually any comm program. This is by far the best protocol to use when you are downloading files from the data libraries of CompuServe's forums. Like ZMODEM, this protocol has the

ability to resume an interrupted download at a later time. Just sign on and start the download again, and it will pick up right where it left off.

The disk also contains several other extremely useful utility programs to make life online easier.

 # CommWin Communications Program

Our current favorite comm program for Windows users is Gerard E. Bernor's CommWin program. It's quick, clean, intuitive, and beats the Windows terminal program all hollow.

 # Encryption Tools

You have to assume that if your e-mail *can* be read it *will* be. Thus, it is always a good idea to encrypt sensitive information before sending it electronically. The programs on this disk can so thoroughly encrypt a binary or text file that cipher experts from the National Security Agency or CIA would have a tough time decoding the results. If you have the key, however, you can decrypt files in an instant.

Among other things, this disk includes Philip Zimmermann's famous *Pretty Good Privacy* (PGP) public key RSA encryption program. For more on Mr. Zimmermann, see the Steven Levy cover story "The Cypherpunks vs. Uncle Sam" in the June 12, 1994, issue of the *New York Times Sunday Magazine*.

 # Idea Processing

PC-Outline is an incredible clone of the commercial idea outlining program, Thinktank. Indeed, many former Thinktank users prefer this shareware product. PC-Outline lets you randomly enter information of almost any type (thoughts, plans, ideas, etc.) and then organize it into a hierarchial structure.

You can then go from viewing the lowest level of detail to a view that shows you only the highest, most important topics. You can also print the outline, copy it into another outline, or paste it directly into

your word processor. Ideal for organizing projects, reports, books, and lists—or just organizing your thoughts!

 # Instant File Management: QFILER, QEDIT, & Associates

QFILER (Quick Filer) by Kenn Flee gives you *complete* control over your files and disk directories. You can tag a group of dissimilar files for deletion or for copying to another disk or directory. You can easily move up and down your directory trees, altering the date and time stamps of files, changing their attributes, compressing, uncompressing, and peering into archives. You can also look at any file on the screen, copy it to your printer, and more. You will find QFILER much easier to use than the Windows 3.1 File Manager or similar DOS-based products.

Also on this disk is WHEREIS, a lightning fast Archie-like file finder. And QEDIT, the famous DOS text-editing program. QEDIT specializes in creating plain text of the sort you must use on the Internet and in most e-mail letters on other systems. Yet it gives you many of the convenience features of a full-blown word processor.

 # Qmodem Communications Program

Here's what a recent issue of *Computer Shopper* had to say about Qmodem from Mustang Software: "This is simply the best DOS-based shareware communications package you can find . . . simple to set up and use, and it features about *every* bell and whistle you expect from a communications package . . . a true powerhouse . . ."

The article goes on to note that Qmodem "bears a great deal of similarity to the ever-popular shareware program Procomm, right down to the key commands . . . This shareware program is superior to the shareware version of Procomm, however, because when Procomm went commercial, Datastorm stopped developing the shareware version. Mustang, on the other hand, has continually updated the free version of Qmodem, and will continue to do so. It's hard to beat the power, and you can't beat the price."

We heartily agree. If you don't have a first-class comm program yet, try Qmodem.

 # System Configuration Tools

This disk includes the UARTTOOLS program (UARTID.EXE) discussed in Chapter 5. This program allows you to find out whether any of your COM ports have the 16550A National Semiconductor UART and if so, what interrupts they are using. Also on the disk are such intriguing DOS tools as BAT2EXEC (converts a batch program to an .EXE file), PopDOS (lets you shell out to DOS from any program), and UMBFILES (a hands-on memory management tool).

TAPCIS for CompuServe

TAPCIS makes it easy to handle electronic mail and get the most out of CompuServe forums. It will automatically sign on, pick up your e-mail, and check forums you have specified for messages addressed to you. Then you can sign off, review the information TAPCIS has gathered, and draft replies using the built-in editor. TAPCIS will then sign on again and automatically upload your e-mail and forum message replies. The whole idea is to make using CompuServe as easy and inexpensive as possible.

TAPCIS can do the same thing when it comes to uploading and downloading files. Just tell it what to do offline, then stand back and let it sign on and zip around the system.

Text Search

This disk contains the programs AnyWord, LOOKFOR, and FGREP. AnyWord by Eric Balkan can parse any text file, build its own index of keywords, and make it easy to search the file using sophisticated search logic. LOOKFOR works even faster. It lets you do AND, OR, wildcard, and proximity searches of text files—with no prior indexing. You can then print (to disk or printer) relevant file excerpts. FGREP

by Chris Dunford operates in a similar way, though it is more UNIX-like and not quite so user-friendly.

⇨ Text Treaters

This disk contains some 45 programs to manipulate, filter, and prepare a text file in virtually any way you can imagine. These programs are particularly convenient when you're dealing with text you get from e-mail correspondents and Internet sites.

For example, a program called TEXT lets you remove all leading white space on each line of a file, remove all trailing blanks, or convert all white space into the number of spaces you specify. CHOP, will cut a file into the number of pieces you specify. CRLF makes sure that every line in a text file ends with a carriage return and a linefeed so it can be displayed and edited properly. There's also a package by Peter Norton to create an index for a report, document, book, or whatever.

⇨ Order Form

You can use the order form on the next page (or a photocopy) to order Glossbrenner's Choice disks. Or you may simply write your request on a piece of paper and send it to us.

We accept Visa and MasterCard, as well as checks or money orders made payable to Glossbrenner's Choice. (U.S. funds drawn on a U.S. bank or international money orders only.) Please allow one to two weeks for delivery. For additional information, please write or call:

Glossbrenner's Choice
699 River Road
Yardley, PA 19067-1965
Voice: 215-736-1213
Fax: 215-736-1031
E-mail: Alfred@Delphi.com

Glossbrenner's Choice Order Form
*for Readers of **Making Money on the Internet***

Name_____

Address_____

City_____State_____ZIP_____

Province/Country_____Phone_____

Payment [ ] Check/Money Order payable to **Glossbrenner's Choice**

      [ ] Visa/MC_____ Exp__/__

Signature_____

Send to: Glossbrenner's Choice   Voice: 215-736-1213
         699 River Road   Fax: 215-736-1031
         Yardley, PA 19067-1965   E-mail: Alfred@Delphi.com

The Internet Toolkit
____Internet 1 Internet Must-Have Files
____Internet 2 FTP Essentials
____Internet 3 Telnet Essentials
____Internet 4 Newsgroup Essentials
____Internet 5 Mailing List Essentials
____Internet 6 Compression Tools
____Internet 7 Just the FAQs
____Internet 8 World Wide Web Essentials
____Internet 9 *Making Money on the Internet* Companion Disk

Other Glossbrenner's Choice Disks
____Communicator's Toolchest
____CommWin Communications Program
____Encryption Tools
____Idea Processing
____Instant File Management: QFILER, QEDIT, & Associates
____Qmodem Communications Program

(Continued)

____System Configuration Tools
____TAPCIS for CompuServe
____Text Search
____Text Treaters

____Total number of disks, 3.5-inch HD ($5 per disk)   _____

Glossbrenner Books (Book prices include $3 for Book Rate shipping.)
____*The Little Online Book* ($21)   _____
____*Internet Slick Tricks* ($19)   _____
____*Internet 101: A College Student's Guide* ($23)   _____
____*The Information Broker's Handbook* ($38)   _____
____*Glossbrenner's Master Guide to GEnie* ($28)   _____

                                              TOTAL   _____

Pennsylvania residents, please add 6% Sales Tax.   _____

Shipping Charge ($3.00 for shipment to U.S. addresses
and $5.00 for shipment outside the U.S.)   _____

                          GRAND TOTAL ENCLOSED   _____

Internet access providers

This appendix is designed to supplement the information found in Chapter 5. It includes the contact information you need to learn more about the services offered by the Internet access providers cited there—and many others besides—in the United States, Canada, and other countries.

As noted in Chapter 5, you will be best off if you first get your feet wet by sampling the Internet via Delphi, America Online, or one of the other large commercial online systems. After you've had some experience, you will probably want to sign up with a company that can provide you with a SLIP/PPP Internet connection. That's the business of the companies you will find here.

⇨ Picking a provider

This is by no means a comprehensive list. As you might imagine, the entire field is exploding, with new providers coming online every day. (Inevitably, there will eventually be consolidations, mergers, and business failures until this market matures.) Our advice is to pick a provider that is located near you. Put them through their paces, testing the software and trying their customer service line.

Take the time to get to know them before committing time and resources to using them for your business and marketing activities. If they aren't up to snuff, cancel your account and try someone else.

⇨ Location considerations: area codes

It's true that on the Internet, all points are the same. Distance and physical location do not matter. But since you must place a call to your Internet access provider to get connected to the Net, the distance separating your computer and theirs does indeed matter. If it's a toll call for you, you'll have to pay long distance charges for each minute you're connected.

That's why the first thing to do when using this appendix is to consult the list of area codes. Under each area code, you'll find the names of access providers you can reach from within that calling area. Next, consult the list of access providers for information on how to contact those specific companies. The list is alphabetized by company name.

Contact several of the firms and request their information packets and rate cards.

 # Toll-free & PDN access

Connecting with your provider by dialing a number within your local area code is probably the least expensive option. But you can also connect with some access providers by dialing either a toll-free "800" number or by using packet-switching Public Data Networks (PDNs) like SprintNet, Tymnet, and the CompuServe Network.

These can be convenient options when you are travelling and thus far from your local provider. (PDNs can be used both abroad and from within North America.) They can also offer a solution if there is no Internet access provider in your local calling area. But neither option is cost-free. Whether you use an "800" number or a PDN, your provider will add a surcharge of some sort to your connect-time bill. So be sure to compare costs and alternatives carefully.

The area code list presented in this appendix begins with companies offering 800-number access and those that can be reached via PDN.

How to find your local PDN numbers

Probably the easiest way to discover which number to dial to connect to your nearest CompuServe Network, SprintNet, or Tymnet node is place a voice call. You can call one of the Internet access providers listed under the PDN heading, or you can call the PDNs directly. Here are the numbers to dial:

CompuServe:	*800-848-8990*
SprintNet:	*800-877-5045, ext. 1*
Tymnet:	*800-937-2862*
	800-336-0149
	215-666-1770
Datapac (Canada):	*800-267-6574*
	613-781-6436

Searching online

You may also find it helpful to know the "secret" numbers and procedures to follow to search for PDN access numbers online. Set your comm program to 2400 baud, 7 databits, even parity, and 1 stop bit (7/E/1). Get into terminal mode, if you're not already there, and key in AT. Watch for an "Okay" on your screen from your modem. If you don't get this response, check your cable connections and possibly the comm port address your software is set to address (COM1 through COM4).

Next, open your capture buffer so you can save the incoming text to a file on disk.

Getting CompuServe numbers

1. *Key in* ATDT 1-800-346-3247.

2. *At the CONNECT prompt, hit your Enter key to generate the HOST NAME prompt.*

3. *At the HOST NAME prompt, key in* phones.

4. *Then just follow the menu that will appear to locate your nearest CompuServe Network number.*

Getting SprintNet numbers

1. *Key in* ATDT 1-800-546-1000.

2. *After "Connect" or something similar appears, key in* @. *You should then see "Telenet" on the screen. (SprintNet used to be called Telenet.) You will be prompted for "Terminal=."*

3. *Respond to the "Terminal=" prompt by keying in* D1. *That's the terminal type for all personal computers, as far as SprintNet is concerned.*

4. *You will next see a prompt like this: YOUR AREA CODE AND LOCAL EXCHANGE (AAA,LLL)=.*

   Your area code is obvious. Your local exchange number consists of the first three digits of your telephone number. So if your area

code is 212 and your phone number is 555-1234, key in
212,555.

5. Key in your area code and exchange, and the Sprintnet "at" sign
(@) network prompt will then appear. Key in mail. Then key in
phones when prompted for a user name and phones again for
your password. (The password PHONES will not show on your
screen.)

6. You will then be welcomed to the system. Some bulletins will
appear. And, finally, you will see a menu you can follow to locate
your nearest numbers.

To get international SprintNet phone numbers in over 100 countries,
key in intl/associates at the "User Name?" prompt. Then key in intl at
the "Password?" prompt. As before, the password will not show up on
your screen.

Getting Tymnet numbers

1. If calling from North America, make a voice call to either 800-
937-2862 or 800-336-0149 to get the number of your nearest
Tymnet local access number. If you have trouble or are calling
from outside North America, call 215-666-1770, the Tymnet
Technical Support number.

2. Use the ATDT command to dial the number of your local Tymnet
node, just as you did when dialing SprintNet.

3. When you see either garbage on your screen or "please type your
terminal identifier," key in A.

4. This will lead to the "please log in:" prompt, at which point, key
in information, and a menu will appear to guide you.

Getting Datapac numbers

If you live in Canada, the Datapac packet switching network is likely
to be your main PDN.

1. Call 800-267-6574 or 613-781-6436, the Datapac Customer
Assistance Hotline, for the number of your nearest Datapac
access number.

If you are already using a system like CompuServe, you may be able to get your nearest Datapac node number from that system. (Keying in go phones *on CompuServe, for example, will take you to a feature that can be used to search for your nearest Datapac number.)*

2. *Once you have the number, see if you can set your comm software to "Local echo" or "Half duplex." The command may be as simple as Alt-E. But it's not crucial. If you can't enable your local echo, you will not be able to see what you type. If you can, you will. That's all there is to it.*

Now use the ATDT command to get your comm program and modem to dial your local Datapac number.

3. *When the connection is made, watch for something like "2400" or "Connect" or a similar message from your modem indicating that the connection has been made.*

4. *At this point, hit your period key (.) three times. Then hit Enter if you are signing on at 2400 baud. (Use two periods for a 1200 baud connection; one period for 300 baud.)*

That will generate the "DATAPAC:" prompt, followed by some numbers.

5. *Now, carefully key in 92100086. This will take you directly into the Datapac Information System menu.*

If you would like to use the French version of this system, key in 92100086,B instead. You will then be welcomed to "Le Systeme d'Information Datapac (SID). Le SID vous informe, sans frais, sur les toutes dernieres nouvelles relatives au Datapac."

Area code summary for providers in U.S. & Canada

This is a list of North American Internet access providers. It starts with companies that are accessible via toll-free "800" numbers and Public Data Networks (PDNs), followed by those that serve a particular area code. You'll find information on how to reach these

companies in the next section, which is organized alphabetically by company name.

Toll-free "800" access
CERFnet Communications
CICNet
CLASS
CNS Internet Express
CR Laboratories
Colorado Supernet
HookUp
IGC
Internet MCI
JVNC
MSEN
OARnet

Public Data Network (PDN) access
Delphi
HoloNet
HookUp
IGC
Merit/MichNet
Millennium
Novalink
Portal
PSI World-Dial Service
PSINet
TMN
WELL
World

201
JVNC

202
CAPCON
ClarkNet
Express Access

Merit/MichNet
TMN

203
JVNC

204
MBnet

205
Nuance Network Services

206
Eskimo North
GLAIDS
Halcyon
Netcom
Northwest Nexus
Olympus

212
Echo Communications
Maestro
MindVOX
PANIX
Pipeline

213
CERFnet Communications
CR Laboratories
KAIWAN
Netcom

214
Netcom
On-Ramp Technologies
Texas Metronet

215
JVNC
PREPnet
VoiceNet/DSC

216
OARnet
Wariat

217
Prairienet

301
CAPCON
ClarkNet
Express Access
IMS Intercom
Merit/MichNet
TMN

302
Systems Solutions

303
CNS Internet Express
Colorado Supernet
Netcom
Nyx

305
Acquired Knowledge Systems
CyberGate

310
CERFnet Communications
CLASS
CR Laboratories
KAIWAN
Netcom

312
InterAccess
MCSNet
Netcom
Xnet

313
Advanced Networks and Services
CICNet
Merit/MichNet
MSEN

401
Anomaly
IDS World Network
JVNC

403
ARnet
PUCnet
UUNET-Canada

404
CR Laboratories
Netcom

407
CyberGate

408
a2i
Netcom
Portal

410
CAPCON
ClarkNet
Express Access

412
PREPnet
Telerama

415
a2i
CERFnet Communications
CLASS
CR Laboratories
IGC
Netcom
Portal
WELL

416
HookUp
Onet
UUNET-Canada
UUnorth

419
OARnet

503
Netcom
Teleport

504
NeoSoft

506
NBnet

508
Anomaly
NEARnet
North Shore Access
Novalink

510
CERFnet Communications
CLASS
CR Laboratories
HoloNet
Netcom

512
Realtime

513
FSP
OARnet

514
CAM
UUNET-Canada

516
JVNC
Network-USA

517
Merit/MichNet

519
HookUp
UUNET-Canada
UUnorth

602
CR Laboratories
Data Basix
Evergreen Communications
Indirect Direct, Inc.

603
MV
NEARnet

604
BCnet
Island Net
UUNET-Canada

609
JVNC

612
MRNet

613
UUNET-CanadaUUnorth

614
OARnet

616
Merit/MichNet

617
Delphi
NEARnet
Netcom
North Shore Access
Novalink
Pioneer Global
World

619
CERFnet Communications
cg57
CLASS
CTS Network Services
Cyberspace Station
Netcom

703
Alternet
CAPCON

ClarkNet
Merit/MichNet
Netcom
TMN
UUNET Technologies

704
CONCERT-CONNECT
Vnet

707
CR Laboratories

708
American Information Systems
Aquila
InterAccess
MCSNet
XNet

709
NLnet

713
Black Box
NeoSoft
South Coast Computing Services

714
CERFnet Communications
CLASS
Express Access
KAIWAN
Netcom

717
PREPnet

718
Maestro

MindVOX
Netcom
PANIX
Pipeline
ZONE 1 Network Exchange

719
CNS Internet Express
Colorado Supernet
Old Colorado City Communications

804
Wyvern

810
Merit/MichNet
MSEN

814
PREPnet

815
InterAccess
MCSNet
XNet

817
Texas Metronet

818
CERFnet Communications
CLASS
Netcom

901
Magibox

902
NSTN

905
HookUp
UUNET-Canada

906
Merit/MichNet

907
Alaska.edu

908
Express Access
JVNC

910
CONCERT-CONNECT

916
Netcom

919
CONCERT-CONNECT
Vnet

 # Internet access providers in the U.S & Canada

a2i communications
E-mail: info@rahul.net
Voice: 408-293-8078

Acquired Knowledge Systems, Inc.
E-mail: info@aksi.net
Voice: 800-930-6398
Fax: 305-462-2329

Advanced Networks and Services (ANS)
E-mail: info@ans.net
Voice: 313-663-7610

Alaska.edu
E-mail: JNJMB@acad1.alaska.edu
Voice: 907-465-6453
Fax: 907-465-6295

Alternet
E-mail: alternet-info@uunet.uu.net
Voice: 800-488-6383
        703-204-8000

American Information Systems, Inc.
E-mail: info@ais.net
Voice: 708-413-8400
Fax: 708-413-8401

Anomaly—Rhode Island's Gateway to the Internet
E-mail: info@anomaly.sbs.risc.net
Voice: 401-273-4669

Aquila
Voice: 708-820-0480
BBS: 708-820-8344

ARnet
E-mail: arnet@arc.ab.ca
Voice: 403-450-5189
Fax: 403-461-2651

BCnet
E-mail: info@bc.net
Voice: 604-291-5209
Fax: 604-291-5022

Black Box
E-mail: info@blkbox.com
Voice: 713-480-2684

CAM (Communications Accessibles Montreal)
E-mail: info@CAM.ORG
Voice: 514-931-0749

CAPCON Library Network
E-mail: capcon@capcon.net
Voice: 202-331-5771
Fax: 202-797-7719

CERFnet Communications
E-mail: help@cerf.net
Voice: 800-876-2373
       619-455-3900

CG57 (E & S Systems Public Access *Nix)
E-mail: steve@cg57.esnet.com
Voice: 619-278-4641

CICNet
E-mail: info@cic.net
Voice: 313-998-6103
Fax: 313-998-6105

ClarkNet (Clark Internet Services, Inc.)
E-mail: info@clark.net
Voice: 800-735-2258
       410-730-9764
Fax: 410-730-9765

CLASS (Cooperative Library Agency for Systems and Services)
Note: CLASS serves libraries and information distributors only.
E-mail: class@class.org
Voice: 800-488-4559
Fax: 408-453-5379

CNS Internet Express
E-mail: info@cscns.com
Voice: 800-748-1200
        719-592-1240
Fax: 719-592-1201

Colorado SuperNet
E-mail: info@csn.org
Voice: 303-273-3471
Fax: 303-273-3475

CONCERT-CONNECT
E-mail: info@concert.net
Voice: 919-248-1999

CR Laboratories Dialup Internet Access
E-mail: info@crl.com
Voice: 415-381-2800

CTS Network Services
E-mail: info@crash.cts.com (auto-responder)
        support@crash.cts.com (human)
Voice: 619-637-3637
Fax: 619-637-3630

CyberGate, Inc.
E-mail: info@gate.net.
        sales@gate.net
Voice: 305-428-4283
Fax: 305-428-7977

Cyberspace Station
E-mail: help@cyber.net

Data Basix
E-mail: info@Data.Basix.com (auto-responder)
        sales@Data.Basix.com (human)
Voice: 602-721-1988

Delphi
E-mail: info@delphi.com
Voice: 800-695-4005
        617-491-3342

Echo Communications
E-mail: horn@echonyc.com
Voice: 212-255-3839

Eskimo North
E-mail: nanook@eskimo.com
Voice: 206-367-7457

Evergreen Communications
E-mail: evergreen@libre.com
Voice: 602-955-8315
Fax: 602-955-5948

Express Access—A service of Digital Express Group
E-mail: info@digex.net
Voice: 800-969-9090
        301-220-2020

FSP (Freelance Systems Programming)
Voice: (513) 254-7246

GLAIDS NET (Homosexual Network)
E-mail: tomh@glaids.wa.com
Voice: 206-323-7483

Halcyon
E-mail: info@halcyon.com
Voice: 206-955-1050

HoloNet
E-mail: info@holonet.net
Voice: 510-704-0160
Fax: 510-704-8019

HookUp Communications
E-mail: info@hookup.net
Voice: 519-747-4110
        905-847-8000
Fax: 519-746-3521
        905-847-8420

IDS World Network
E-mail: info@ids.com
Voice: 401-885-6855

IGC (Institute for Global Communications/IGC Networks)
E-mail: support@igc.apc.org
Voice: 415-442-0220

IMS Intercom
E-mail: led@imssys.com
Voice: 301-856-2706
Fax: 301-856-5974
BBS: 301-856-0817

InterAccess
E-mail: info@interaccess.com
Voice: 800-967-1580
Fax: 708-671-0113

Internet Direct, Inc.
E-mail: info@indirect.com (auto-responder)
        support@indirect.com (human)
Voice: 602-274-0100 (Phoenix)
        602-324-0100 (Tucson)

Internet MCI
Voice: 800-779-0949

Island Net
E-mail: mark@amtsgi.bc.ca
Voice: 604-479-7861
BBS: 604-477-5163

JVNC (John von Neumann Computer Network)
E-mail: info@jvnc.net
Voice: 800-358-4437
609-897-7300
Fax: 609-897-7310

KAIWAN Public Access Internet Online Services
E-mail: info@kaiwan.com
Voice: 714-638-2139

Maestro
E-mail: info@maestro.com (auto-responder)
staff@maestro.com (human)
rkelly@maestro.com (human)
ksingh@maestro.com (human)
Voice: 212-240-9600

Magibox
E-mail: net.info@magibox.net
Voice: 901-757-7835
Fax: 901-757-5875

MBnet
E-mail: info@MBnet.MB.CA
Voice: 204-474-7325
Fax: 204-275-5420

MCSNet
E-mail: info@mcs.com
Voice: 312-248-8649
Fax: 312-248-8649
BBS: 312-248-0900

Merit/MichNet
E-mail: info@merit.edu
Voice: 313-764-9430
Fax: 313-747-3185

Millennium Online
E-mail: jjablow@mill.com
Voice: 800-736-0122

MindVOX
E-mail: info@phantom.com
Voice: 212-989-2418

MRNet
E-mail: dfazio@mr.net
Voice: 612-342-2570
Fax: 612-344-1716

MSEN
E-mail: info@msen.com
Voice: 313-998-4562
Fax: 313-998-4563

MV Communications, Inc.
E-mail: info@mv.com
Voice: 603-429-2223

NBnet
E-mail: info@nbnet.nb.ca
        nbnhelp@nbnet.nb.ca
Voice: 506-458-1690

NEARnet
E-mail: nearnet-join@nic.near.net
Voice: 617-873-8730

NeoSoft
E-mail: info@neosoft.com
Voice: 713-684-5969
Fax: 713-684-5922

Netcom Online Communication Services
E-mail: info@netcom.com
Voice: 800-501-8649
        408-554-8649
Fax: 408-241-9145

Network-USA
E-mail: Finger guest@netusa.net
Voice: 516-543-0234
BBS: 516-543-0240

NLnet
E-mail: admin@nlnet.nf.ca
Voice: 709-737-8329
Fax: 709-737-3514

North Shore Access
E-mail: info@northshore.ecosoft.com
Voice: 617-593-3110

Northwest Nexus, Inc.
E-mail: info@nwnexus.wa.com
Voice: 206-455-3505

NovaLink
E-mail: info@novalink.com
Voice: 800-274-2814

NSTN
E-Mail: info@nstn.ns.ca
Voice: 902-481-6786
Fax: 902-468-3679

Nuance Network Services
E-mail: staff@nuance.com
Voice: 205-533-4296 (voice recording)

Nyx, the Spirit of the Night
(Free public Internet access provided by the University of Denver's
Math & Computer Science Department.)
E-mail: aburt@nyx.cs.du.edu

OARnet
E-mail: nic@oar.net
Voice: 614-292-8100
Fax: 614-292-7168

Old Colorado City Communications
E-mail: dave@oldcolo.com
         thefox@oldcolo.com
Voice: 719-632-4848
         719-593-7575
         719-636-2040
Fax: 719-593-7521

Olympus—The Olympic Peninsula's Gateway to the Internet
E-mail: info@pt.olympus.net
Voice: 206-385-0464

Onet
E-Mail: herb@onet.on.ca
Voice: 416-978-4589

On-Ramp Technologies
E-mail: info@onramp.net
Voice: 214-746-4710
Fax: 214-746-4856

PANIX
E-mail: info@panix.com
Voice: 212-787-6160

Pioneer Global
E-mail: info@pn.com
Voice: 617-375-0200
Fax: 617-375-0201

Pipeline
E-mail: info@pipeline.com (auto-responder)
         staff@pipeline.com (human)
Voice: 212-267-3636

Portal System
E-mail: cs@cup.portal.com
         info@portal.com
Voice: 408-973-9111

Prairienet Freenet
E-mail: jayg@uiuc.edu
Voice:　217-244-1962

PREPnet
E-mail: prepnet@cmu.edu
Voice:　412-268-7870
Fax:　　412-268-7875

PSINet
E-mail: info@psi.com
Voice:　800-827-7482
　　　　703-620-6651
Fax:　　703-620-4586

PSI's World-Dial Service
E-mail: all-info@psi.com
　　　　world-dial-info@psi.com
Voice:　703-620-6651
Fax:　　703-620-4586

PUCnet Computer Connections
E-mail: info@PUCnet.com (auto-responder)
　　　　pwilson@PUCnet.com (human)
Voice:　403-448-1901
Fax:　　403-484-7103

RealTime Communications
E-mail: hosts@wixer.bga.com
Voice:　512-451-0046
Fax:　　512-459-3858

South Coast Computing Services, Inc.
E-mail: sales@sccsi.com
Voice:　713-917-5000
Fax:　　713-917-5005

Systems Solutions
E-mail: sharris@marlin.ssnet.com
Voice:　800-331-1386
　　　　302-378-1386

Teleport
E-mail: info@teleport.com
Voice: 503-223-4245

Telerama Public Access Internet
E-mail: info@telerama.pgh.pa.us
Voice: 412-481-3505

Texas Metronet
E-mail: info@metronet.com
Voice: 214-705-2900
        817-543-8756
Fax: 214-401-2802

TMN (The Meta Network)
E-mail: info@tmn.com
Voice: 703-243-6622

UUNET Canada, Inc.
E-mail: info@uunet.ca
Voice: 416-368-6621
Fax: 416-368-1350

UUNET Technologies
E-mail: info@uunet.uu.net
Voice: 800-488-6384
Fax: 703-204-8001

UUnorth
E-mail: uunorth@uunorth.north.net
Voice: 416-225-8649
Fax: 416-225-0525

Vnet Internet Access, Inc.
E-mail: info@char.vnet.net
Voice: 704-374-0779

VoiceNet/DSC
E-mail: info@voicenet.com
Voice: 800-521-2733
        215-674-9290
Fax: 215-674-9662

WELL (Whole Earth 'Lectronic Link)
E-mail: info@well.sf.ca.us
Voice: 415-332-4335

Wariat
E-mail: zbig@wariat.org
Voice: 216-481-9428

World
E-mail: info@world.std.com
Voice: 617-739-0202

Wyvern Technologies, Inc.
E-mail: system@wyvern.com
Voice: 804-622-4289
Fax: 804-622-7158

XNet Information Systems
E-mail: info@xnet.com
Voice: 708-983-6064
BBS: 708-983-6435

ZONE 1 Network Exchange
E-mail: info@zone.net
Voice: 718-549-8078
Fax: 718-884-7998

 # Internet access providers in other countries

 ## Australia

Aarnet
E-Mail: aarnet@aarnet.edu.au
Voice: +61 6-249-3385

Connect.com.au
E-mail: connect@connect.com.au
Voice: +61 3 528 2239
Fax: +61 3 528 5887

 # Germany

Individual Network
E-mail: in-info@individual.net
Voice: +49 2131 64190 (Andreas Baess)
Fax: +49 2131 605652

Individual Network—Rhein-Main (Frankfurt/Offenbach)
E-mail: info@rhein-main.de
Voice: +49-69-39048413

Inter-Networking Systems (Ruhr Area)
E-mail: info@ins.net
Voice: +49 2305 356505
Fax: +49 2305 25411

muc.de e.V. (Munich/Bavaria)
E-mail: postmaster@muc.de

 # Greece

Ariadne
E-mail: dialup@leon.nrcps.ariadne-t.gr
Voice: +301 65-13-392
Fax: +301 65-32-910

 # Netherlands

Knoware
E-mail: info@knoware.nl
Voice: 030 896775

Netland
E-mail: info@netland.nl
Voice: 020 6943664

Simplex
E-mail: simplex@simplex.nl

 # New Zealand

Actrix
E-mail: john@actrix.gen.nz
Voice: 04 389-6316

 # United Kingdom

Almac
E-mail: alastair.mcintyre@almac.co.uk
Voice: +44 0324-665-371

Cix
E-mail: cixadmin@cix.compulink.co.uk
Voice: +44 49 2641 961

Demon Internet Systems
E-mail: internet@demon.co.uk
Voice: +44 (0)81 349 0063

Direct Connection
E-mail: helpdesk@dircon.co.uk
Voice: +44 (0)81 317 0100
Fax: +44 (0)81 317 0100

IBMPCUG
E-mail: info@ibmpcug.co.uk
Voice: +44 (0)81 863 6646

IEunet Ltd.
E-mail: info@ieunet.ie
        info@Ireland.eu.net
Voice: +353 1 6790832

Index

Boldface numbers indicate illustrations.